The Public and t

The Public and the Private

Edited by

Eva Gamarnikow
David H.J. Morgan
June Purvis
Daphne Taylorson

Heinemann · London

Heinemann Educational Books Ltd
22 Bedford Square, London WC1B 3HH
LONDON EDINBURGH MELBOURNE AUCKLAND
HONG KONG SINGAPORE KUALA LUMPUR NEW DELHI
IBADAN NAIROBI JOHANNESBURG
EXETER (NH) KINGSTON PORT OF SPAIN

© British Sociological Association 1983
First published 1983

British Cataloguing in Publication Data

The Public and the private.
1. Sexism—Great Britain—History—Congresses
I. Gamarnikow, Eva
    305.3′09   HQ1075

    ISBN 0-435-82334-5
    ISBN 0-435-82335-3 Pbk

Phototypesetting by Georgia Origination, Liverpool
and printed by Biddles Ltd, Guildford, Surrey

Contents

1 Introduction
   Eva Gamarnikow and *June Purvis*   1
2 Social Sciences and the State: Fighting like a Woman
   Meg Stacey   7
3 Public and Private: Marking the Boundaries
   Linda Imray and *Audrey Middleton*   12
4 Blowing the Cover of the Protective Male: A Community Study of Violence to Women
   Jalna Hanmer and *Sheila Saunders*   28
5 Men and War: Status, Class and the Social Reproduction of Masculinity
   Patricia Allatt   47
6 Women and Caring: Skills, Tasks and Taboos
   Clare Ungerson   62
7 'It's a pleasure to cook for him': Food, Mealtimes and Gender in some South Wales Households
   Anne Murcott   78
8 'Women and Old Boats': the Sexual Division of Labour in a Newfoundland Outport
   Marilyn Porter   91
9 Dividing the Rough and the Respectable: Working-class Women and Pre-school Playgroups
   Janet Finch   106
10 Purification or Social Control? Ideologies of Reproduction and the Churching of Women after Childbirth
   Peter Rushton   118
11 Do Her Answers Fit His Questions? Women and the Survey Method
   Hilary Graham   132
12 Interviewing Men: 'Taking Gender Seriously'
   Lorna McKee and *Margaret O'Brien*   147
Notes on Contributors   162
Bibliography   166
Index   177

1 Introduction
Eva Gamarnikow and June Purvis

The papers in this volume (together with its companion, *Gender, Class and Work*) were presented at the Annual Conference of the British Sociological Association in 1982 which had as its theme Gender and Society. This selection is by no means representative of the variety of topics discussed at the Conference. Instead, this collection concentrates on the public/private split – a theoretical framework which informed many papers and much of the discussion.

The inspiration for this theme, and indeed the 1982 Conference, came from Meg Stacey's *Two Adams* paper (presented at an earlier BSA Conference) in which she addressed the persistent absence of considerations of gender in sociological theory. She argued that such an absence stems from the legacy of the past. Thus, in the mid nineteenth century, it was men who dominated the development of sociology and who gave exclusive attention 'to the public domain, to affairs of state and the marketplace' (1981, p. 173) – in other words, social institutions and activities from which women, by and large, were excluded. In so far as women featured at all in sociological accounts, they were consigned and confined to the private realm of the family. The concerns of the past still inform the present and thus the sociological paradigm has, at its very core, the public/private split.

Since the focus of male (main) stream sociology is on the public sphere of male concerns, the private realm of the family occupies a contradictory theoretical niche. On the one hand, if the public realm alone is seen as the main concern for the sociological construction of what is social, then the private realm, by definition, lies outside the boundaries of the social. In this case, male–female relations, or the gender order, become conflated with biological sex, located in a naturalistic and timeless reproductive dualism. On the other hand, because the private sphere also encompasses the social organisation of family life, it enters the social through the family–society relationship.

Feminist contributions to sociology, especially over the last ten or so years, have, to some extent, succeeded in challenging many of the assumptions that have been made about the private sphere. Feminist studies on housework, motherhood and violence in the family have illustrated only too well that notions of the family as a 'unit', of conjugal relations as 'complementary', and of motherhood as a 'biological function' derive from a patriarchal view of the world.

However, we still need to examine critically the 'oversocialisation' of the public sphere. Without that gender will remain a marginalised area in sociology, forever confined to the family.

Traditionally, sociological theories of the relationship between society and family have established a conceptual hierarchy which places the 'family' in a subordinate or determined position in relation to 'society'. This hierarchical structuring also produces a picture of the family as a unit 'made up of more or less social parts'.

This is especially true of structural-functionalism, a theoretical perspective which sees society as a social system that has various interrelated parts (such as the family) which contribute to the functioning of the whole system by socialisation processes which teach people acceptable ways of behaving. Talcott Parsons, for example, argues that the nuclear family developed in response to the needs of industrial society for small, mobile units. Female nurturing roles ensure biological reproduction and socialisation, and male instrumental roles link the family to society. Furthermore, Parsons presumes that the explanation for such a division of labour within the family must relate to the primacy of biology. Despite the fact that structural-functionalism has been subjected to much criticism, the notion of the 'family' and its 'functions' for the wider society still pervade sociological thinking.

In this account of the family–society relationship the family form does not develop (relatively) autonomously. It is an effect created by an external force – society – and is linked to this determining external force by male instrumentality – or the public domain of work. Thus only bits of the family are 'social': the breadwinner role of the husband and the marriage relationship which binds women to society through the breadwinner.

This unilinear determination of the private sphere of the family by society is also a feature of another influential perspective in sociology – Marxism. Here the family-society relationship is analysed through the concepts of production and reproduction. Of the two, it is production which is primary: it constitutes modes of production and class-structures. Reproduction is secondary in that its role is to recreate materially, politically and ideologically the social relations of production. Since the family lies in the sphere of reproduction, the activities and relations within it are not autonomously generated, but geared towards sustaining the realm of production.

The family is excluded from production because it is the site of privatised, unwaged labour. It is connected to production through the social labour power it either creates or regenerates. In other words, production and reproduction are linked to each other by the wage-earner, as in the Parsonian model.

In both cases society is defined by the public sphere of male activities, institutions, hierarchies and conflicts. The family, which perches uneasily between the social and the non-social, is a subsidiary, supporting institution with no independent or determining role.

Critically examining the public/private dichotomy may provide a way out of this sociological, conceptual straitjacket. It is, by no means, a tidy, theoretical framework; public/private offers, rather, an open and flexible perspective. It derives its unity and analytical force from constituting the gender order as integral to the concept of society, and as, potentially, primary. By addressing the most basic social division of patriarchy, male and female spheres, we begin to ask fundamental questions about the social patterning of gender.

The papers in this volume demonstrate, for example, that the private realm is by no means a sociological 'puppet regime' installed by the public domain. Porter shows how a rigid division of labour and separation of spheres between fishermen and their wives, in which the male activity of fishing predominated socially and economically, shifts under the impact of changes in the position of, and opportunities for, women. As women acquire education and enter clerical and/or industrial occupations, so they transform their role from fisherman's wife to that of wife–housewife and/or worker, thus crucially altering the way in which the public male sphere intersects with the private realm of the family.

In his discussion of the churching of women, Rushton shows how the male ritual of purifying women polluted by childbirth has been subverted through incorporation into, and redefinition by, the female culture of motherhood. This process has resulted in the ritual being characterised by a lack of doctrinal and theological clarity and ambivalence on the part of the Church hierarchy.

Finch's working-class mothers who take their children to playgroups actively use the playgroup structure, and their own definitions of what constitutes good mothering, to construct a powerful form of social stratification in the private sphere. This social hierarchy exists independently of stratification systems which arise out of occupation, work and class in the public sphere, but assists in spelling out and refining social divisions in the public domain.

Another way of addressing the family–society relationship is to look at men as the recipients and controllers of female servicing. Imray and Middleton's wives have responsibility not only for housework and child-care, but also for producing the material conditions of their husband's leisure. In this case the recipients of leisure services, or the cricket team, define their leisure as a public activity, although, technically, cricket is played outside the confines of work and the marketplace. Murcott is concerned with the social significance of cooking which, she argues, is not a description of transforming groceries into meals, but entails a concept of service performed by wives for husbands. Ungerson examines the role of female kin in caring for dependent relatives. She unpacks the contradictions in the ideologies of motherhood which are used to justify community care (or unpaid service work in the private realm), but which are deemed inappropriate for underpinning and guiding caring behaviour.

Allatt approaches this issue by examining educational programmes set up for the armed forces during the Second World War. She demonstrates how the ideologies of 'morale' were utilised to perpetuate a vision of the private as a male right, and how the reasons for fighting were subtly transformed from exclusively public ones, to do with the state and relations between states, to preservation of the conditions of the private, or family life. By focusing on what all men possessed, the army attempted to obscure that which divided them, thus constructing consensus in the public sphere of war by uniting soldiers around the issue of their place in the gender order.

These papers pose a feminist critique of the sociological common-sense notion which claims that industrialisation or capitalism 'eliminated' a large number of family functions and that, by corollary, the impersonal public nature of industrial society has all but eradicated kinship structures, and the personal rights and obligations associated with them, as determinants of social behaviour. Indeed, to present the issues in their boldest form, the thrust of the argument in these papers is that male rights to female servicing unite all men on one common dimension to the private realm. To stretch the argument even further, one could claim that the public sphere, characterised by male competition over resources and power, is made possible not by that competition and conflict, but through the advantages that men gain through female servicing. It is the flow of services from women to men (especially, but not exclusively) in the marriage relationship which creates that time, space and energy for men in the public sphere and unites them all. Female servicing constructs a firm base for male social solidarity; it defines the common interests of men otherwise divided by class and power.

This transvaluation of the public/private relationship is emphasised further by the discussion of the boundaries between the two spheres. Imray and Middleton argue that the public sphere is the social and physical space occupied by men, from which women are actively excluded by male bonding rituals which stress and reproduce gender divisions.

They show how men attribute public (and private) status to structures and processes, and how women constantly threaten this definition by intruding into public space.

Hanmer and Saunders address this issue of boundaries by focusing on male violence and its effects on women. They are concerned with practical effects on women's lives, and with the way in which women define male violence as a feature of the public rather than private sphere. It is this definition of violence which ideologically separates the two spheres, and which thus obscures violence in the private sphere by defining it out of existence. Thus the notion of the private realm of the family as the safest and best space for women is reproduced in ideology.

But the social construction of boundaries does not imply social separatism. Male rights to female servicing constitute the private as controlled by men. Men actively circumscribe women's leisure (Imray and Middleton), the public sphere of male work regulates cooking and mealtimes (Murcott), and the public sphere of welfare provisions dictates the content of female tending activities (Ungerson). The public sphere intrudes into the private sphere by means of the power attributed to men as recipients of female servicing.

Sociology partakes of this contradictory and shifting social construction of the public/private dichotomy. McKee and O'Brien focus on the problem of doing sociological research, especially when this occurs at the intersection of the public and private domains. They discuss female sociologists interviewing fathers, both husbands and single fathers. The husbands, located unambiguously in the public realm, and therefore in possession of the rights of service Murcott and Imray and Middleton discuss, and Allatt depicts as central to the post-war welfare state consensus, respect the women's public sociological persona. On the other hand, the single fathers, who straddle the public/private divide and who have lost their right to unpaid servicing, privatise this public encounter between interviewer and interviewee as a way of asserting rights over the private.

Graham discusses in detail the sociological survey method and argues that it is a methodology derived from features that characterise the public sphere of male work. Since the private sphere is organised around entirely different sets of social relationships, she questions the suitability of public methodologies for describing and explaining the social realities of women's lives. She claims that the methodological privileging of public structures and processes contributes to the silencing of women in sociology.

The public/private split is a metaphor for the social patterning of gender, a description of sociological practice, and a category grounded in experience. As a model, it directs us to the structure of gender relations, as expressed in institutional, spatial, symbolic and controlling mechanisms. Clearly gender is mapped both onto and across the divide.

Sociology has, until recently, taken for granted the existence of this divide, by concentrating on the public sphere and by conforming to patriarchal ideologies in its treatment of the private realm as (more or less) unproblematically subordinate. As a result it has, to a large extent, defined gender out of existence. Considerations of gender, therefore, cannot simply be grafted onto existing models and theories. Gender can only become an integral part of sociological analysis if we adopt conceptual spectacles which will cure our theoretical tunnel vision which, as mentioned earlier, vastly oversocialises the public sphere and cannot embrace the social significance of the private. We hope that the papers in this volume, which confront sociology with feminist insights and thus stretch its conceptual frontiers, will assist in clarifying how the traditional concerns of sociology have reproduced the gender order through the categories of the public and the private. Sociology cannot continue to ignore the female majority of the population, as Stacey points out in her presidential address (in this volume), and to treat the male minority as a genderless norm. We, therefore, hope also that this collection will show how theorising gender, or socialising the private sphere, can expand and enrich sociological practice.

Acknowledgements

To Anne Dix, the BSA Secretary, whose efficiency and long experience of BSA Conferences made the organising of the Conference a pleasure rather than a task.

To Mike Milotte, the BSA Publications Officer, for his effective mediation between ourselves and the publishers.

To all our Colleagues on the BSA Executive for their support and encouragement in preparing these volumes.

And most of all, to the BSA Women's Caucus, without whose militant concern to inject feminism into sociology the 1982 Conference would never have taken place.

2 Social Sciences and the State: Fighting like a Woman*
Meg Stacey

In front of my desk there is a card on which is reprinted a short poem from *Hens in the hay* (1980). The poem, by Stephanie Markman, is called 'the male tradition' and it runs:

> standing-up-and-fighting-like-a-man is a good deal
> easier than sitting down and writing like a woman.

A gender-bound discipline

There is no doubt it is difficult to write like a woman. The problem is that we lack the terms to express the concepts which we as women understand. They are not in the literature or in the conceptualisation of a male-dominated discipline. Sociological concepts and terms, as I have explained in the 'Two Adams' paper (Stacey, 1981) and as others, notably Smith (1974), have also pointed out, were devised by men about the male world of the public domain and about the family as it was seen by those men. Those concepts and terms have a crippling effect on any attempt to understand the world of women and men and not just the world of men. This effect is found in all schools of sociological thought, whether they stem from Marx, Durkheim or Weber. These concepts and terms are quite inappropriate to deal adequately with the private world of the family. They are also inappropriate to deal with all those tasks of education, nurture and care when these move from the private to the public domain, from the historical domain of the women to that of the men. The concepts are also inappropriate to deal with those tasks which, like nursing, are undertaken in both the private domain (unpaid) and in the public domain, where they are paid at market rates depressed because they are 'women's work'. The confusions which abound in the analysis of professions can be related to

---

* From the BSA Presidential Address, delivered at the *Gender and Society* Conference. Selections reprinted from *Sociology*, Vol. 16, no. 3, by kind permission of the author and Editor.

this conceptual lacuna and result in such awkward notions as the 'semi-professions', not only an unhelpful concept but insulting to those (mostly women) in the occupations so labelled.

There was a second reason why in that 'Two Adams' paper I called for a fundamental rethink of the sociological concepts associated with the division of labour: the male domination of sociological terms and concepts and the partial nature of the associated theories actively contributes to the continual re-creation of the male dominated gender order and thus to the continued oppression of women.

A time to fight

The problems that are associated with sitting down and writing like a woman are thus becoming clearer, but there are times when it is necessary to stand up and fight. As sociologists, as social scientists, as human beings and as women, we have one of these times upon us now. We are experiencing in this country a serious attack upon the knowledge base of the entire society, upon academic freedom and particularly upon the social sciences and sociology among them. This attack is part of a new immiseration being imposed upon our entire people, as the welfare state is run down and government permits the highest rates of unemployment we have experienced since the 1930s. In these circumstances we have to fight, not only for ourselves but for the continuation of what we hold valuable in our society. The battle is taking place in the public domain, a domain, which despite our legal rights, is still dominated by men. Too many of the very few women in the public domain have learned to think and act like men.

The need to fight in this man's world poses a new problem for women. If it is hard to sit down and write like a woman, it is even harder in my experience, to stand up and fight like a woman. Since fighting has been man's work there is a grave danger that we shall all, women and men alike, fight like men. If so our fight will be in vain. There is no point in fighting for a world which will continue the oppression of women, of the relatively poor and powerless, of the working class, of the ethnic minorities. In any largely defensive struggle, fought on ground chosen by others, there is the danger that conservative positions are taken up and that a reactionary outcome will ensue: the paradoxical danger is that in fighting we betray that for which we fight.

If we are forced to fight it is essential therefore that we should be clear what it is we are about. One of those things has to be to establish a more just and equitable gender order and also to continue to work to refurbish our sociological concepts, terms and theories, in such a way that they are more capable of the task of analysing society than they are at present. This is why I say we have to find out what it is to fight like a woman. One of the ingredients has to be that the fight is not conducted so that the outcome is in the interests of men and of elite, upper class men at that.

The role of sociologists
What part then do sociologists have to play in all of this and how is it that I say we should learn to fight as a woman would?

Taking the sexism out of sociology
One of our major tasks is to continue to put our own house in order, vigorously to go about taking the sexism out of sociology. There are, as Roberts and Woodward (1981) have pointed out, two related but distinct aspects to this problem. One I have already alluded to: the gender-bound construction of sociological knowledge. The other is the problem of sexual divisions in the sociological labour force. On this score the account which can be made of sociology is a good deal more creditable than that of many other academic disciplines, notably than the physical sciences and even some of the social sciences such as economics and political science. However, as Roberts and Woodward say 'while there has been some movement in the employment of women in British sociology over the last thirty years, their representation in the profession is not as great as one might expect from the undergraduate numbers, ability and performance' (p. 544). Nor is this, as plenty of evidence now shows, because of any lack of industry or production on the part of those women who have survived into higher levels of academic employment including those who are married and with children (Blackstone and Fulton, 1975, 1976).

The contribution of women
There are alternative ways of approaching change, the restrictive and the imaginative. And it is here that I think we women probably have something important to offer. We have not been involved in these last years in accepting the society we find ourselves in. We have been engaged in finding ways to recreate society so that it shall be more human. We have had to work our imaginations hard to think of ways in which good aspects of women's experiences, for example the joyous parts of motherhood, the rewarding facets of family life, can be retained and enhanced at the same time as we shed what Rich has called 'the institutionalized violence of patriarchal motherhood' (1977, p. 263). Women have had to work their imaginations hard to think of ways in which (whether we want to have children or not) we can live without male domination and without oppressing other women, or live as lesbians and yet have and rear children. We have not found all the answers, but we are used to looking beyond the frontiers of our society and trying to imagine a world in which women might be liberated.

There is nothing naturally inherent in women as biological beings which necessarily makes us behave differently from men in administrative, academic or political office. The structural position asserts its imperative on women just as much as on men. Our great ability to conceive and bear children does make fundamental differences, but need not lead to the assumptions that are at the base of the patriarchal family: other arrangements are possible. The potential we have as women at this historical moment comes from our collective situation. Our potential is not only negatively to resist being pushed back into an alienating private domain. It comes from a vision which may well be a new transcendentalism. Those of us who have understood feminism in collectivist rather than individualistic terms have a concept of womanhood which embraces all women in all conditions in all places. The notion of liberation for us is something which transcends our own particular experience although each of our experiences is one with it. It is the shared experience of motherhood, of daughterhood and sisterhood, in a variety of patriarchal societies which have been variously oppressive. It is the consciousness of belonging to a movement of women. It has no place for any supine or passive attitudes.

My proposal about what women have to offer is not without empirical referent. Pauline Hunt (1980) has shown how women, fresh from and still linked to the domestic experience, less subjected than men in their previous work to the calculative relations characteristic of capitalism, are not prepared to accept the unpleasant working conditions that men have come to expect over the years. Women, that is, in Audrey Wise's words, are putting up a fight to stay human. Pauline Hunt argues that precisely because women are out to find satisfaction in their place of work they are more likely to be politically assertive. The women may be inexperienced in trade union matters, less schooled in the ethos of capitalism, but may take a more positive view of work and thus be more obstinate, more aggressive and carry with them a greater potential as fighters for change.

What is true of women workers may also be true of women academics. We have fought hard for the places we have got; some of us have had to deny ourselves children for them; many carry the double burden, but we want our paid work. Women's jobs may be more at risk even than those of the men, but women know what we have to fight for and why it is worth it.

It is well for the British Sociological Association that it accepted the challenge presented to it by the women in 1974 and that it has (despite difficulties and oppositions) supported the struggle of women to play a full part in the discipline. Sociology needs women at this time. But women will only join cause with those who accept the unity of human kind (without which concept as Morris Ginsberg long ago pointed out, none of the social sciences is possible); who accept the equivalent worth of women and men. We will not be happy to engage in a fight for our continued oppression. If the struggle for academic freedom and for the social sciences is predicated upon liberation and imagination, then it may well be possible to recruit the anger that women have learned from oppression and the creativity they have developed in aiming to emerge from it. Women will not be supine. We have our own struggle anyway. The struggle to preserve and improve the social sciences and the institutions of learning is part of that same struggle. Civilisation and human dignity are both involved. Let us all continue to fight 'like a woman' with vision, courage and determination in the common struggle.

3 Public and Private: Marking the Boundaries
Linda Imray and Audrey Middleton

> Men may cook, or weave, or dress dolls or hunt hummingbirds, but if such activities are appropriate occupations of men, then the whole society, men and women alike, votes them as important. When the same occupations are performed by women, they are regarded as less important.
>
> Margaret Mead, *Male and Female*

Introduction

Athough the concept public and private is increasingly popular in sociology, it seems to us that its contribution to the analysis of women's subordination is being obscured. In her ovular work, Michelle Rosaldo indicated the importance of the value which attaches to each sphere and it is this strand in her work which we shall focus on in this chapter.

We want to deal first with what we consider a major contradiction in her chapter in *Women, Culture and Society* (1974). She starts off by asserting, in our view correctly, an asymmetry in the cultural evaluation of male and female, in the importance assigned to women and men which appears to be universal.

> male, as opposed to female, activities are always recognised as predominantly important, and cultural systems give authority and value to the roles and activities of men (p. 19).

Everywhere, from societies that appear most egalitarian to those that demonstrate a marked degree of sexual stratification, men are the locus of cultural value. Some area of activity is always seen as exclusively or predominantly male and, more importantly, this activity or group of activities has a meaning within the society which is associated with prestige. This observation has its corollary in the fact that everywhere men have some authority over women, that they have a culturally legitimated right to their subordination and compliance. At the same time, women themselves are far from helpless. They can and do exert pressures on the social life of the group, whether or not their influence is acknowledged.

Rosaldo goes on to site her argument fairly and squarely in, what she calls, a near-universal fact of human experience, that 'a good part of a woman's adult life is spent giving birth to and raising children' (1974, p. 23). Thus there is an opposition between what women do and what men do, which she expresses in terms of domestic and public orientations and which provides the basis of a structural framework necessary to identify and explore the place of female and male in psychological, cultural, social and economic aspects of human life.

It is the definition of what constitutes the domestic which seems to us to confound her analysis. Domestic, for Rosaldo, 'refers to those minimal institutions and modes of activity that are organised immediately around one or more mothers and their children' (p. 23). This definition leads her into the trap of implying the immutable, unchanging nature of women's activities. Although we would not deny that everywhere women do bear and rear children, not all women do it and for those who do it does not necessarily take up all of their adult lives. In any case there is no reason to suppose that the meaning that attaches to women as bearers and rearers should not change. Because she defines the domestic so narrowly and rigidly, she is moving away from the opposition between what is valued and what is not valued and its relevance for gender asymmetry towards a simplistic division between what women do as 'nature' and what men do as 'culture'.

Her article in *Signs* (1980) indicates her awareness of the dangers in assuming that the meaning attaching to women as reproducers remains constant, and she is concerned to refute her earlier claims for the analytical importance of concepts that have a universal application. She warns us of the dangers of thinking about a social world in ultimately dichotomous terms, where woman is universally opposed to man in the same ways in all contexts, which prevents us from asking questions about the varying social contexts within which gender differences are pepetuated. This universal application, she says, traps us within a conceptual tradition that discovers 'essence' in the natural characteristics which distinguish women from men.

The trap which Rosaldo is aware of is not one which is set by using the concept private/public, but rather by an assumed split between women as natural, reproductive beings and men as cultural, economic, political beings. For Rosaldo, reproduction and lactation have provided a functional basis for the definition of a domestic sphere. Moreover, it is these activities of bearing/rearing *only* which belong in the domestic sphere. But, in our view, she is mistaken in rejecting the concept of private/public as one which leads us merely to construct assumptions about how gender really works.

We will argue that a model based on the concept of private and public spheres may throw light on the universality of male dominance and show

how the boundaries between what is valued and what is not valued change over time and between and within cultures. We hope to demonstrate that an analytical separation of the spheres can clarify the meaning of the activities which take place in concrete social situations. Throughout human societies, what men do is valued above what women do, even if both women and men do the same things in the same places at the same time. The opposition between private and public, then, is not seen as opposed activity, but rather in terms of power relationships which are thrown into sharp relief by rituals that mark these boundaries.

The economic boundary
Just as Rosaldo's analysis of what constitutes the private and the public is inadequate because of her emphasis on the significance of reproduction for gender asymmetry, so we see Marxist analyses of women's position as equally inadequate because they take as their central tenet the relationship of women to the economic system. Perhaps the most stark example of this tendency can be found in the domestic labour debate (e.g. Dalla Costa and James, 1972; Gardiner, 1975; Seccombe, 1973). Marxism enables us to understand many aspects of capitalism, but in the same way as capital creates 'empty places' and is indifferent to the individuals who fill them (Braverman, 1974), so the categories of Marxist analysis do not explain why particular people fill particular places. As Hartmann (1981b) observes, they give us no clues about why women are subordinate to men inside and outside the family and why it is not the other way around.

If we use a Marxist analysis in our attempts to explain gender asymmetry we are not only limited to a discussion of the sexual division of labour, i.e. a discussion of what people *do*, but we are also left searching around for a material base upon which we can build explanations of patriarchal structure. The blinkered nature of Marxist categories and the Marxist method of social analysis insist that the only valid analysis of women's oppression is one which is grounded in materialism. Thus we are prevented from asking questions about the enduring nature of patriarchal power. For example, although material bases may change from society to society, male violence against women is constant.

While not denying that the economic may be of great relevance when we talk about women's position, to argue that it has always, throughout history and across cultures, had the same degree of relevance is an assumption which has led to an Engelsian prescription for women's emancipation: namely that capitalism would abolish sex differences and treat all workers equally; that women would become economically independent of men and would participate on an equal footing with men in bringing about the proletarian revolution; and that after the revolution, when all people would be workers and private property abolished, women would be emancipated from capital as well as from men. Whatever may be the arguments that state socialist societies fall far short of a Marxist ideal, evidence from the USSR, China, Vietnam and the GDR suggests that despite women's full entry into the labour force they are not only under-represented at the top of professional and political pyramids but that patriarchal power is alive and flourishing (Rowbotham, 1972; Einhorn, 1981).

Violence against women belongs to a whole area of continuing social reality to which the GDR has difficulty in admitting. This situation results from the mechanistic view that with the abolition of private ownership of the means of production, *all* forms of exploitation would automatically disappear. Thus rape, mugging and other forms of violence against the person have no official existence in the GDR (Einhorn, 1981, p. 449).

This would suggest a return to the tried, tested and partially successful patriarchal strategy of denying the existence of male domination, denying women access to the means of recording the substance of male power and then telling women that it's all in our heads. Moreover, it demonstrates the way in which concepts and systems of analysis developed to explain the world as men see it confound explanations of the world not only as women experience it but also the meaning of those experiences. As Dale Spender observes, 'the world of women is defined out of the subject matter and the devaluation of women is thereby doubly enforced' (1980, p. 68).[1]

We do not deny that capitalism, in common with other economic and political formations,[2] has made use of patriarchal structures in instances of mutual benefit.[3] Cultural expression of sexual asymmetry may indeed be associated with economics, but it is often found in other domains of activity as well. Among the Yoruba of Nigeria, women may control a good part of the food supply, accumulate money and travel long distances to trade in important markets. Yet, before going out to spend the day in the marketplace, the Yoruba wife curtsies deferentially to her husband. When approaching her husband, she must feign ignorance and obedience and kneel to serve him as he sits (Lloyd, 1965; Callaway, 1981). In the Jewish ghetto communities of Eastern Europe, women had great influence. They were strong and self-confident mothers, receiving loyal support from their sons; through their close contacts throughout the community they shaped most political events. In the household a woman kept control of the income and dictated family spending, and in wealthy families it was women and not men who ran the family business. Yet wives would still defer to their husbands, were still segregated in the upper galleries of synagogues, and their greatest joy was to have a male child (Zborowski and Herzog, 1955, quoted in Rosaldo, 1974). And Marilyn Strathern (1972) found that although the women of Mount Hagen in the Western Highlands of New Guinea are responsible for production, they are considered the servants of men, they have no political power, and they do not control valuables. Hagen men evaluate women's activities as producers in terms of low status: production is not as valued as making transactions (men's work). Prestige derives from being able to influence people and from demonstrating power over exchange partners and clansmen alike. In Mount Hagen, then, 'producers' (women) are located in the private sphere while 'transactors' (men) are in the public.

The association of the private sphere with what is done inside the household and of the public sphere with what is done outside the household is, we suggest, a reflection of the currency Marxist and much sociological analysis has in the conceptualisation of women's subordination. This synonymous use of the concept has been instrumental in its devaluation as a possible explanatory tool since it perpetuates the assumption that it is the activity which characterises the sphere rather than the actor. Activities in themselves have no absolute and unchanging value, be they economic, political, cultural. Rather, value accrues to activities by virtue of who performs them and more importantly who controls their social meaning and importance. We seek to demonstrate that it is not work *per se* which is valued and which is part of the public sphere, but rather that it is work done by *men*.

The role of trade unions
Within systems of waged labour, one of the means by which the value of work is illustrated is in the levels of cash paid. Before the Equal Pay Act, women were consistently paid less for doing the same jobs as men. Establishment by employers of an all-female workforce was a strategy used to buy cheap labour, thus keeping wages low for everyone, men included, since occupations in which women predominate were (and still are) low value occupations. The fact that women could earn wages separately from men also undermined authority relations between the sexes: not only were women cheap competition but also working women were men's 'very wives, who could not "serve two masters" well' (Hartmann, 1981b, p. 20). Thus male workers marked the boundaries between men's work and women's work by resisting the wholesale entrance of women into the workforce and seeking to exclude them from union membership.

The union fight for protective labour laws for women limited the participation of adult women in many 'male' jobs[4] and the demand for a family wage not only raised male wages generally and so reinstated the cash value of labour, but also firmly established a private sphere for each individual male wherein he was serviced by his wife. Of course, women were not forced out of the labour market completely but only out of certain sections. Catherine Hall's work on the Birmingham middle class between 1780 and

1850 shows a significant shift towards a concentration of women in certain trades (Hall, 1981).

The growth of the female occupational ghetto is such that if we look at the present day distribution of women in the labour market we find that in Great Britain 68% of women who work full or part-time are found in three service and four manufacturing industries. Within these industries the sorts of jobs that women do further illustrates the extent of segregation. According to the 1966 Census, 2.8 million women, nearly a third of the female workforce, were working in occupations where women constituted 90% of the workforce.[5]

Thus we see a shifting of the boundaries: a pattern of women's employment where women, by and large, are structured out of men's jobs and channelled into industries and into occupations within industries where their value as workers so far as financial reward is concerned is minimal. And of course the Equal Pay Act is ineffective as far as individual claims in these areas are concerned since a woman needs to be able to compare her work tasks with those of a man, a requirement which has rarely been challenged by unions. In sum, then, the wage differential is one of the ways women's work in the labour force is defined as being of less value than men's work.

Demands for higher wages are made through trade unions, where women are notoriously under-represented, both as members and as officials. Women *themselves* are frequently blamed for their lack of participation in union affairs.[6] We would contend, however, that it is precisely because trade unions exist to represent male interests that women have either been excluded or, if they are union members or officials, are actively prevented from participating fully.[7] If we look at trade unions as sites of patriarchal bonding which serve to make public space for men to gather as *men* in order to maintain and perpetuate the boundary between the public and private spheres, this may throw some light on the strategies unions and unionists adopt to exclude or peripheralise women.

One woman Imray interviewed told of her experiences as the only female union official in her branch. She made elaborate child-care arrangements so that she could attend union meetings, making sure she had the entire evening free. She learnt the official union language so that she could interrupt proceedings with 'points of order' in the same way as her male colleagues. She learned to play the male game. She was frequently surprised, however, that decisions seemed to be made without the full discussions they merited, unless they happened to be concerned with women's affairs such as nursery provision. She became increasingly aware, also, of the solicitousness with which, after meetings had formally ended, the male officials ensured she caught her bus home. On several occasions she was given a lift home in one of the men's cars – a considerable distance out of his way. The consideration turned out not to be an example of male 'chivalry' but one of male exclusion, since having seen her safely home, the male officials repaired to the club and proceeded with the *real* union meeting. It was in the club that full discussions took place, that decisions were made which were merely ratified in the official meetings. When she realised the relevance of her exclusion from the unofficial club meetings and challenged the men, they responded by saying that all decisions that concerned her were made at the official meeting. The get-together in the club was just to talk about 'general' matters which would bore her anyway. They assured her that they all tried very hard to fit discussions of issues that would interest her into the official meeting so that she could get off early, back to her child. This woman's experience indicates the control that men exert over women who invade the public sphere. They relegate to women those issues they define as women's affairs, which belong to the private sphere, and they protect the boundaries they themselves set between the two.

The political boundary

We have so far concentrated on the private and public spheres as they affect women at the lower end of the labour market. We are now going to look at what happens to women who invade the 'male territory' of political life at the highest level. The seats of power are everywhere a 'male preserve'. Silvia Rodgers (1981) makes this point when she compares an Iatmul Men's House in New Guinea and the Askwẽ-Shavante Men's House in Brazil with the British House of Commons, basing her analysis on the work done by Bateson (1967) among the Iatmul and Maybury-Lewis (1967) among the Askwẽ-Shavante. Bateson found that among the Iatmul, the men occupy themselves with aggressive and public activities 'which have their centre in the ceremonial house', while the women quietly carry out the mundane activities concerned with food preparation and child-rearing 'which centre around the dwelling house and gardens' – the domestic space (1967, p. 123). Women are *never* allowed into the Men's House, but they are expected to listen outside when the men are preparing for the most important rituals. For women to be found inside the Men's House would be symbolic of the disintegration of the community.

The Askwẽ-Shavante of Brazil show similar divisions between the sexes. Here, too, women are forbidden to enter the Men's House and to see full ceremonies but they are allowed to listen.

Until the old House of Commons was burned down in 1834, women in Britain were allowed to hear the activities going on in the Chamber from the roof space where they were concealed. After the fire, the building was redesigned but it was still basically a Men's House with no provision for women *inside* the Chamber. 'The role of women who were wives or friends of the political élite was acknowledged in their special assignment to the peripheral Ladies Gallery' (Rodgers, 1981, p. 53).

In the new House, rebuilt after the Second World War, there is just one space in the House which is used by all women members irrespective of party, and *only* by women, and that is the toilet just outside the Chamber. There are in addition two sets of rooms, each marked 'PRIVATE, LADY MEMBERS ONLY'; one set of these is used by women members of the political left and the other by women of the political right[8]. Men's toilets are simply marked 'MEMBERS ONLY' which has led new women members into embarrassing mistakes. There would seem to be an implicit assumption, even though the House was rebuilt at a time when women were eligible for election to membership, that members are men. As Shirley Williams commented in 1979, this 'tells one quite a lot about the House of Commons' (*Guardian*, 10 October 1979).

Rodgers points to the sacred nature of the Chamber in the Durkheimian sense of being a 'place apart'. To those on the floor of the House, people sitting in the galleries are, in theory if not in fact, *invisible*. They are not seen, but like the women outside the Men's Houses in New Guinea and in lowland Latin America, not only can they hear but they are *expected* to listen. Shirley Ardener (1981, p. 20) comments: 'University wives, Jewesses and nuns in Church provide us with similar cases.' Rodgers says that the basic division between Members and Strangers is exemplified by this premise of invisibility which implies that business should be conducted as if no one were watching. The sacred nature of the Chamber is emphasised through its links with established religion: the daily procession and prayers conducted by the Speaker with his regalia (and witnessed only by members) echoes the rituals of the church; the neo-Gothic architecture closely resembles churches of the same period; and the protection afforded by parliamentary privilege is a conceptual reflection of the spatial dimension of the church sanctuary. This does not mean, however, that profanity and bawdiness are unknown in the House.

Membership of the House of Commons, which is in principle open to both women and men, in practice is far from being shared equally. Rodgers estimates that women members have less than 3% of the space in this legislature. Nevertheless, women *are* allowed this tiny piece of public space in what is constantly referred to by members as 'a men's Club' and Rodgers suggests that this is done by re-classifying women as men. This enables those women who are elected to the House to be absorbed into the political body, while preserving its masculinity.

However, as women in this Men's House, they are 'matter out of place' (Douglas, 1970) and as such are a threat to its purity and integrity. The men of New Guinea and lowland Latin America protect the boundaries of their Men's Houses with the threat of rape and assault. The men of the House of Commons are a little more subtle: 'Common practices include attempts to throw doubt on a woman's femininity, to question her legitimacy in the House, to place her on a different plane of reality' (Rodgers, 1981, p. 59). Nancy Astor was treated as though she were invisible: 'Men whom I had known for years would not speak to me if they passed me in the corridor' (Brittain, quoted in Vallance, 1979, p. 23). Some women members are reclassified into the category of men, given the status of 'honorary man' and gain the approval of male members for what are deemed male characteristics – ranging from clarity of mind to the capacity to drink beer. Other women members are seen as ruthless, tough and aggressive, characteristics which presumably also fit them into the category of men. Nancy Astor, however, 'who succeeded as a feminist rather than a parliamentarian' (Rodgers, 1981, p. 59) was described as a 'witch' and a 'termagent' – female creatures with negative powers. In entering the House of Commons *as a woman*, Nancy Astor constituted a threat similar to that posed by a woman entering the Iatmul Men's House and thus symbolising the disintegration of the community.

One problem the House of Commons has in reclassifying women members as fictive men is that women members sometimes become pregnant and are patently *women*. Women members who make no attempt to conceal their pregnancy evoke negative feelings from other members, although these feelings are seldom expressed directly but communicated obliquely through joking.

If pregnancy is out of place in the House of Commons, the more so is breastfeeding; to breastfeed openly is a flagrant admission of womanhood. The knowledge that a woman member is breastfeeding provokes sniggers from some men and overt and covert hostility from some women members who fear that in being associated with someone who is breastfeeding they will be identified as 'women' and therefore 'out of place' in this male club. One woman member who breastfed in the House of Commons, and then had the nerve to campaign for a crèche in the House, was criticised as having 'gone too far'. Pregnancy, breastfeeding and child-care taking place within the House of Commons may be seen as the most private part of the private sphere moving into the most public part of the public; a rejection of and a challenge to the validity of the boundaries.

These boundaries of public space are often preserved by the deterrent of violence, as with the Men's Houses of New Guinea and lowland Latin America. Another, more subtle, mechanism used to keep women out of men's space is joking behaviour (Whitehead, 1976; Middleton, 1981). In the House of Commons, ribaldry based on women's physiological and anatomical features is used as 'an attempt to mark out the invading category as unsuitable, and to render it harmless and ineffective' (Rodgers, 1981, pp. 63-4). Rodgers suggests that joking is a method by which a dominant category defends itself against a disadvantaged but threatening category, the dominant category reinforcing its boundaries by joking about women's sexual features. In the House of Commons, joking is the symbolic and acceptable way of stating that members of the private sphere have no place in this public institution. Most of the joking is directed at those women members most resistant to reclassification as social males.

Significantly, on one occasion, the jeering was directed at a *group* of women members. Women members usually avoid sitting in a group because to do so categorises them as women rather than as members; but a group of women from the political left did so during the debate on the 1980 Corrie Abortion Bill Amendment Act (Stacey and Price, 1981, pp. 168-9). This defiant display of women occupying space *as women* who shared a common concern led to a barrage of ribald abuse from the men.

Another technique of male control of women in the public sphere is that of exaggerated courtesy. Middleton (1981) for example found that the male clique in the village where she was working defined the boundaries of the public sphere by at times displaying excessively chivalrous behaviour when she ventured into it. This controlled her behaviour in the public sphere and defined her as a member of the private sphere who needed the 'ticket' of a man to gain admission. In the House of Commons, displays of excessive courtesy are seen by Rodgers as yet another method of undermining the confidence of women MPs.

To reach the House of Commons in the first place and then to withstand such male attempts to erode their confidence, women members have to be strong. They have indeed succeeded in gaining places on the front benches. These are, however, in departments usually associated with women's issues. Education has been represented more frequently by a woman than any other department, and Rodgers suggests that this is because the traditional role of woman as educator and socialiser of children in the private domain has been transferred to the public domain.

The most valued offices of state have never been held by a woman. Departments that deal with finance, law and order, and relations with foreign powers – departments which handle the most secret materials – are closed to women. This exclusion of women from top secrets seems just as obvious and natural to one male Minister as to men in New Guinea and lowland Latin America; when asked why no woman had ever been Chancellor of the Exchequer, Home Secretary, or Foreign Secretary, he replied with the tautology: ' "None of the women are senior enough" ' (Rodgers, 1981, p. 66). Women members are excluded too from the positions of Leader of the House and Chief Whips. Considering the sacred nature of the House, it is interesting to note the explanations given for the exclusion of women from these offices: ' "A woman may be Prime

Minister, but she would never be able to have one of the jobs which deal with the internal arrangements by which the House conducts its affairs".[9] She would not be "on the right wavelength for the heart of the mystery"; "certain aspects of that inner mystery within a mystery could never be fathomed by a woman"; "that inner sanctum which no woman could penetrate" ' (p. 67).[10]

Rodgers concludes that Britain shares the belief with other societies that women should not be prominent in positions of power and control in the public domain. Having a woman Prime Minister cannot change the essential nature of the British Men's House. Only through a group of women acting as representatives of their sex might this be possible.

The social boundary: cricket in a Yorkshire village

We have discussed the marking of the boundaries in the areas of work and parliamentary politics but in order to indicate the ubiquity of these boundaries between public and private, we turn now to research being done by one of us (Middleton) in a small Yorkshire village. In this rural community, the reflection of the public and private spheres in geographical space is clear, and Middleton as a member of the private sphere who rejected reclassification as an honorary male found herself trespassing on public space and, as a result, being subjected to a continuum of male control ranging from courtesy, through gossip and ridicule, to violence and its threat (Middleton, 1981).

For the purpose of this chapter, however, we will concentrate on one activity in the village to illustrate the reflection of public and private spheres in village space. The activity is village cricket. The cricketers are a team of men from both middle and working-class backgrounds whose ages range from 14 to 60. They are the 'prima donnas' of the community: other village events are arranged around their fixture list. They give no support to other village activities and yet expect support from the community; they dominate the bar area of the sports and social club; and no other sport is allowed to take part on 'their' pitch – even in the off-season.

The cricket pitch is situated in the centre of the village, adjacent to the river. The clubhouse of the village sports and social club was designed so that the verandah overlooks the cricket pitch and not the tennis courts which stand in its shade. And the benches that stand on the clubhouse perimeter of the pitch have their backs fixed so that, sitting on them, one *has* to face the cricket field rather than the tennis courts.[11]

On a fine day when the cricket team is at home it seems as though the whole village turns out to watch. This may be because the cricket field is the best piece of public land in the village and does have access to the river, but the effect is of support for the cricket team. The verandah and steps of the clubhouse are packed with spectators; looking from the cricket field, men sit on the right of the french windows with women on the left.[12] Other spectators sit on benches or on the grass while, outside the token fence which marks the perimeter of the pitch, women push their prams, this evidence of female fecundity framing the purity of the male ritual within. No woman is allowed to set foot on the pitch.

But in the private sphere, women are hard at work producing leisure for men. Besides being responsible for maintaining the 'whites' of the team, there is a rota of women who provide teas for the cricketers. From early afternoon onwards, women may be seen arriving at the village hall, adjacent to the clubhouse, with plates of sandwiches and cakes which they carry into the kitchen. In the hall itself, they set up trestle tables onto which they load the food they have brought. They are not seen, nor do they see, but they are as vital to this production of a cricket match as are the women listeners outside the Iatmul and Askwē-Shavante Men's Houses.

When the men have been playing for a couple of hours, a woman emerges from the kitchen with a tray of drinks which she carries to the edge of the pitch where it is taken from her by a man who carries it to the 'square'.

At five o'clock, the teams leave the field for the village hall where the women serve them the food they have prepared. And after the return of the men to the field, the women clear the tables, dismantle them, wash up and go home where eventually they will be handed the grass-stained 'whites' to prepare for the next match.

After the end of the match, the two teams return to the clubhouse for showers. The corridor in which the men's changing rooms are located is forbidden to women, even though this corridor leads from the bar to the kitchen. Women who want to enter the bar from the kitchen have to walk around the outside of the building. However, most women are not usually to be seen in the bar after the match; having provided leisure for their men, they are not welcome. Later in the evening some wives do reappear in order to drive home husbands who have had too much to drink. Middleton has, however, stayed on in the bar on such occasions and has been subjected to the same sort of treatment as women members of the House of Commons who have ventured into the public sphere. She has either been reclassified as 'not there' by fellow officers and committee members[13] or subjected to the sort of joking that defines her as an 'object to be screwed'.

Once a year, however, women are allowed onto the 'square' on the occasion of the men versus women cricket match. This takes place on a weekday evening so that it does not interfere with the fixture list, and usually lasts between two and three hours. The men field a young, inexperienced side while the women's team comprises the wives of young cricketers plus young women from the village. They wear a 'uniform' of brief badminton skirts, tan coloured tights, men's cricket sweaters which reach almost to the hemline of their skirts, and plimsolls. They are watched from the club verandah by the established cricketers on the right and their wives on the left.

The play is accompanied throughout by a barrage of obscene comments on the play of the male cricketers from their more experienced colleagues on the balcony. The women, aware of the exposure of their legs, run awkwardly to field the ball to the accompaniment of sexual banter from the male spectators. To Middleton, sitting with one ear tuned in to the comments of the men, it seemed as though there were a *double entendre* a minute.

In this match, right-handed men have to play with their left hands and left-handers with their right, but the men still have enough control of the game to ensure, aided by instructions from the 'elders' on the balcony, that the game comes to its ritual end of the women winning by one run. Long before that point is reached, however, the men on the balcony show their impatience and contempt for their junior colleagues by shouting at them to 'get on with it' so that they can retire to the clubhouse for an evening's drinking.

Once a year, then, members of the private sphere are allowed onto the 'square' where they are encouraged to flaunt their femininity and where inexperienced cricketers are defined as 'women', being beaten by them. We see this event as a calendrical rite of status reversal, similar to the *Nomkubulwana* ceremony of Zululand[14] where 'a dominant role was ascribed to the women and a subordinate role to the men' once a year (Gluckman, 1954, pp. 4–11). The Yorkshire village ritual, in which the male cricketers are deliberately made weaker and the women are made to look strong has the long-term effect of emphasising the strength and permanence of the usual order. As Turner (1974, pp. 165–6) observes:

> Cognitively, nothing underlines regularity so well as absurdity or paradox. Emotionally, nothing satisfies as much as extravagant or temporarily permitted illicit behaviour. Rituals of status reversal accommodate both aspects. By making the low high and the high low, they reaffirm the hierarchical principle. By making the low mimic (often to the point of caricature) the behaviour of the high, and by restraining the initiatives of the proud, they underline the reasonableness of everyday culturally predictable behaviour between the various estates of society. On this account, it is appropriate that rituals of status reversal are often located either at fixed points in the annual cycle or in relation to movable feasts that vary within a limited period of time, for structural regularity is here reflected in temporal order.

After watching the men versus women's game in 1981, Middleton, as secretary of the sports and social club, decided to try to make some space for women in the village to play seriously as a team. Discreet enquiries in the village elicited the information that some women were keen to play hockey. It was about this time that the cricket club refused to pay an increase in 'rent' which had been imposed on all sections by the sports and social club. Middleton used this dispute to get support from the committee for her suggestion that hockey be played on the outfield of the cricket pitch during the winter. Support was given in the belief that the suggestion of a women's hockey team was merely a stick with which to threaten the cricket team into payment of 'rent' rather than a reality of eleven women wanting actually to play hockey. When this was realised, support was withdrawn. Not, however, before Middleton had had the matter discussed in several meetings, the minutes of which were posted out to committee members and passed from them to members of the cricket team.

Walking into the sports and social club bar one evening, Middleton was greeted with overt hostility – not even disguised as humour. Comments recorded included: 'I've no time for strangers who come into this village and try and change it'; 'Women will never be allowed to play on that field, it's ours by right of usage'; and – most tellingly – 'if women are allowed on the cricket pitch, this village will fall apart'. Compare this remark of a non-cricketing male villager with Bateson's comment on the Iatmul – that for a woman to be found inside the Men's House would be symbolic of the disintegration of the community.

The issue of a women's hockey team continues to be put on the agenda of committee meetings at which women are outnumbered fifteen to two. At the time of writing, consideration is being given to letting a hockey team play on the old school playing field which is unusable: it is adjacent to a busy trunk road, is uneven, gets flooded at certain times each year, and slopes down to the river. The football team has refused to use it as a practice ground, and the children's swings have recently been moved to a safer part of the village. A request for goalposts to the village charitable trust, which owns all the recreation grounds and which provided the cricket team with its roller and scoreboard, has not been acknowledged to date. The message is clear both from the committee of the sports and social club which has withdrawn its support for a women's hockey team now that the cricket team has paid its 'rent' and from the charitable trust which is effectively denying women access to public ground. Women, as a women's team, would be seen as 'matter out of place' (Douglas, 1970) on public land in this Yorkshire village.[15]

Conclusion

In this chapter, we have attempted to reassert Rosaldo's argument that an activity when performed by men is always more highly valued than when performed by women. When men act it is defined by them as acting within the public sphere; when women act men define it as acting within the private sphere. In doing so, we have focused mainly on institutions located in the public sphere to see what happens when women attempt to gain entry. We found that the public sphere has access to a plethora of resources to deal with such eventualities which together constitute control of the private sphere and, moreover, uses such control to mark the boundaries between the two.

Our work points to the need to study male institutions in order to uncover the ways in which patriarchal systems operate as well as concentrating on the effect on women of patriarchal domination. Put another way, we must study not only how women are constructed as subordinate but how male structures operate to keep them this way. However, as our illustrations have shown, access to 'the heart of the mystery' is denied women and we must therefore persuade our sympathetic male colleagues to turn their attention away from the study of the oppressed to a study of the powerful.

Notes
1 This 'double enforcement' of the devaluation of women is apparent in the structural absence of women from traditional stratification theory. This issue is addressed in the companion volume, *Gender, Class and Work*.
2 There is some evidence to suggest, for example, that with the institutionalisation of patriarchy in emerging state societies, ascending rulers literally made men the heads of their families (enforcing their control over their wives and children) in exchange for the men's ceding some of their tribal resources to the new rulers (Muller, 1977).
3 Hartmann (1981b) argues that union demands for the family wage are an instance of the partnership of capital and patriarchy.
4 For a discussion of the case of the 1842 Mines Regulation Act, see Jane Humphries (1981).
5 For a discussion of the 'feminisation' of certain categories of service work, see Fiona McNally (1979).
6 For a discussion of the myth of women as passive workers, see Kate Purcell (1979).
7 For further discussion of women in trade unions, see Cunnison and Pollert in the companion volume, *Gender, Class and Work*.
8 Rodgers was writing before the election of Shirley Williams as an SDP member; one assumes that she has no room of her own.
9 For a discussion of Mrs Thatcher's position in the House, see Rodgers (1981, p. 67).

10 Compare these remarks with those made by members of male secret cults that centre around sacred musical instruments and exclude women, e.g. the Mbuti (Turnbull, 1961) and the Mundurucú (Murphy, 1958).
11 Women, of course, are allowed to participate in tennis and thus pollute it so that within the sports and social club it has relatively low status. For an analysis of the concepts of pollution, see Mary Douglas (1970).
12 Hertz (1973b, p. 10) writes, 'Society and the whole universe have a side which is sacred, noble and precious and another which is profane and common: a male side, strong and active, and another, female, weak and passive; or, in two words, a right-side and left-side.'
13 Middleton is secretary of the village sports and social club.
14 Status reversal rituals are not confined to Zululand but take place in many southern African societies.
15 Middleton's suggestion that a women's hockey team should play on the outfield of the cricket pitch was greeted with incredulity by some male sociologists when she presented a paper on her work at a BSA Ethnography Study Group meeting in January 1982 (in Lancashire).

4 Blowing the Cover of the Protective Male: A Community Study of Violence to Women
Jalna Hanmer and Sheila Saunders

Violence to women from men is an intensely political area in which to undertake research. We conclude from the history of research funding on violence to women in Britain to date that social interests are served by knowing as little as possible about this widespread social phenomenon. Funding, when available, is for double checking the accuracy of information generated by agencies that serve women rather than attempting to assess the extent of the problem, how the work of effective groups can be extended and how poor quality state intervention can be improved (Hanmer and Leonard, forthcoming).

The study was a pilot in the conventional use of that term and also a way of developing research ideas that could be pursued by unfunded groups. We decided to seek interviews from every woman in six adjacent streets in an inner city area of Leeds, but not the most deprived. We wanted to ensure that the selection of women in and of itself would not define the type of violence, or its amount, and a neighbourhood study suited our limited funds. While we did not assume that we could find out the true incidence of violence to women, we wanted to gain as much information as possible about the 'dark figure' of violent crime, as well as ways of gaining information.

The survey area of six adjacent streets had 171 houses from which we obtained 129 interviews. The streets had a mixed population of single and married people, with and without children, living in multiple-occupied as well as single-family houses. The streets chosen had a minimum of non-white residents as we felt it was important to focus on the problem of the dominant cultural group. The sample was skewed towards the younger, highly educated and childless woman, but 10% were elderly women. The refusal rate from all sources was 16%. Although we varied the times of calls and never made fewer than three, we still did not find anyone at home at some of the houses in our area. In this paper we describe the results obtained, while the research problems and issues involved in the study are discussed elsewhere (Hanmer and Saunders, forthcoming).

First we describe how women perceived violence to themselves and other women. We were concerned to unpack a central paradox in the thinking and behaviour of women, i.e. that women expect and seek protection from men, the very group which abuses them. Next we describe the ways in which the state intervenes when men attack women. Our aim was to increase understanding of how male violence to women is socially constructed to perpetuate itself. Given the data collected we conclude that the perpetuation of violence from men to women is a circular system rooted in the division between private and public spheres of life for women. We analyse the importance of this division to the processes by which women are driven into greater dependency on men both individually and collectively and how this serves to make women more vulnerable to attack.

How do women define violence?

We could not assume agreement on which behaviours under which conditions constitute violence. The cultural consensus contained in generalities about the inappropriateness of using force in interpersonal relations quickly disperses into exceptions to the rule and variations in response once confronted with specific situations. This variable response has been observed in the criminal justice system, among other professionals who provide services for victims of violence such as doctors and other medical personnel, health visitors and social workers, and also the general public, as well as parties actually involved in violent encounters (Borkowski, Murch and Walker, 1981; Maynard, forthcoming). We were less concerned with defining a particular term than with locating the experiences and parameters within the general area. We therefore used a variety of words to trigger responses on aggressive episodes moving from what we thought would be more to less acceptable kinds of disclosure; that is, from threats, to violence, to sexual harassment.

The apparently simple device of accepting the criminal law with its various subdivisions as the sole criterion of violence would be a tidy solution only if there were consensus about the categories of behaviour to be labelled violent, their seriousness, and easily achieved agreement about whether or not actual situations are criminal offences. All these areas, however, are problematic. Wesley Skogan (1981, p. 10) sums up victimisation research in the US and Europe: 'that we are not agreed on what a crime is or how it may be isolated for measurement and analysis is indicative of how far victimisation research has yet to proceed'.

Most importantly, the type of aggression, the dominant organising principle for the criminal justice system's typology of crimes against the person, is not the major criterion used by the women interviewed. Because the criteria for defining behaviours as violent differ, the woman interviewed classed as threatening, violent or sexually harassing situations that fell outside the criminal law as well as within its categories. Further, there were some reports of situations where the criminal justice system would have prosecuted the woman as well as, or rather than, the man if the offence had come to their attention.

The women we interviewed reported a wide range of behaviour as threatening, violent, or sexually harassing. Two-thirds of our sample reported one or more incidents that they had experienced, witnessed or overheard happening to other women during the past year, a total of 211 incidents. Table 4.1 summarises the incidence and distribution of violent experiences.

Table 4.1 Incidence of reports of violence to self and others

	Violence experienced or witnessed		No violence experienced
	Number of incidents	Number of women	Number of women
To others	70	47 (36%)	82 (64%)
To self	141	76 (59%)	53 (41%)
Total	211	84[a] (65%)	45[a] (35%)

Note: [a] As some women reported violence (and no violence) both to themselves and others the total number of women is less than the sum of the column.

The number of women and incidents recalled were higher in relation to oneself than others. Women tend to see violence not only as their problem but also as one not shared by others. These results can probably best be explained as selective attention, but they are also consistent with the myth that violence is an unshared personal problem.

The common strand running through these reports of violence is the inability of the woman to control the initiation of the behaviour and the subsequent interaction. While we did not attempt to measure how frightened or out of control of the situation the women were or believed themselves to be, it seemed that the greater the uncertainty about the outcome the more terrifying the encounter. For example, visual violence where no, or minimal, words are exchanged, and no physical contact occurs can be amongst the most frightening of incidents. Genital exposure or being chased or followed were common visual encounters which were interpreted as violent. Exposure of the male genitals, or flashing, to a woman on her own in an isolated part of an open space or deserted street may engender fears of injury and death because of the uncertainty about what may happen next. It is only after the encounter that the label, flashing, or 'only flashing' is put upon the event. Murder or rape or being seriously beaten up and/or sexually assaulted may be the feared outcome while the encounter is going on.

Uncertainty about the outcome is influenced by a number of factors such as previous experience, how those interviewed were feeling about themselves and the world, interaction within the encounter, especially behaviour on the part of the aggressor that leaves room for speculation about his intentions, and the context itself. Important contextual factors are the climate of fear concerning violence from particular groups or individual men, whether or not the parties knew each other, the time and place of the encounter, and whether or not others are present. But these factors are not weighted equally. Because of the association of the private domestic world with known others and the public outer world with strangers there is a conflation of the location of a violent event with whether or not the victim and aggressor know each other which intensifies their relevance.

To look first at the encounters with strangers, in addition to the visual events of following, chasing and sexual exposure there were a number of accounts of women's inability to avoid verbal approaches by men while in public places, particularly the street, which were described as indecent, or sexually harassing or threatening. Verbal assaults from strangers could be accompanied by physical touching, bumping into, grabbing and there were also assaults that were primarily physical, including sexual attacks. Stranger assault also is repeated, but by different men. Women's sense of personal security and behaviour is profoundly shaped by their inability to control interaction with strangers.

Threatening and violent situations between people known to each other also can be of more than one type, with women reporting verbal and physical encounters including sexual attacks. An example of a less obvious and non-criminal experience that illustrates both individual variation and the difficulty of defining behaviour as threatening or violent when the parties know each other was given by a young woman who lived in a bed-sitting room house with a shared kitchen. She reported that a young man, also resident, made advances to her that included reading her a story that she thought pornographic. She considered moving in with a girlfriend until her absent boyfriend returned, but decided to stay and lock her door instead.

In this example the outsider to the event might interpret the woman's behaviour as collusive, but one may become involved in ways not intended or anticipated, given assumptions about shared understandings that often exist between people known to each other. The essential aspect was that she could not stop the approach being made nor terminate it at will.

This example also illustrates the relative ease of restricting encounters with the same man when it is possible to exclude a person from one's living space. The following archetypal example, already exposed by the work of refuges for battered women, illustrates how difficult this can be

(Binney, Harkell and Nixon, 1981). One woman, married for 22 years, whose recently-left husband had been violent for years reports,

> I stood it for my kids. He began hitting me when I was pregnant. He was arrogant, ignorant and violent. He fractured my nose, broke my ribs, nearly strangled me, smashed up the furniture.

In the past year he came to her place of work to threaten her which resulted in the involvement of her employers and police as well as being violent at home. Over the years her attempts to gain help from public agencies, including the church, proved fruitless.

Home, the location of known others and assumptions of shared values about social behaviour, is well illustrated by this woman,

> Everyday life is different. You argue for a little while. It does not mean he is going to murder you. It is different to what happens outside. Nothing wild. Just arguments.

This view is, of course, completely at odds with statistical fact, as he is more likely to murder her than a stranger, but often it feels safer to be injured, and possibly murdered, by someone known than not known as we do not believe anything really serious will happen. Minimising the importance of being attacked by someone a woman knows is not uncommon. For example, a woman reporting on an argument with her husband:

> I was beaten up, but not very much. I didn't suffer much from this.

Table 4.2 presents the relationship of the victim to the aggressor. More incidents with known aggressors were reported as witnessed or overheard in the neighbourhood between others than in self-reports. Comparing the percentages, 18% of all violence to the self was by a known other while 69% of all violence witnessed or overheard in the neighbourhood involved parties known to each other. This provides a partial cross-check exposing massive survey error. The prevalence of attack by strangers and known others, however, are similar to those obtained by US national crime surveys (Skogan, 1981). As would be expected women were less certain of relationships when reporting on incidents witnessed or overheard in Leeds generally.

While we do not know the true incidence of violence from known others or strangers, police and court data indicate that women are much more likely to be seriously assaulted or murdered by men known to them (Dobash and Dobash, 1980; *Criminal Statistics England and Wales*). That there are more known aggressors in violence to others than to oneself is consistent with the myth of the protective male; that is, the individual known other with whom the woman lives or sees more or less often is

Table 4.2 *Incidence of violence and the relationship of self and other women to aggressor(s)*

	Relationship to aggressor			
Incident occurred to	Known	Unknown	Do not know	Total
Self	25 (18%)	110 (78%)	6 (4%)	141
Others				
Neighbourhood	29 (69%)	2 (5%)	11 (26%)	42
Leeds generally	9 (32%)	5 (18%)	14 (50%)	28
Total	63 (30%)	117 (55%)	31 (15%)	211

protective while strangers are not to be trusted.

Table 4.3 presents the location of the violent event. Almost half of the women reported that incidents took place in streets and open spaces. When other public locations are included, more than half of the reported encounters took place in public. More incidents occurred at home to neighbours than self, illustrating the same cross-check and survey error mentioned above. The results shown in Table 4.3 are consistent with the myth that the home is safe while public places are not.

Public space includes pubs, clubs, railway stations and other buildings. Women described verbal incidents some of which escalated into physical encounters. An example, involving a known man,

> I went to a pub with a woman friend. Her ex-husband drinks there. He asked her to leave. He was drunk and got vicious and abusive to her and me. He didn't actually hit her but it got very close. We stayed in the pub and sat it out.

But this woman has not returned to that pub and the curtailing of move-

Table 4.3 *Incidence and location of violence to self and other women in past year*

	Location of the incident					
Incident occurred to	Home	Work	Public bldgs pub, clubs, transport stations, etc	Street and open spaces	Not clear	Totals
Self	30 (21%)	15 (11%)	16 (11%)	67 (48%)	13 (9%)	141
Others						
Neighbourhood	15 (36%)	— —	— —	25 (60%)	2 (4%)	42
Leeds generally	6 (21%)	— —	6 (21%)	11 (39%)	5 (19%)	28
Total	51 (24%)	15 (7%)	22 (10%)	103 (49%)	20 (10%)	211

ment is a not infrequent response to violent and threatening encounters in public.

While the context was used by the women interviewed to define violence and threatening situations and to grade their importance, we were struck by the similarity of the types of violence, including the intensity, that occurs in the public and private spheres, and how an encounter begun in one context can spill over into another. Thus violence at work may or may not be related directly to the work environment. For example, obscene and threatening phone calls from strangers reached into the work environment and husbands harassed women at their place of work. Many women were in occupations that serve the public such as barmaids in pubs or behind social security counters, where verbal abuse from customers and clients is seen, in practice, as part of the job.

Violence at home may or may not be directly related to the home environment. Our respondents report that violence may take place between members of the household or guests, that is friends, acquaintances, other family members, or it may come from total strangers. Violence from strangers in the home took many forms, from obscene and threatening phone calls, peeping Toms, to physical and sexual assaults.

And finally, violence in the street and public places may or may not be related to the public environment in the sense that it is the place where strangers meet. The expectation and fear is of attack from strangers, yet disputes also occur between people who know each other. Arguments and assaults between acquaintances, friends or married couples may begin and/or end outside the home or in any public location. We conclude from our evidence that the same types of interpersonal violence may occur in the street, or in the home, or in the workplace, and that specific violent events are not sealed off into private versus public domains.

But in order to discuss the relevance of this to understanding violence to women, we need to look at the experiences of our respondents in relation to the criminal justice system.

Views and experiences of the criminal justice system

With the assistance of the local law centre, the experiences of the interviewed women were categorised as criminal offences (Table 4.4). Where detail was sufficient to establish that an offence had taken place, but there was doubt as to the exact crime because of inadequate detail, the event was categorised as a minor crime.

The interviewed women suffered ten major crimes: one robbery, three rapes, two indecent assaults, three offences of grievous bodily harm and one of aggravated bodily harm. The 116 minor crimes (Table 4.5) were allocated to four categories: indecent exposure; obscene or threatening phone calls; assaults, battery, technical battery, breach of the peace

Table 4.4 Incidence of major-minor crimes to self and other women as defined by criminal law

	To self	To others	Total
Major crimes	10 (7%)	3 (4%)	13 (6%)
Minor crimes	116 (82%)	52 (75%)	168 (80%)
No crime and insufficient information to categorise	15 (11%)	15 (21%)	30 (14%)
Total	141 (100%)	70 (100%)	211 (100%)

A total of 84 women reported incidents. The column totals are more than the sum because some women reported more than one offence.

offences, loitering; and insulting or threatening behaviour. There were 15 events that could not be categorised as offences either because no crime had occurred or there were insufficient details.

With witnessed or overheard crime there were three major offences: one a Ripper-type attack and two assaults occasioning actual or grievous bodily harm, one by a husband and the other by a son-in-law. The minor crimes involving others could not involve indecent exposure, as to observe is to experience the incident, and there were no overheard obscene or threatening phone calls although in theory this is possible. The latter two categories contain all 52 observed minor crimes, i.e. assault etc. and insulting or threatening behaviour. There were 15 incidents involving no crime or insufficient details. The abstract right of women to redress through the criminal law should not be taken literally, however. If attempts were made to encourage the police to press charges, many of these offences might well be dismissed as no crime.

One question raised by our data is why do women report crimes of

Table 4.5 Types of minor crimes and their incidence

	To self	To others	Totals
Indecent exposure	22 (19%)	—	22 (13%)
Obscene or threatening phone calls	13 (11%)	—	13 (8%)
Assault, battery, technical battery, breach of peace, loitering	29 (25%)	27 (53%)	56 (33%)
Insulting behaviour or threatening behaviour	52 (45%)	25 (47%)	77 (46%)
Total	116 (100%)	52 (100%)	168 (100%)

violence against them? Even if an act of violence is perceived as a crime the victim or witness may prefer to confide solely in family and friends as did many of our respondents. It seems reasonable to assume that to report a crime one must expect to derive some benefit from doing so. This may explain the differential reporting rates between property theft and damage and acts of violence experienced by our respondents where insurance claims depend on reporting and the crime may be seen as particularly appropriate for police involvement. Of the 23 property crimes within the past year a minimum of 11 (48%) and a maximum of 19 (73%) were reported to the police. (It is unclear whether they were or not in eight.) This compares with 13% of crimes of violence.

The commonly held view expressed by Sparks, Genn and Dodd (1977, p. 116), '... the victim will presumably not notify the police if he regards the incident as too trivial to bother about', does not explain the experience of our respondents. To recognise an act as threatening, anti-social or hostile, which includes an assessment of the severity of the incident based upon the woman's experience and feelings and perhaps the response of known significant others, is only the first step in defining an event as a crime against the person. The next step is to define crime according to her understanding of the response of the criminal justice system. She may simply ask herself, 'Is this against the law?'

Our data indicates that women are more likely to base their actions on whether or not they think the police will consider the incident too trivial. For example, one respondent experienced three incidents. One of which, an indecent exposure, she reported to the police; the other two, an obscene telephone call and an assault (a youth kicked her while she was in a theatre queue), were not reported as she thought they were too trivial. She did, however, report these incidents to us which suggests that she perceived them as hostile acts against her. We suggest that her category, too trivial, is based upon her understanding of the likely social response to her victimisation.

The memory of previous experience with the police will influence a decision to report another. For example, a 17-year-old woman was raped on two separate occasions, but only the first, when she was raped by her uncle, involved the police. She said that she felt too ashamed to tell the police as they had not believed her the first time.

Women also accept responsibility for crimes of violence against them thus influencing decisions to report. For example, women who are raped may share the frequently held cultural view that the victim must have done something to provoke the attacker, even when he is a stranger. Another respondent, an expert in karate, large and physically able said that she had not contacted the police for,

Lots of conflicting reasons. I felt guilty. I felt that it was my fault because I had been drinking. I felt angry at myself for not having fought or screamed louder. I thought that I was really strong and that I could fight and was tough. But the violence that was coming from this man really frightened me. He really paralysed me. Now I actually view men with suspicion. All men I see as potential rapists and violent. I have since talked about it to friends who have had similar experiences.

Only 26 offences experienced or observed involved the police (Table 4.6). As might be expected, the proportion reporting violence to themselves was somewhat greater than that reporting violence to others. Of the major crimes to women only the robbery and one rape were reported. Women were more likely to report the legal minor crime of indecent exposure than any other crime. It seems that neither the women interviewed nor the police (see below) were guided in their actions by the legal distinction between major and minor crime to the extent that might have been expected. However, with witnessed crime the distinction between major and minor crime appears to be operating as all major assaults to others were reported while very few minor crimes were. The conclusion we draw from the experiences of women is that they are much more likely than the police to conceive of violence to themselves as serious. While this is a common-sense finding, the discrepancy is greater than might be expected.

Of the 26 only two women reported that a man was caught and charged, a prowler and a notorious rapist known as the Chapeltown rapist. The

Table 4.6 Offences reported to police

Type of offence	To self	To others	Proportion of total reported
Major	2	3	5/13 (38%)
Minor			
Indecent exposure	8	—	8/22 (38%)
Obscene or threatening phone calls	1	—	1/13 (8%)
Assault, battery, breach of peace	4	3	7/56 (13%)
Insulting or threatening behaviour	4	1	5/77 (6%)
Proportion of total reported	19/141 (13%)	7/70 (10%)	26/211 (12%)

repeated assaults of these men led ultimately to their arrest. Our respondent interrupted the rapist by coming in the front door before he attacked a woman living in the house, and as he had done nothing, this is categorised as a minor crime as is the prowler incident. Only 8% of reported crime led to an arrest so far as our respondents know, and none involved a major crime.

We asked two questions about satisfaction with police action. Table 4.7 presents the views of respondents on reported violence in the last year and Table 4.8 on the last contact with police. Just under half in both groups were satisfied when the report was of a violent crime. Satisfaction rates increased with reports of other offences. A recently completed British study of the views of victims on the criminal justice system response to interpersonal crime found that 85% were satisfied with police response (Shapland, Willmore and Duff, 1981). As with our study the crucial factor was police attitude at first interview, which also affected their decisions to report on other crimes. Satisfaction declined, however, as the victims of crime passed through the system, largely because of lack of information about how their cases were proceeding. In comparison, the women we interviewed were less satisfied, but our samples differ as it is not clear if the incidents reported to us were recorded as crimes by the police nor, if so, how far they had proceeded. In the study of Shapland and his colleagues informants were gained from police records, thus only those individuals the police had decided to treat seriously were interviewed.

Three complaints about police action stand out: not responding quickly enough to calls, not knowing the outcome of complaints, and the seriousness (or lack of) with which women were treated. Slowness to respond meant that several offenders left before the police arrived. After having given their account most respondents heard nothing more from the police, although in several incidents it is clear that something was noted in writing because the police returned at a later time. Women were concerned to be taken seriously and to be dealt with in a sympathetic manner. One woman, reporting an indecent exposure, said the police searched the streets, but although the offender was not found,

> I was much comforted and calmed by their [the police] behaviour. I was not made to feel it was a trivial incident or a waste of their time. The seriousness with which it was handled was most important.

Another women reporting the same offence was dissatisfied:

> They were not bothered, very disinterested. They took a statement and followed it up two months later with a visit from the vice squad. They wanted a better description. They asked if he had a beard.

The implication is that the incident was followed up because bearded

Table 4.7 *Satisfaction with police action - violence reported within past year*

	Violence to self		Violence to others		
	Major crimes	Minor crimes	Major crimes	Minor crimes	Total
Satisfied	—	9 (53%)	1 (33%)	1 (25%)	11 (42%)
Not satisfied	2 (100%)	8 (47%)	2 (67%)	1 (25%)	13 (50%)
Left before police arrived	—	—	—	2 (50%)	2 (8%)
Total	2 (100%)	17 (100%)	3 (100%)	4 (100%)	26 (100%)

Peter Sutcliffe (the 'Ripper') had been arrested. Our respondent was indignant because her experience was not treated with concern; interest was shown only when it might be linked to a major crime.

While there were a number of indecent exposure offences within a small geographical area, none of the offenders were apprehended so far as the women knew. For example, one woman said that the man who had exposed himself to her could be identified easily as he 'had a big belly, funny hat and limps'. Upon recounting the incident it emerged that two of her friends also had seen this man but so far as she knew the police had not picked him up. Satisfaction with police action did not seem to depend upon catching and prosecuting offenders, as women responded as if that would be expecting too much. 'What can the police do?' and 'They are doing as much as they can' are two comments which typify this attitude. Another way of viewing this is to say that male violence to women is not seen as contestable.

Table 4.8 *Satisfaction with police action - last contact initiated by woman and/or others on her behalf*

	Reasons for contact		
	Burglary and theft of own and others' property	Other misc. (e.g. missing dog)	Violence to women
Satisfied	28 (70%)	6 (100%)	10 (40%)
Not satisfied	10 (25%)	—	13 (52%)
No answer or not applicable	2 (5%)	—	2 (8%)
Total	40 (100%)	6 (100%)	25 (100%)

40 The Public and the Private

> A flasher, wearing a funny hat, with a long white beard and a wooden leg? I'm sorry, madam, that description doesn't give us much to go on!

If we look at what police do, on the whole we observe a pattern of minimal intervention. Both victims of major crimes were dissatisfied with police action. The raped woman said the hospital doctors called the police who took her to the station where she was questioned for approximately six hours and further examined medically. She said the police told the church sisters, who had taken her to hospital, that there was proof of rape but that her uncle had denied it. The police told the respondent that there was no proof and that she should let it drop for the family's sake. The outcome was that the aunt threw her out of the house and she was living alone in a bedsitting room at the time of interview.

The other major experienced crime was a robbery. A woman and her friend were pushed to the ground by a gang of youths who ran off with her handbag. Although dissatisfied the respondent expressed anger over the incident and a determination to contact the police again if she saw any of these youths. She had reported one man earlier who was interviewed but not charged.

In one witnessed crime as the respondent and her male friend turned a corner, they saw a woman lying on the pavement as a man fled. Her friend went to telephone the police while she stayed with the unconscious victim.

> The police came in fifteen to twenty minutes. One policeman asked my male friend some questions and took his address. I asked if he wanted mine which he took down reluctantly, and improperly as I later found out. The victim was taken away by ambulance and the police let us go home but they turned up at 3 a.m. saying that the first policeman should not have let us leave the scene of the incident. They said they didn't know as yet if the attack was connected to others in the area, but it seemed likely. They left saying, 'If we decide to treat this incident seriously, we may interview you again.' Three weeks later Jacqueline Hill was murdered in what seemed to me to be rather similar circumstances, i.e. not very late at night, a student, just off a main, well-lit road, hit on back of head, etc. The *Yorkshire Post* reported that the police said the attack I witnessed was not connected to other incidents in the area, but when the Ripper squad was increased, they said the case was 'being reviewed'. I never heard anything more, but Sutcliffe has not been charged with this assault. However, I believe that this was a Ripper attack and that if the police had decided to treat the incident seriously, Jacqueline Hill's murder might have been prevented. I should like this to be public knowledge.

In the two home-based assaults the women turned to neighbours for help. In one the woman left before the police arrived, while in the other the police tried to get the woman to charge her husband. This is customary in so-called domestics. The police do not arrest the man or take any action except perhaps move him on. They tell the woman that it is her responsibility to prosecute, which in this case, as in many others, she did not do. For many reasons a woman may not want to press charges; not least being that he will be on remand and at home until the case comes up, which could be months.

The experience of the women we interviewed with the criminal justice system leads to the conclusion that it does not interfere in any serious way with male violence to women. The role of the police can be likened to gatekeepers who only allow a few through the system. The police can be seen as standing between abused women and violent men, severely rationing the number of these men to be prosecuted. This is true even if the police only reflect accurately what they know would happen if more cases went to court; that is, nothing or next to nothing. It is not necessary that the police be particularly hostile to enforcing the criminal law in relation to abused women not to do so. There is some recent work in the US on how decisions to prosecute men who have been violent to women are made (Stanko,

1982). The filtering processes are based on very fundamental values about men and women. Our data illustrate that the police as the protective male collectivity of women is a myth.

Private-public divide and the perpetuation of male violence to women

The experience of public violence and the fear of public stranger violence, which women define much more strictly than private home-based violence from known others, is having an effect on their sense of freedom and regulating – by restricting – their movements. The so-called Ripper murders and the resulting publicity intensified these feelings and behavioural outcomes. The vast majority of women were scared and more frightened than usual of going out at night. Most said they had not always been frightened to do so. Over the year the majority of women restricted their movements in a variety of ways. The most frequent was to never walk alone, followed by changing their mode of transport. Women acquired bikes and cars, used public transport, including taxis, for the first time or more frequently, and women students used the University mini bus service provided by the students' union. (This worked like a taxi service.) When not going out alone if possible is combined with never walking alone, 83% of the women interviewed were restricted in this way. The Ripper scare did not change behaviour for a substantial minority (18%), however, as they already were not going out alone, or at all, at night.

While these major changes in attitude and behaviour were occurring, they could not be as great in respect of the neighbourhood itself. The majority of women regarded the neighbourhood as a safe place to walk around alone in during the day while the reverse was true after dark. When asked if the neighbourhood had become more or less safe in the last twelve months, half said it was more or less the same even though the question had not offered that option.

While the neighbourhood was not defined by the questionnaire, from the replies it is possible to work out that its area is approximately a quarter of a mile square. The area consists of quiet residential streets with brief early morning and evening traffic as people go and return from work. There is a block of little shops and the open space known as the Moor borders one side. The Moor contains a few trees and allotments and has a gentle slope leading to higher ground in the middle. Because of these factors it is possible to be out of sight of others when walking even though it is a relatively small space. There is no lighting on the Moor, and the street lighting is dim as is usual in residential areas. The Moor at night was already a no-go area for women before the Ripper began his series of murders.

When asked how the neighbourhood could be made more safe and later, more specifically, if there was anything the police could do, just over half recommended increased police activity, particularly foot patrols, but also changes in police attitudes and a quicker response to calls. Almost a third thought the police could do nothing either because they were doing what they could or it might be unwise to have too many police about. The remainder did not know or did not reply. Thus a majority of women, in terms of attitudes, look to the collective organisation of men, i.e. the police, to protect them from individual male attack. But as once attack occurs, the reporting rate is low, we conclude that the vast majority of our respondents do not think the police *in practice* either able or willing to protect them.

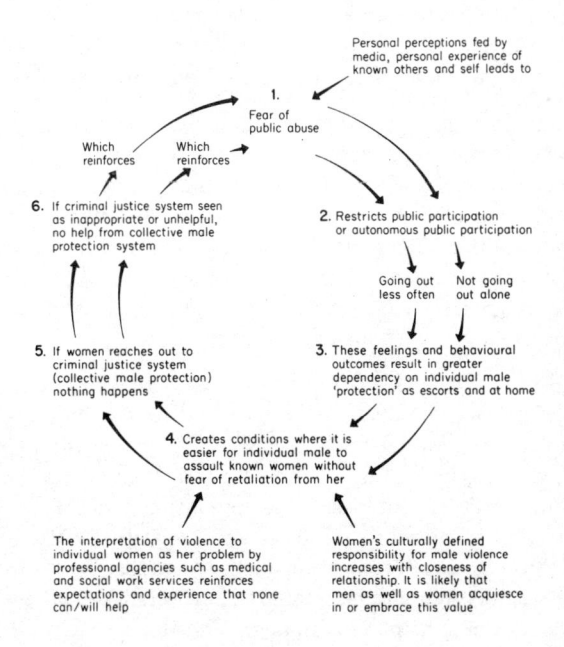

```
                            Personal perceptions fed by
                            media, personal experience of
                            known others and self leads to
                                  1.
                              Fear of
                          public abuse
         Which       Which
      reinforces   reinforces

6. If criminal justice system seen          2. Restricts public participation
   as inappropriate or unhelpful,              or autonomous public participation
   no help from collective male
   protection system
                                          Going out    Not going
                                          less often   out alone

5. If women reaches out to              3. These feelings and behavioural
   criminal justice system                 outcomes result in greater
   (collective male protection)            dependency on individual male
   nothing happens                         'protection' as escorts and at home

                4. Creates conditions where it is
                   easier for individual male to
                   assault known women without
                   fear of retaliation from her

The interpretation of violence to      Women's culturally defined
individual women as her problem by     responsibility for male violence
professional agencies such as medical  increases with closeness of
and social work services reinforces    relationship. It is likely that
expectations and experience that none  men as well as women acquiesce
can/will help                          in or embrace this value
```

The way in which these patterns interact to drive women into greater dependency on men both individually and collectively which makes them more vulnerable to attack can be described by means of the diagram. Male violence to women is enclosed within a circular system. We are able to describe this by a diagram in a series of steps that return to reinforce the starting point.

1. Fear of public abuse is fed by the media, informal rumour, personal experience of women, their friends and acquaintances. The public world is seen as the place of strangers who may not share the same social values

about appropriate social behaviour. Women are expected to be more circumspect in their public behaviour than men and, when attacks occur, they are often held at least partially responsible for them. Women's fear of public abuse is socially sanctioned.

2. Fear of public abuse leads to a lessening of public participation. This can be total in the sense of not going out alone, or partial by going out less often. Each woman works out, possibly only semi-consciously, the places, times and means governing her use of public space. For example, a woman may not feel able to use the local public open space, even during the day, except to walk across, unless someone is with her, either a child or an adult. She may feel she can enter some pubs, but not others, on her own, or some, but not others, with other women, or some only with a male escort. It is not a simple matter of being able to go anywhere during the day but highly restricting one's mobility during the hours of night.

3. No matter how variable a woman's response, restrictions on public access result in greater dependency on male protection both as escorts and in a more general sense. The pressure from the outside, or public world, creates the feeling of dependency which helps to structure the actual dependency of women on men in their homes. (Dependency of women on particular men is furthered by other structural factors, of course, such as economic dependency on male wages and state support for the nuclear family through various systems of state benefit, housing policies, etc.)

4. Dependency on the men with whom women live creates the conditions where it is easier for individual men to assault 'their women', secure in the knowledge that they cannot retaliate easily. These structural conditions are supported by a general cultural understanding which defines women as responsible for male violence, and this responsibility increases with the closeness of the relationship (Dobash and Dobash, 1980). If women attempt to object by turning to state agencies, by and large the medical and social work services response is to reinforce expectations and experiences that no one can or will help. The problem of male violence is turned back upon the woman who becomes labelled inadequate or deviant (Stark, Flitcraft and Frazier, 1979; Maynard, forthcoming).

5. Our study illustrates that if women reach out to the criminal justice system – the police – nothing happens, or nothing happens that women can understand as being the result of their actions. If men are penalised for their crimes it occurs in some obscure way, divorced from the action and participation of women in curtailing the violence of particular men. This encourages dependency on the collective male protection system which has the effect of reinforcing a state of dependent helplessness. It does not reduce women's fear of public violence. If women decide the police will

not or cannot help, or are inappropriate to involve, once again fear of public abuse remains unchallenged.

6. Unchallenged public abuse reinforces fear as nothing stands between women and attack by unknown men in public places except the careful monitoring of access and the means by which this is to be accomplished. And around the circle we go again.

But other pressures make it necessary for women to go out at times and in ways they think inappropriate as well as appropriate. As we have discussed, women work in situations where harassment is part of the job, or must do night shifts, or attempt to work in or train for employment defined as male. This necessity to go out is a constant reminder of vulnerability. Women cannot relax their vigilance, and this serves to remind them that they are tolerated in these settings on certain conditions. The need for male protection is reiterated in the deepest layers of the self.

During the five years when the so-called Ripper roamed the North, women's consciousness began to be transformed. Women began to call on women to depend on each other and not men. The widespread rumour that the Ripper was a policeman, along with their inability to capture him, began to invalidate the belief that the collective male system, the police, is one of protection of women. In our study women recognised the part women's groups had played in helping victims of violence and made suggestions for the extension of voluntary and self-help organisations such as rape crisis centres, self-defence groups, safe house programmes, women's advice centres, neighbourhood and women's groups, and escort and transport services. Three-quarters of our respondents had heard of the major groups working against violence to women, that is Women's Aid, Rape Crisis, and Women Against Violence Against Women, although fewer knew how to contact these organisations if needed.

The feminist response to male violence is that women should develop ways of depending on each other for protection. Women began to argue that women should accompany each other when out at night and set up women operated transport systems. This demand is radical as it is not based on deference to and dependency on men. Quite the contrary, the aim is to break the connection. Further, when the demand for a curfew on men first surfaced, it was met with shock and disbelief that such a statement could be made, so strong is the system of dependency and male privilege. A curfew on men after dark by and large would make the streets safe for women. Curfews on men do occur when law and disorder is threatened, for example, some young blacks had to be indoors at night after the Moss Side riots, as a condition of bail.

Force and its threat is used to maintain power differentials between subordinates and superordinates in many groups, e.g. social classes, races, countries. The maintenance of power differences between males and females is no exception, but each system has its specific forms to be analysed (Hanmer, 1978).

The division of women's lives into public and private spheres is central to the process of ensuring dependency on men, both as individuals and as collectivities, and the greater the threat of attack, the more intense this is, thus ensuring the perpetuation of the system.

Social systems, however, can be challenged and changed. The process begins with transformations of consciousness generated by experience of the material world. The exceptional conditions arising from the Ripper reign of terror, by exposing the contradiction in depending upon the abusing group for protection, has played an important role in fuelling a demand for an end to male violence to women. The process of challenge and change has begun.

Acknowledgements
We wish to thank all the women who contributed to this study. With special thanks to Ruth Bundy, Al Garthwaite, Marianne Hester, Diane Hudson, Lesley Kay, Sandra McNeil, Jenny Wardleworth, and also the South Headingley Community Association, the Bradford Law Centre and the Ella Lyman Cabot Trust.

5 Men and War: Status, Class and the Social Reproduction of Masculinity
Patricia Allatt

The class divisions amongst the British armed forces in the Second World War were seen by elements in the military hierarchy as not only a threat to the pre-war social order, but as counter-productive to the war effort itself. Modern warfare required male solidarity.

The texts of the Forces' Education Programme in citizenship reveal how such solidarity was encouraged by the explicit construction of a male status group. In a period of social disorganisation, the divisions amongst men were blurred not only by the call to men and women as responsible and participatory citizens of a democracy who could and should by their intelligent contribution shape a more equitable post-war world, but also, and in contradiction with this ideology, by the overt reaffirmation of that which all men shared, their superior property rights in the system of gender relationships both in the private domain of family and the public domain of waged labour and politics. In this paper I describe how the components of a traditional socially constructed masculinity were reaffirmed in the interests of the state.

At issue for the military were the interrelated problems of morale and efficiency arising from the constitution of a mass conscript army and the changed conditions of modern warfare. Low morale was grounded in boredom, outmoded conceptions of the fighting man and cynical expectations with regard to the aftermath of the present war in view of the empty promises of the First World War.

Yet, for the progressives in the military hierarchy, the commitment of the soldier to what he was fighting for was essential to a modern war machine which demanded technical skill and a high degree of cooperation on the part of all ranks in combat alternating with long periods of boredom in military bases. Consequently the rigid hierarchical divisions and the old forms of motivation through harsh discipline were neither productive nor did they control or, alternatively, harness to the war effort, that undercurrent in the armed forces denoted as the mood of popular radicalism

(Summerfield, 1976, p. 18) – the urge towards a more egalitarian society encapsulated in the war-time phrase 'Post-War Reconstruction'.

While, however, the debate on social justice was predominantly articulated around the theme of economic class, the problem of morale was compounded by a challenge inherent in the concept of equality itself – the logic of its extension to women. Whether or not such an extension was deemed preposterous it was nonetheless a source of some anxiety. That men felt their position in the labour market, control over women and sense of superiority threatened was apparent in a war-time survey of soldiers and their wives (Slater and Woodside, 1951) and in the popular press (*Picture Post*, 1941; 1944; *Home Chat*, 1942; *Woman's Outlook*, 1942; *Good Housekeeping*, 1943). Such anxiety was, moreover, exacerbated by the sense of powerlessness consequent upon conscription (the state itself had removed men from the locale of the action), coupled with an awareness that national, and indeed personal, survival depended upon female labour and a relaxation of former normative controls.

The disruption of war was exposing the conceptual and material frailty of the boundaries between the masculine public domain of war and work and the feminine private domain of home and family. The family unit was atomised by conscription, women's war work, child-care provision outside the home and evacuation, a situation accentuated by bomb damage to housing stock. Further, following the Blitz in 1940, the provision of communal feeding in Local Authority British Restaurants and in industrial canteens and by the expansion of the school meals service (Price, 1981, p. 2) encroached upon, drawing into the public domain, that function *par excellence* – wifely service in the provision of meals – which underpinned the ideology, indeed spirituality (Allatt 1981a), of the family and the power relations within it (Murcott in this volume).

There were associated changes in the objective experiences of women and new patterns of daily behaviour which were conducive, at least, to a questioning of hitherto accepted ways and assumptions. Demands for and appreciation of the women in formerly male-defined jobs (Bullock, 1967, p. 63; Douie, 1949, p. 19) and enforced separation from husbands in the armed forces, or working away from home in key occupations, gave them new or renewed experience of social and economic independence which many had never expected to taste again once married. Moreover, irrespective of entry into the labour force, women had to assume responsibility for family affairs previously held to be the sphere of men, and some experienced a new independence in the regularity, irrespective of its adequacy, of the dependants' allowances compulsorily deducted from servicemen's pay.

It was against this turbulent background that the Forces' Education Programme in citizenship emerged. There were two prongs to the scheme.

The first, the Army Bureau of Current Affairs (ABCA), sanctioned in September 1941, was to educate men in the aspects for which the war was being fought through discussion of current events. Discussion material in the form of a bulletin, *Current Affairs*, was to be supplied by a central directorate, and W.E. Williams, a civilian, a radical (Calder, 1981, p. 252), former head of the British Institute of Adult Education and on the editorial board of Penguin Books, was appointed director. The second prong was the establishment in November 1942 of a scheme entitled the *British Way and Purpose (BWP)*, the most important component of which came to be education in citizenship, comprising subjects concerned with British society and government 'for which it was worth fighting' (Wilson, 1949, p. 60), again taking the form of regular pamphlets produced by the Directorate of Army Education. To be effective and counter the resistance of the rank and file, this education was to be compulsory, to take place in duty hours and to be 'served up like rations' (Williams, cited in Summerfield, 1976, p. 15). Elements within the origin, structure and content of this programme, in Weberian terms, rendered men a status group: the demarcation of membership; the way membership cut across memberships of other groups, allegiances and divisions; and the affirmation of that which was held in common.

Boundaries of membership
First, boundaries were raised which marked off the male group from women. Women comprised a small but significant proportion of the army, approximately 9% (470,000) of the Forces in September 1943, at the peak of recruitment (Summerfield, 1981, p. 151). Moreover, although defined as supportive, their work – predominantly in administration, communications, long-range reconnaissance and machine maintenance – was vital. It would seem, therefore, that their morale too must be important to the war effort (Summerfield, 1976, p. 291).

The women, however, were conceptually and physically screened out. That the scheme was perceived, if not intentionally conceived, as an exercise in the mass education of the male is apparent amongst those responsible for the material, commentators and those with power to implement the scheme.

Firstly, because men greatly outnumbered women, men's needs were seen as predominant with the result that educational work with women was slow to develop and the material was written primarily for men (Wilson, 1949, p. 89).

Women's education was further circumscribed not only by the later than in the case of men recruitment of educated women to the services – predominantly composed of young, single, ill-educated and unskilled girls – but by discriminatory practices. Thus whilst the men received ABCA and *BWP* sessions in work time as part of their duty, the male commanding officers, under whose jurisdiction the ATS (Auxiliary Territorial Service) largely fell, often refused to allocate any duty hours to education. Consequently, to avoid encroaching upon leisure time, the ABCA and *BWP* sessions took place on the night of the week when they had to be 'in' for their personal chores – a nice symbolic and material comment on gender and education. For men education resides in the public domain as an integral part of their role; for women it is relegated to the private domain as an additional chore, overburdening their role.

Secondly, implicit in the above, women were perceived as a special category requiring different treatment both by way of their needs and method of instruction. Difficulties were anticipated in the raising of interest in abstract concepts, international affairs and even citizenship unless the material was intimately related to a woman's experience. Although recognised as only a matter of degree (indeed it was the basis of the adjutant-general's rationale for the structure of the material), that lectures and discussions for men were also enhanced by relating them to men's personal experience, Wilson observes that 'a more simple and nearly always a more personal approach was necessary than with a male audience'. Thus, 'Prospects for Poland' was replaced by 'Would You Marry a Pole?' (Wilson, 1949, p. 91)

A mild astonishment is expressed by historians when such expectations are not fulfilled and 'a larger number of girls than might have been expected' showed a deep interest in 'the subjects which had hitherto been regarded as the province of men' (Hawkins and Brimble, 1947, p. 149). Nonetheless, domestic subjects were deemed to have greater appeal and the concept of citizenship was channelled through an introduction to those institutions with direct links to domesticity – education, child welfare, social welfare and health (Wilson, 1949, p. 93).

Homogeneity and cohesion

Although the masculine bonds were thus delineated, the conscript army comprised many, potentially antipathetic, social and economic groups. Taking account of officers and men, these encompassed differing economic classes, age, regional and occupational groups and the spectrum of political allegiances. The military hierarchy, responsible for the emergence and control of the programme, accommodated progressive and conservative upper class elites; and the civilian educationalists associated with the production and presentation of the material were intellectuals and teachers drawn from universities and the Workers' Education Association. Despite such heterogeneity two factors contributed to a climate favourable to the welding of a more solidary group: the teaching methodology and the reservoir of latent assumptions.

In an attempt to combat the social and military divisiveness between officers and other ranks, recognised by military progressives as interfering with the war machine, every low ranking officer was under orders to give the ABCA classes (Summerfield, 1976, p. 15). In a complementary fashion, however, in the later *BWP* scheme, instructors were also drawn from civilian personnel and service personnel from other ranks (Wilson, 1949, p. 60). Expertise, therefore, was seen to cut across many boundaries. Additionally, audience involvement was specifically encouraged and emphasised in notes to instructors. Thus, in an attempt to assuage the anxiety of inexpert officer instructors, one directive runs, 'It is the duty of the Group as a whole to provide answers; it is not one man's job.' (ABCA, 1942, **20**, p. 2).

There was further an underlying accord, totally unconscious, between conservatives and progressives in the military establishment, liberal educationalists, and the radical soldiery. Thus although the material was subject to censorship from the war office and criticism by the radicals, no critique emerged of the material on the family and women.

Censorship by the War Office centred on the detection of 'politics', that is, any hint or postulation of change in the distribution of wealth, power or opportunity and any criticism of the status quo. For instance, although references to worker participation in industry, trade union participation in government, the unequal distribution of wealth and income in British society, the possibility of full employment and a growing equality in postwar society were ultimately incorporated (*BWP*, 1942, **2**, pp. 50–51), Lord Croft, parliamentary under secretary, initially commented in the proofs that the texts contained 'definite propaganda wholly of "left-wing" character' (PRO, 1943, cited in Summerfield, 1976, p. 26).

In contrast, the material on family and gender aroused no criticism. Thus the adjutant-general, Sir Ronald Adam, pressing for a radical approach in *BWP*, argued and won the case for a series centred on the individual's relationship to the wider social units in which he found himself – the nation, Europe and Empire. He claimed that the most expedient way to raise morale was to arouse soldiers' interest by instruction in matters which affected them personally (Summerfield, 1976, p. 32). In November 1943, this was adopted starting with the individual's relation not to the nation but to the family and neighbourhood. This material is heavily infused with traditional familism (Allatt, 1981a).

The civilian 'watchdog', the Central Advisory Committee for Adult Education in His Majesty's Forces, composed of civilian educationalists liaising with Army educational personnel, criticised the material from the opposing perspective – for supporting the status quo and omitting all critiques of capitalism (ABCA, 1941, **3**) and race. No inadequacy, however, was seen in the material on the family and women.

Finally the extent of the radicalism of the soldiery is suggested by a comment made by a sergeant (close to the Communist party and who, with others, decided to initiate informal political activity) on the debates stimulated by ABCA; included were the Public Control of Banks, the Beveridge Report, 'and then we had some lighter topics like should women be nationalised' (Summerfield, 1981, p. 154).

The affirmation of masculinity

Within this climate a male status group was constructed by the articulation of that which all men shared, the right to the occupancy of the public and the control of the private realms. Two themes around which male superiority is affirmed are extracted.

The challenge of logic

The first theme is the containment of the feminist challenge to traditional gender relationships. That the challenge was based upon logical deduction and arose within educational material premised upon the canon of intellectual integrity (a situation made more ironic by the liberal reputation of W. E. Williams) meant that it had to be met within the convention of balanced argument.

Pivotal to both challenge and strategies of containment is a bulletin written for ABCA by Phyllis Bentley, 'Women in the Post War World' (ABCA, 1943, **44**). Bentley raised issues that counter the entire import of the texts: the logic of the extension of equality to women, the inherent conflict between equality and the traditional family structure, the conflict between citizenship and motherhood, and the unsatisfactory nature of the traditional conjugal relationship.

The issue of equality is taken up by Williams. The logic is uncontested but the case demolished by the representation of feminists as an unrepresentative group, intellectually ill-equipped for the public domain of political debate. Two strategies are employed: a reorientation from a structuralist to an individualistic perspective and a redefinition of equality.

The shift in perspective serves to empty Bentley's argument (and feminist intellect) of any claim to authority. First, an individualistic cast is implied by subsuming Bentley's visionary title under the more prosaic and limited 'Women After the War'. The topic itself is then accorded a special status, heralded in the discussion guidelines for officers by the introductory heading 'A Controversial Subject'. The ensuing directives contrast markedly to those in other bulletins. Whereas elsewhere officers are enjoined to encourage the appropriate perspective, for example, to 'ram home...crucial points' (ABCA, 1942, **20**, p. 1) or 'to get into the right perspective that pattern of reconstruction of which social security is only one of the pieces to be fitted together' (ABCA, 1943, **45**, p. 2), the teaching notes for Bentley's article emphasise not only the presence of opposing views but their equal status. Thus, the directive for the treatment of 'Women After the War' is specifically to leave the issue open and unresolved, 'Let your ABCA session on this topic be a reconnaissance rather than a legislative assembly' (ABCA, 1943, **44**, p. 2). Paradoxically this lack of prescription simultaneously facilitates and disarms a challenge.

Bentley's argument is further debased by implying it to be not only individualistic but idiosyncratic. Thus, rather than introducing the subject as full of debatable matter, as Williams does of his own pamphlet (ABCA, 1943, **48**, p. 2), it is stressed that the author,

> in presenting the topic, sometimes underlines her own views. But these views need not be yours or your man's...read in a mood of critical alertness what Miss Bentley writes (ABCA, 1943, **44**, p. 2).

And mention of Bentley's occupational status, 'the well known author' (ABCA, 1943, **44**, p. 4), an occupation which Williams later debunks as 'one of the more elegant professions' (see below) providing only a partial world view, undermines any claim to authority. In this context it is perhaps significant that a bulletin on this theme was not commissioned from feminists with a more legitimate public status: MPs, trade unionists, barristers, academics. Indeed, most pertinently for such educational material, Margaret Mead (1943), was then publishing and lecturing on her anthropological studies on the social construction of gender.

Direct editorial intervention in the text furthers the idiosyncratic image crucial to the demolition of the feminist challenge. As noted, Bentley's logic is uncontested; implied, however, is the inadequacy of feminists as logicians and advocates and, because of their socio-economic position, their misinterpretation of the issues.

One of Bentley's major advocacies is the reconciliation of marriage and career for women by the systematic re-entry of women into the workforce through a scheme of registration for use by employers. With skilled domestic help, women in the early years of motherhood could retain their occupational skill, first, by practising it as a hobby, then by working on a part-time basis and, with increasing availability as their children grow, then gradually return to full-time employment.

While Bentley's treatment of class, like that of other middle class women's groups (Pierce, 1979), is inadequate, the 'part-time solution' (ABCA, 1943, **44,** p. 15) does connote economic independence for all classes of women. Williams, however, not content to leave the inadequacy to discussion, seizes upon the oddity rather than the import of the argument. The editorial asterisk accompanies the word 'hobby' and the footnote runs,

This is all very well for the minority of women who enter a profession. But how does this prospect of part-time employment after marriage look to *the majority* of the women whose work consists of putting lids on tins or pressing buttons? Editor, *Current Affairs*. (emphasis original).

By introducing the dimension of class, one form of inequality is contained by the use of another, confining a potentially universal criticism of family structure to a specific group of women in a class specific location. This underlines both class antagonisms and antipathies between women while simultaneously affirming the cohesion of the male status group in their intellectual superiority to even educated women.

Eight months later, in his bulletin 'Woman's Place' (ABCA, 1944, **61**), Williams extinguishes the feminist case. Under the 'challenge: to whom is it "unfair" if a married woman works', the following advice appears whereby Phyllis Bentley's authority, along with that of other women who venture into the public domain, is incidentally rejected and the underlying antagonisms and threats of gender are both made explicit and subdued within the convention of balanced presentation.

'A Counter-Balance'
If you find that "Woman's place is the home" is rousing a one-sided opposition you might find it salutary to balance things up by taking a familiar feminist slogan to pieces.

"A Woman has a Right to a Career"

This slogan is usually repeated by upper-class feminists whose women friends practise the more elegant professions – novelists, actresses, staff managers and so on. It ignores the grim fact that most women who work are inevitably employed on rather wearisome jobs such as filling bottles in factories. The feminist extremists always overlook this fact and consequently glamourise the whole discussion. Is there really anything more attractive to a woman in the prospect of a job of her own than in the prospect of a home of her own? Is this alleged "right to a career" moreover to apply in a sex-combative way?...' (p. 5).

Finally, the premises upon which feminists base their argument are defined as false by fiat. Equality is redefined.

'Some Generalisations about Women'
In most discussions about women there comes a point at which someone throws a hand-grenade into the debate. The well-known phrase "woman's place is the home", can be depended upon to make the argument really explosive, for it develops extremism on both sides. On the one hand it makes the Grand Turk positively livid in his affirmation that he is the superior sex and that women's role is subordinate to his. On the other hand it goads the Ultra-Feminist

into the preposterous position that women have a right to do everything that men do (p. 3).

The poverty of the feminist case, where the challenge to the traditional family structure and power relationship between men and women is at its most articulate and formal, is established. The treatment defines, to the detriment of women, the intellectual imbalance between the sexes and the inappropriateness of women in the public domain of political debate, a process which was underway in the political arena itself (Allatt, 1981b, pp. 180, 198).

A second stand drawn from the latent bond of masculinity is the pivotal position of the male. That it comprises small and apparently trivial detail serves to provide a cumulative and sustained infusion of male superiority, lasting over a period of years, into the articulation of citizenship. These orientating assumptions fall into three major categories: the centrality of the male; ownership, control and power; and women as problems.

The centrality of the male
Given the origin of the scheme, the male orientation of the texts is unsurprising. Thus a directive to officers runs, 'The purpose of the discussions ... will be to clarify men's minds about the world we are fighting for ...' (ABCA, 1943, **48**, p. 2). Again, the linguistic convention of the use of the masculine to encompass both male and female would seem normal, although the Director General of Manpower of the Ministry of Labour and National Service drew attention to its potential dangers for the manpower needs of total war. 'Into the term man-power', he instructs, 'please read also woman-power' (ABCA, 1942, **20**, p. 2).

This orientation and the patterns of language, however, help to mask underlying conceptual distinctions between the sexes. In the texts universal categories emerge as not universally applicable, and relegate women to minority status and a lower order of citizenship; further, a conceptual structure is erected of separate public and private spheres respectively inhabited by men and women.

At the simplest level, discussions of citizenship include such phrases as 'What a man wants [is the] health and happiness of his children and a constructive leisure for himself' (ABCA, 1943, **48**, p. 10); 'a decent standard of living, a nice house and a bit of a holiday now and then with the wife and children' (*BWP*, 1943, **12**, p. 363); and 'a happy life depends as much on choosing the right job as the right wife' (*BWP*, 1942, **2**, p. 75). These examples also illustrate how women appear as male appendages, defined by their relationship to men. Even the absence of men places a woman by such evocative phrases as the 'so-called million surplus women' between the wars (ABCA, 1944, **61**, p. 7) and their enforced state as 'childless spinsters' (*BWP*, 1943, **6**, p. 205).

More seriously, however, women's statuses are conflated or lost. In a discussion of citizenship woman becomes synonymous with housewife (ABCA, 1944, **61**, p. 12); and in the account of social security, a key document in the debate on equality, the relationship between the state and individual is transported to that between the state and the family man.

> Social Security must be achieved by co-operation between the State and the individual... The State... should leave room and encouragement for voluntary action by each individual to provide more than that minimum for himself and his family. (ABCA, 1943, **45**, p. 14).

Conflation of a different type takes place in the area of values. Thus the universal rules which the 'Just Man' must observe are, according to A. D. Lindsay, 'not confined to any single group or country [but] are human, universal'. One such rule, however, is 'protecting women and children'. Natural justice and masculinity are merged (*BWP*, 1943, **12**, p. 365).

Lost also are inequalities of gender which, although raised elsewhere in the texts, do not constitute one of the divisions that must be looked to in a definition of democracy.

> Democracy... implies that every man – whatever his race, colour or creed – should be given an equal opportunity of realising the best that is in him (*BWP*, 1942, **1**, pp. 14, 17).

And even when inhabiting the same structures women's tasks or contribution undergo crititical redefinition. For example, constant distinctions are drawn between the soldier and the auxiliary. Although indispensable to the war effort, auxiliary means helper, despite the claim that, by virtue of being the only country to conscript women, Britain was demonstrating its belief in equality – 'we really believe in the quality (sic) of rights and duties between men and women' (ABCA, 1942, **20**, p. 1). In the sections on industry a distinction is nicely implied between workers and women in the headings, with accompanying male and female stick figures, 'What has happened to the Worker' and 'What has been the effect of women in Industry' (*BWP*, 1944, **14**, pp. 416, 418). And when women form part of a mixed audience for an ABCA session, while their contribution to the balance of the debate is welcomed by Williams, balance is seen to consist of women arguing about the height for a kitchen sink and men concentrating upon the placing of garages and arterial roads, thereby implying discrete spheres of male and female competence (ABCA, 1944, **61**, p. 2).

Such venturing of women into the public domain, whether into industry or community, is partially controlled by the use of the male as the normative criterion, irrespective of its adequacy, against which women are measured. For example, although acknowledged that in both skills and attitudes women in industry have achieved and in some cases surpassed the competence of men (ABCA, 1943, **44**, p. 13), and despite the bad industrial relations of the period, only partly reflected in the increase in strikes which, although made illegal in 1940, had by 1942 increased the number of 'man-days' (sic) lost beyond the total for 1939 (Calder, 1981, p. 299), G.H. Ince writes,

> all of them are doing work that was usually thought of as men's work, and all of them doing it just as cheerfully and efficiently as the men did (ABCA, 1942, **20**, p. 4).

And while acknowledging, both in the text (ABCA, 1944, **61**, p. 14) and in published comments, the apathy of men regarding the responsibilities and knowledge of citizenship (Hawkins and Brimble, 1947, p. 160), Williams retains men as the standard rather than advocating a higher general standard for all. Thus, on women's attitude to community responsibilities and education he observes,

> What is too often lacking is the social conscience and the civic determination to apply (their capacities) to the job of making a better village or a better world. To suggest that this dereliction is solely a woman's weakness would be absurd, for men as a whole are also a long way from the fulfilment of their minimum civic duties, and responsibilities. But men are less liable to plead, when pressed, that 'they aren't up to it' or 'they can't understand it'. If women are to play their part in government, local or national, they must bestir themselves to make no less an effort than men to keep in touch with the issues of the day. But the emphasis must be on effort. (ABCA, 1944, **61**, p. 14).

Moreover, assumptions about the biological chasm of innate gender differences support this normative masculine standard. These assumptions are explicitly grounded in authoritative, high status (pseudoscientific) knowledge, for example, theories of child development. This approach contrasts starkly with advice to soldiers to draw on their own personal experience and common sense in their assessments of Phyllis Bentley's argument, or the *BWP* sections on the family.

Ownership, control and power
Intimately linked to this latent standard is the assumed legitimacy of male power, manifest in a recognition of male ownership, control and arbitration in public and private domains – major attributes of traditional masculinity.

Ownership of the occupational world
The pivotal nature of male employment is related not only to the role of breadwinner but men's sense of ownership of the occupational world.

This dominance combines a control of male occupational territory, that is, of distinct traditional labour markets protected by formal war-time agreements between unions and government (Douie, 1949, p. 10), with a control over women as wage-earners. This control over the public domain of the marketplace coincides with male rights to personal service in the private domain.

That waged work is personal male property becomes apparent where officers are 'urged to ram home to their men [that] by sharing our work with women, we may rid ourselves of nonsensical notions about them' (ABCA, 1942, **20**, p. 2). The duality of the fear of losing power is encapsulated in the following,

> Thousands of soldiers are going about believing that their jobs have been permanently taken from them by women and that women will not be able to look after them on this account. (ABCA, 1943, **48**, p. 9).

Their rejection of women in industry, is moreover, phrased in terms of male personal costs, 'If you don't want women in industry you'll have to lower your standard of living'.

Male possession is, moreover, subtly advanced by the imagery and by defining women's physical presence in the public domain in a manner which conceptually retains it within the private. Thus men leave empty places in industry which others temporarily fill. The purpose of the Schedule of Reserved Occupation, it is explained, is,

> to reserve skilled men who could train other men and especially women, so that the latter would be ready to take the empty places when the time comes to call up more men (*BWP*, 1944, **14**, p. 405).

Further, women's industrial contribution is always defined as helping their men, '... it is their way of helping their men in the forces to fight with better equipment and to come home sooner' (ABCA, 1942, **20**, p. 12). (This image is strongly represented in the civilian and official advertisements and posters of the period.) The definition is further sustained by the emphasis given to the maintenance of a woman's traditional role and by stressing the abnormality of war. Thus 'women are running homes and taking the place of men in industry' (*BWP*, 1943, **8**, p. 250) and their child-rearing responsibilities are aided by the provision of nurseries. Women's roles therefore are not to be reassessed but the content altered by including additional elements while retaining the old patterns of identity.

Male control over women
That women are subject to control by both state and men is explicit. This is not to deny that men were massively subject to state control but rather that, in the concern with male morale and the need for woman-power,

gender relationships with the male as dominant are constantly affirmed. Consequently, the thrust is not merely for men to relax their control over women but to transform the nature of that control to further the war effort.

In these documents, there is an assumption (held also by civil servants)[1] that men not only control women's activity but that control extends to women's opinions. Furthermore the legitimacy and validity of male knowledge of the domestic is given credence. For example, a crucial point officers are asked to 'ram home' to their men is that, 'Much of the dislike many women have of going to war work is due to the fact that their men don't approve', that 'if the men will back the women ... the women will go to it gladly' (ABCA, 1942, **20**, p. 2). Certainly, at the time, women were conscious that their activities were subject to constraint by husbands, even in their absence; this is apparent in letters to women's magazines (see, for example, Home, 1942, 1943).

Loss of male control over women's physical mobility, and its latent association with loss of control over female sexuality, has also to be assuaged. In the case of women with husbands in the Armed Forces or Merchant Navy this is met with assurances that the state will protect the 'home' by not directing married women, even without children, to undertake work beyond daily travelling distance of their home (ABCA, 1942, **20**, p. 7); and that 'single women and women without home responsibilities will be called for service before the married with husbands and homes to look after' (p. 6).

The sexual fears in the relaxation and reorientation of normative control to facilitate female participation in the industrial workforce are met by chiding male adherence to the old fashioned notion that 'Woman's place is in the home', or feeling 'aggrieved because a sister or girl friend has had to leave home to go to work in a factory 100 miles away' (p. ii), or 'giving themselves needless headaches about the calamities which, they imagine, might befall [young married women without children if conscripted to] the services' (p. 1). The ATS in particular had a bad reputation for moral laxity, but no doubt the fear could be generalised to all instances where women now entered the public domain.

Finally, while the presence of women in the ABCA discussion groups is alleged to add a new dimension to the debate, men are nonetheless considered capable of responding to a questionnaire in lieu of their wives but 'which many ATS can answer for themselves' (ABCA, 1944, **61**, p. 12). The questionnaire refers to the housewife's daily round, covering facilities in the home, public utilities, health service and schools. Yet Spring-Rice (1939, p. 104) notes that men, however well-intentioned, had little idea of the burden of daily life for the housewife.

It could be argued that, to boost male morale, the State merely sought to maintain a fiction of male dominance. However, at the same time in civilian life, the Beveridge (1942) proposals for social insurance also reflected these traditional patterns of dominance, and the long-term future of male dominance was about to be structurally secured by legally supported sanctions (Allatt, 1981b).

Women as a problem

Finally, women, unlike men, can be raised as a social problem and isolated as an object for discussion. The issue of women entering the public domain, citizenship in fact, is detrimentally linked to the societal role of the family.

> after all, no matter how we develop the wide community sense we must remember that the basic social unit is, in fact, the family (ABCA, 1943, **48,** 14).

The oportunity for moral pronouncements is provided in such questions as, 'Do you approve of married women having independent careers?' (*BWP*, 1943, **13,** p. 383); and room for value judgements on the position and role of women in, 'Before we pronounce on what she ought to do...' (ABCA, 1944, **61,** p. 16).

Titles and subheadings are suggestive: 'Women at War', 'Women after the War', 'Woman's Place', 'The Woman Bogey', 'Hitler and the Gentle Sex', this latter an awesome warning about the fate of women (German or otherwise) in the hands of the German male (ABCA, 1942, **20**; 1943, **44**; 1943, **48,** p. 9; 1943, **49,** p. 13; 1944, **61**); and, where women are part of the audience, they are orientated to objectifying themselves rather than towards questioning the social structure.

In sum, 'women as a problem' unifies men and displaces women, already established as a fragmented group, to a different place of discourse; fragmentation and displacement are powerful tools of ideological control (Allatt, 1981b).

Conclusion

The debate on equality during the Second World War was set within the dual context of the power relationships of class and gender. For opposing reasons the coincidence of these two sets of relationships as factors influencing the morale of the armed forces posed a threat to the efficient pursuit of the war. The material of the Forces' Education Programme provides a unique opportunity to examine the attempt of liberal military and educational elites to resolve these tensions. Attention has been paid to women as a minority group (Hacker, 1951) and as a class (Morgan, 1975). Here the obverse side is revealed in the construction of men as a status group and the social reproduction of masculine attributes of power and prestige when under serious threat.

In this process class and status become specially articulated, dissolving and appearing in the pursuit of ideological maintenance, drawing, as appropriate, upon the reality of shared attributes or the divisions within groups. Thus, conceptually at least, the class position of women can be used as a means of fragmenting women as a group while simultaneously consolidating and affirming the masculine intellectual superiority of men as a status group. Similarly the status attributes of men can be drawn upon to dilute the antagonisms of class. Additionally, irrespective of what people actually do, public and private domains remain conceptually unscathed in terms of occupants and tasks.

These constructs of masculinity and femininity also provide continuous referents in the texts infusing any debate at a level which rarely needs to be articulated. They can be implicitly drawn upon as commonly held ground when discussing any subject and provide an 'unquestioning' support when other rationales are not easily available. Furthermore, they infuse an orientation into apparently neutral statements and concepts such as citizen, equal opportunity and individual development, thereby comprising a sustained defence against any challenge.

Of the situation obtaining today, it is perhaps a similar sense of shared identity (unchanged, at least in part, on the evidence of the regular *Guardian* feature, 'Naked Ape') which is latent in contemporary debate and practices and which sustain resistance to change.

Acknowledgements

The author gratefully acknowledges the permission of the Keeper of the Public Record Office to reproduce Memoranda.

Notes

1. In a letter to Sir Thomas Phillips concerning the White Paper on Social Insurance, P. N. Harvey of the Government Actuary's Department broached the idea of 'ascertaining the views of women on paying an additional contribution to enable spinsters to have a pension at 55'. '... Another point which occurs to me is that to the extent that any of the women included in the sample population are married their husbands may take the view that they have an interest in the matter; in other words the question is not wholly one for women' (*PRO*, 1945).

6 Women and Caring: Skills, Tasks and Taboos[1]
Clare Ungerson

While researching the relationship between women's paid work and the 'caring capacity of the community' (Ungerson, 1981) I became convinced that, despite women's increased participation in paid work the ideology of housework and caring was so strong that women would continue to work their 'dual roles' largely irrespective of their changing material circumstances. It was within that context that I became interested in the implications of such sex-based caring for the relationships within the 'private domain' (Stacey, 1981). This paper attempts to spell out some of those implications.

The interest in the relationship between women's paid and unpaid caring work is a form of recognition of the significance of women's unpaid contribution to the welfare state. But this recognition has been slow in coming, despite some excellent research in the area (Bayley, 1973; Wilkin, 1979; Nissel and Bonnerjea, 1982). The reason for this lack of recognition is that, like housework, informal caring takes place in the 'private domain' where the sexual division of labour is still imbued with naturalism or functionalism. This view has remained remarkably impervious to the claims of the women's movement that domestic labour bears a striking affinity to work (and, arguably, *is* work). Such conservatism has also been reflected in mainstream sociology (Stacey, 1981). Feminist sociologists, on the other hand, have redressed the balance a little, but in so doing they have tended to focus on the role of women's domestic labour in the 'reproduction of *labour* power' thus largely ignoring the work of caring for the potentially or actually unproductive labour of the sick, the elderly and the handicapped, and stressing instead the role of women in child-care and the problems and contradictions arising therefrom (Wilson, 1977; Oakley, 1974b). Those academic feminists who have discussed caring for people other than normal children or husbands have focused on the intervention by the state into domestic relationships, and as far as caring is concerned, largely confined their discussion to an analysis of the state itself (Land,

1978; McIntosh, 1978) or consideration of the impact of recent public expenditure cuts on women's lives (McIntosh, 1981; London Edinburgh Weekend Return Group, 1979). While this work is very important, not least because it does discuss the relationship between public and private domains, it omits an analysis of the caring role itself. In this paper, I want to do the latter: in other words, I shall take as given the argument that the major determinants of the supply of and demand for domestic labour lie outside the private domain and begin, instead, to unravel the actual tasks of caring, the skills involved in carrying them out, and the implications of the fact that informal caring, almost by definition, *is* private.

A recent article by Roy Parker (1980, p. 3) has taken us in the right direction for such an analysis of caring relationships. He points out that the word 'caring' has two elements. In one sense it means 'caring about' while in another

> it describes the direct work which is performed in looking after those who, temporarily or permanently, cannot do so for themselves. It comprises such things as feeding, washing, lifting, protecting, representing, and comforting. It is the active and personalised manifestation of care.

In order to distinguish this task-orientated concept of 'caring for' a person from 'caring about' them, Parker argues for the use of the word 'tending' to describe 'caring for'. This new vocabulary has two very important implications. First it clarifies the idea that caring *about* someone and caring *for* them are not necessarily or logically linked. They do not share the same affective basis; one can perfectly well care *for* a person without caring about them, and similarly one can care about them without doing a great deal to care *for* them.

Secondly, Parker's analysis has drawn attention to the *tasks* of tending. Using this word has two implications: first, according to the Shorter Oxford Dictionary, a 'task' is 'a piece of work imposed, exacted or undertaken as a duty or the like' and thus its use implies a set of obligating norms. Secondly, the carrying out of tasks has an implication that whoever does this job is bringing to bear a set of skills, learnt either through training or experience. The obligations to care, both for children and for adults, appear still – and for the foreseeable future – to devolve upon women (Ungerson, 1983). The point I want to concentrate on here is that the *skills* regarded as necessary to carry out those tasks are themselves imbued with sex-role stereotyping. It is not at all difficult to see why this should be so, since so many of the tasks of tending seem, superficially, to have a great deal in common with the tasks of parenting – and parenting, in its turn, is conventionally regarded as motherhood (Graham, 1979). The process and skills of mothering and caring have much in common; for instance:

1 Time, available at short-notice and in flexible lumps;
2 High levels of skill in domestic tasks – e.g. cooking, cleaning, washing;
3 High levels of social skill in, for example, talking to their clients – be they very young or very old – and in listening to their clients in order to assess their present and future needs;
4 Skills in information gathering about other services, and ability to manipulate other services on the client's behalf;
5 Ability to act autonomously over a wide range of tasks of widely differing skill level;
6 Punctuality and reliability;
7 Ability to operate over long periods in fairly isolated circumstances, engaging in routine and often unpleasant tasks, with – particularly in the case of the very old, the mentally handicapped and mentally ill – very little measurable 'success', let alone positive response from the client.

Such attributes are not confined to paragons from another planet. They are the socially expected attributes of women in Western European society, and most mothers attempt to fulfil them daily through the medium of housework and child-care.

It is this notion of skills in relation to tending and motherhood which poses a central problem for feminists. For the feminist critique of domestic labour, which partially argues that housework is akin to paid work and can very easily be substituted for it, can be combined with the feminist critique of the medicalisation of health care in general and child-bearing and rearing in particular (Ehrenreich and English, 1979; Donnison, 1977) to present a powerful argument that women do have, as a result of their experience of sex roles, now and in the recent past, a considerable body of knowledge that is largely unrecognised but nevertheless unique to their gender. Indeed, it is very tempting for feminists to make these claims, for in so doing they elevate the status of motherhood and other aspects of tending. Moreover, the view that mothering and housewifery constitute a set of skills accords with the reported views of women themselves. Many women evidently feel that in these areas of their lives they excel and, indeed, this may be the only area of their lives where they get the sense of a 'job well done' (Oakley, 1974b, p. 105). The difficulty for feminists is that these views (whether based on arguments about experience or biologically determined instincts) seemingly trap men and women into their socialised gender roles: Oakley's sample themselves argued that their greater domestic efficiency was the reason why men could not take over the housewife role. It seems important, therefore, if one is going to make a link between motherhood and tending, both at an experiential and at a conceptual level, to consider motherhood critically as a model for other forms of tending.

Motherhood as a model for tending

There are a number of issues here concerning both the carers and the cared for, but the central question is whether motherhood is an appropriate model for all caring, irrespective of the needs of the cared for and the nature of the history of the relationship between the carer and his or her charge. It is in fact the maternal model as a *relationship*, rather than a set of skills and aptitudes, which complicates matters. For maternity is a reciprocal relationship: it implies infancy, and it is the role of the cared for as 'infants' which introduces the chief ambivalence about the motherhood model.

As far as the cared for are concerned, it is immediately obvious that there is a very wide range of disabilities and disabled people, all of whom need tending, but many of whom will resist attention based on a mother/child relationship. At one end of the spectrum lie the severely mentally handicapped, for whom infancy remains a permanently ascribed state. (In a recent BBC2 programme – *The Silent Minority* – severely mentally handicapped adult men were referred to as 'the babies'.) At the other end of the spectrum are the physically handicapped who, through accidents of birth, life, or the degeneration of old age, remain able-minded but have severe mobility problems. For them, the mother/child model seems particularly inappropriate; indeed, the physically disabled have recently mounted a vigorous campaign against the infantalising attitudes held towards them by the able-bodied. The title of the Radio 4 programme for the physically handicapped – 'Does he take sugar?' – is an ironic echo of these objections, while the recent growth of literature on sexual relations between handicapped people (e.g. Stewart, 1979) is part of their pressure to gain legitimate adulthood. Not all these handicaps are due to accidents of birth or life and hence restricted to a small minority. Towards the centre of the spectrum are those who have some physical or some mental disabilities or a combination of the two and, most typically, the group in this category are the elderly and very old. Thus all of us are highly likely to move on to this spectrum at some point in our lives.

The fact that there is a spectrum of dependency along which most of us move has two important implications. First, where care is carried out by people who have known us over a long period, the nature of our relationships with those who care for us will be partially determined by the *history* of our relationships with those carers. Secondly, we do not grow old 'gracefully' in, as the phrase implies, a linear and coherent way. Instead, we lose some faculties and feelings and retain others: elderly 'infants', entering Shakespeare's 'second childishness', can mourn their past as adults, and other adults such as children and spouses with whom they have established long-term relationships will themselves find it difficult to adjust old feelings to new tasks.

There is an issue, then, about whether the extension of motherhood into tending insults and hurts the cared for, and at the same time creates complex emotional problems arising out of role adjustment for the carers. There are likely to be wide differences in attitude to this maternal model of caring amongst the cared for themselves. Some of these differences will arise out of objective differences in circumstances. For example, for people born severely mentally handicapped infantalisation will probably be their only human experience, except possibly where efforts have been made at school to develop their potential. For others, affected by sudden disability as a result of accident or illness, or by the slow process of ageing, the adjustment to increased mothering by carers may well be strongly resisted. Alternatively caring through mothering by strangers within an institutional or personal social service setting may be more acceptable than mothering by close kin who may at one time have been the lovers, siblings or children of the cared for. And, finally, mothering may be more acceptable to men than to women, since tending as mothering, in many respects, bears similar characteristics to the human servicing element of domestic labour conventionally carried out by wives (Evers, 1981).

Objective factors are not necessarily the only ones that matter. It is also likely that people in similar circumstances use, negotiate and resist the motherhood model according to their own personal characteristics and biographies. In a recent study by Helen Evers (1981) of 86 geriatric patients in 8 wards she outlines three different ways in which the patients negotiate (not necessarily in a consciously manipulative way) the motherhood model widely used by the nurses. The first stereotype patients she calls 'Dear Old Gran'.

> When speaking of patients of this category, and sometimes also when speaking to them, the nurses would implicitly ascribe child-like qualities to patients, or treat them like children (p. 120).

The result for these patients was extra privileges and extra attention:

> Patients who fitted this category were often the recipients of any 'treats' which might be available, e.g. clothes arriving on the ward which were judged to be particularly nice by the nurses... They had a higher rate of interaction with the nurses, on average, and a proportion of these interactions appeared to be purely social, rather than being structured around some identifiable task being performed by a nurse (pp. 118-19).

A second category of patient – 'Poor Old Nellie' – was more likely to be senile than the Grans.

> Nellies were regarded not as sweet children as with the Grans, but as unfortunate, helpless children. In the main, they presented the

nurses with care problems in the form of an immense burden of work, much of which was distasteful, but which could be tolerated because patients were not on the whole to be held responsible for their parlous state (p. 121).

A third category Evers terms 'Awkward Alice'. These patients were, on the whole, rather more mentally alert than the others – in other words, they had not made the uncomplicated and final shift into 'second childishness'. They still had personal biographies, and felt they had certain tending skills left over from their own careers as informal carers at home. Thus they were 'critical of staff, particularly nurses, and the way they went about their work, not only as it affected them, but also other patients' (p. 122).

> As for their ward careers, these could be described as a running battle, which was sometimes overt, and sometimes featured a truce... the patients resisted the pressure to hand over their autonomy to the nurses, and to 'fit in', to the routine and the ward community (p. 123).

The result for Awkward Alice and her male equivalent – 'Churlish Charlie' – was lack of nursing attention, threats of, and occasional acts of, punishment.

Thus, according to Evers and the evidence of campaigns by the physically disabled to overturn their image as infants, the motherhood model of caring is only variously enjoyed by many people in need of tending. Evers' work has been carried out in an institutional setting: I suspect that the difficulties are considerably amplified when it comes to tending at home. There the history of longstanding relationships determines the ease and difficulty with which carer and cared for adjust to their new roles:

> Tea time, and twelve hours up. Granny said, 'This is a very smooth cup of coffee'. 'Well, tea, actually', I said as I sat sewing. She added, 'But really, dear, I should be doing that.' How to avoid saying, 'You can't, and I wish to hell you could'? It's three years since she was able to sew, and then she managed to cut holes all down the back of my work dress while 'taking out the zip' (Flew, 1980).

Heather McKenzie (1980) in her book *You Alone Care*, which is intended as advice to informal carers (whom she assumes, rightly, to be daughters), goes into these problems of adjustment in some detail. She suggests two kinds of difficulty: in the first case, the mother as the person who is being looked after resents giving up her maternal power to her daughter.

It is not uncommon in a strict parent–child hierarchy for the parent quite bluntly to refuse to do what the daughter suggests, because she maintains that 'she will not be guided by her child'. Some elderly people can be steadfast in this attitude, and it can make the caring role very difficult. If your mother reacts in this way, bring the GP, the health visitor or the social worker on to the scene. They will probably tell your mother a few home truths (p. 53).

Alternatively, she suggests that successful exchange of mothering roles is itself problematic:

> A number of middle-aged women 'baby' their mothers, and subconsciously try to satisfy the unfulfilled mother instinct through their parents. If this happens it can produce a premature dependency on the part of the old person and become a burden on the daughter herself (p. 56)

Thus the use of the motherhood model in tending creates tension and difficulty for some people both in institutions and at home. But it is also clear that other people are happy to revert to infancy, particularly if, as in the case of the 'Dear Old Grans', the effect is to generate extra attention and special treats. But it is at this point that professional advisers themselves begin to object to mothering, on the grounds that by encouraging dependency it is actually *bad for the client* (Bentovim, 1972).

In short, then, there are real problems about the extension of motherhood into tending. Many of the cared for dislike it intensely, and in certain respects the professionals themselves advise against it. Moreover, it may well create more problems at home than it does in institutions largely because the problem of role adjustment is likely to be more difficult between people who have had a totally different kind of relationship in the past. The difficulty, of course, is finding an alternative model, particularly when the mothering model is one which we are all familiar with and have, as children ourselves, almost certainly experienced in our early lives. Indeed, it seems that the motherhood model is so convenient as a guide to the techniques of tending that it may act to exclude men from many caring tasks; for it seems from the sparse literature available, that women themselves dictate and uphold the mothering model in a way which, probably unconsciously but certainly in effect, tends to exclude men from important aspects of tending.

This is hinted at, though not developed, in David Wilkin's (1979) valuable study *Caring for the Mentally Handicapped Child*. Wilkin found that, except for babysitting and lifting, fathers made relatively low contributions to tending their children. For example, only 17% were responsible for dressing and 54% gave the mothers no support with this task; 14% were responsible for changing nappies but 60% gave no support. However, when Wilkin asked the mothers what help they themselves would have liked he found that they least wanted help with housework and the physical care of their children compared with greater demand for help with child-minding. In any case, only a small minority of the mothers wanted more help with almost all domestic labour tasks. Wilkin (1979, pp. 173-4) states:

> Most [mothers] accepted that physical care was something for which they should be responsible and which, in any case, *they felt they were better able to do than others*. They did not identify these tasks as in themselves restricting and did not therefore feel that extra help would have made a very great difference to their lives. *Of course, this is not to say that increased involvement of other family members would have been rejected had it been offered.* (emphasis added).

Table 6.1 Felt needs of all mothers with physical child-care, child-minding and housework (all children mentally handicapped)

Task	No help wanted
Physical child-care	
Dressing and undressing children	77%
Washing and bathing children	84%
Changing nappies	76%
Taking children to toilet	94%
Feeding or supervising children at meal times	85%
Lifting and carrying children	69%
Minding	
Day care	64%
Minding children after school	72%
Minding children at weekends	52%
Minding children in school holidays	32%
Babysitting	54%
Housework	
Cleaning and tidying the house	82%
Cooking and preparing meals	96%
Washing dishes and laying the table	96%
Washing and ironing clothes	86%
Shopping	90%
Transport	49%

Source: Wilkin (1979), Tables 8.1, 8.3, 8.5.

What we do not know is whether – implicitly or explicitly – these offers of help had in fact been turned down, because – as Wilkin points out – the mothers themselves felt that physical caring – and housework – was something they could do better themselves. Nor do we know on what basis mothers thought they could do it better themselves – whether as a result of instinct (as Oakley's sample indicated) or experience. Moreover, some of Wilkin's sample derived great satisfaction from 'a job well done':

> The comprehensive care of a severely mentally handicapped child often requires nothing less than devotion on the part of the person bearing the major responsibility. Many mothers... expressed this sort of devotion, often saying that they lived for their handicapped child. They obtained a sense of fulfilment through caring for him or her and from completing the daily round of routine domestic chores... They saw themselves as wives and mothers, and were content to derive their status from fulfilling to the best of their abilities, the arduous duties of caring for their family and their handicapped child (p. 182).

Thus, certainly as far as caring for mentally handicapped children at home is concerned, tending as mothering seems the obvious and most attractive model for parents themselves to follow. That is how David Wilkin's sample of mothers themselves appeared to want it and the consequence is that caring becomes predominantly woman's territory. But mental handicap is only one of many conditions that need tending, and it has the unique feature of retarded development – in other words, extended infancy. Thus it may well be the case that the mothering model is more appropriate in this particular case than in any others. We have already examined, in a limited way, the problems of role adjustment in tending the elderly and the physically handicapped and there is reason to think that for these groups in particular mothering is inappropriate – or at least has unintended, insulting, and often unhealthy consequences.

Tasks and taboos

Recent research (Wilkin, 1979; Nissel and Bonnerjea, 1982) has unravelled a great many of the tasks actually involved in tending. Wilkin uses the three broad headings of 'physical child-care', 'minding children', and 'household tasks' within which are subsumed tasks such as 'toiletting', 'minding children after school' and 'washing dishes' (see Table 6.1). Nissel and Bonnerjea (1982, Appendix B) use an even longer list of activities which comprise caring for the elderly or handicapped:

> Bathing and washing cared-for
> Dressing cared-for, including undressing or dressing for bed
> Getting into or out of bed
> Lifting, turning, assisting with stairs or getting about house
> Putting on, helping with or taking to commode/toilet
> Giving, overseeing or helping with medication in home (includes exercises)
> Feeding, including a snack, when it means actually physically feeding or assistance, not merely placing tray in front of cared-for

Shopping, specifically for cared-for
Listening out for
Accompanying cared-for in travel
Obtaining medical care in home for cared-for
Obtaining medical care outside the home
Toilette: hair care, nails, shaving, make-up, etc.
Attending to correspondence, bills, paperwork, etc. of or for cared-for
Meal or snack preparation specifically for cared-for
Cleaning specifically for cared-for
Care of clothing of cared-for
Leisure activity performed with or on behalf of cared-for

These tasks they group into five categories according to the 'difficulty' of the task and the extent to which carrying it out excludes the possibility of carrying out any other task. Thus tasks such as dressing, lifting and washing the dependent relative are seen as one grouped activity since they involve the relative's presence, while getting medical care, and administering the affairs of the invalid is another activity since these tasks can be carried out in conjunction with other tasks. There are, then, fairly close relationships between Nissel's overall classification and Wilkin's: both tend to group 'physical care' activities together and have a certain similarity over the classification of 'minding' activities.

But it seems to me that there is an alternative way of classifying these tasks which – for our purposes – is of greater use. The clues for this alternative classification lie in Wilkin's empirical data, which in turn echoes Michael Bayley's work on *Mental Handicap and Community Care* (1973). Wilkin found clear patterns of 'male' and 'female' care, revealed by a close scrutiny of his data on the father's participation in child care and household tasks (see Table 6.2).

On the whole, Wilkin's data shows the low contribution made by the fathers to both the physical care of their children and the other jobs of 'minding' and more general domestic labour. When he looked at father's age, social class and whether or not he was employed, Wilkin found some indication that unemployed fathers gave more support overall, as did fathers aged 31–40. But it seems to me that of at least equal importance in furthering analysis of caring is the clear division of labour between fathers and mothers over particular tending tasks. For certain tasks, limited in number, many fathers were chiefly responsible: over half were mainly responsible for lifting the child (53%), about half (49%) and two-thirds (68%) were responsible respectively for minding the child at weekends and babysitting, and about one-third (31%) were mainly responsible for washing the dishes. In contrast, fathers were on the whole not responsible for other physical care tasks, in particular changing nappies, where 60% of fathers gave no help at all, and dressing and toileting, where 54% and

53% respectively of fathers gave no support. Only very small minorities of fathers were mainly responsible for these physical caring tasks. Wilkin (1979, p. 134) points out that these differences reflect a sex-role stereotyped division of domestic labour and that neither mothers nor fathers thought the situation could or should be much altered.

Table 6.2 Father's participation in child-care and household tasks

Task	Participant	Support helper	No support	Total (100%)
Physical child-care [a]				
Dressing	17 (17%)	30 (30%)	54 (54%)	101
Washing	21 (21%)	29 (29%)	51 (51%)	101
Nappies	9 (14%)	17 (26%)	39 (60%)	65
Toiletting	11 (20%)	15 (27%)	29 (53%)	55
Feeding	20 (24%)	32 (39%)	31 (37%)	83
Lifting	30 (53%)	19 (33%)	8 (14%)	57
Minding children				
After school	15 (14%)	28 (27%)	62 (59%)	105
Weekends	51 (49%)	24 (23%)	30 (29%)	105
School holidays	7 (7%)	15 (14%)	83 (79%)	105
Babysitting	71 (68%)	12 (11%)	22 (21%)	105
Household tasks				
Cleaning	10 (10%)	23 (22%)	72 (69%)	105
Cooking	7 (7%)	28 (27%)	70 (67%)	105
Washing dishes	33 (31%)	23 (22%)	49 (47%)	105
Washing clothes	3 (3%)	10 (10%)	92 (88%)	105
Shopping	24 (23%)	29 (28%)	52 (50%)	105

Note: [a] Includes only those fathers who had a child who required the task performing or who required close supervision.
Source: Wilkin (1979), Table 6.1.

But what are the origins of this clear sexual divison of labour in the tasks of tending? Why is it that fathers (or men) help most with lifting, and least with washing, toiletting and changing nappies? What is it about these particular tasks that so dictates a particular division of labour between the sexes? And if it is apparent that there are general rules about the distribution of particular tasks, do these rules extend into the caring of people other than children, both at home and in institutions? If they do apply in all human tending situations, how does that determine the suitability of caring for a particular individual at home or in an institution?

Lifting the handicapped, which as both Wilkin and Bayley found is largely a male preserve, is, in fact, a question of technique which women as much as men can learn (Chartered Society of Physiotherapy, 1975). The existence of these techniques – largely developed to aid female carers working in institutions – demonstrates that the sexual division of labour is imbued with mistaken views of what constitute male and female aptitudes. But these aptitudes *may* have had a concrete basis in the recent past before reasonable handling skills were developed.

It is when we turn to the other physical caring tasks, particularly those concerned with removing human dirt, that we find more than just a residual view of 'aptitude'. Clearly, the division of labour over managing human dirt owes a great deal to the motherhood model of tending. Like the Newsons (1965) before her Ann Oakley (1974b) found that nappy changing was a central issue in establishing the boundaries of fathers' willingness to help in child-care.

As I have already suggested, crucial aspects of the image of mothering are translated into tending handicapped adults; dealing with incontinence and other human excreta is doubtless another of these aspects. The fact that women have a virtual monopoly in dealing with these aspects of tending can be most easily ascribed to a system of taboo in contemporary British society about the management of human excreta. I use the word 'taboo' rather than 'norm' in order to convey the idea that the transgressing of the system is polluting and dangerous. It is interesting to note that one of Ann Oakley's respondents, in answer to her question 'Does (or did) your husband change the baby's dirty nappy?' replied:

> No! He absolutely refuses. He says 'no thank you, goodbye, I'm going out!' If I'm changing a nappy, he runs out of the room, it makes him sick. He thinks it's my duty. (1974b, p. 154.)

It is, of course, foolhardy to generalise from a sample of one, but it seems to me that this hypothesis raises a number of interesting issues. Does the taboo system exist and what is its origin? How can we explain it? Clearly hygiene has little or nothing to do with it, since otherwise one might expect that women, who are the cooks as well as the cleaners, would be excluded from the kitchen particularly when rearing small children. Is the fear of human excreta and emphasis on its control relatively recent in our society – possibly since the introduction of the flushing cistern and the discovery of public health – and how is it that women have come to be the managers of it in the 'private domain'? Is it simply the fact that the job is unpleasant and women carry it out because men have used their power and refused to do it? As the chant of the women's movement would have it:

> When Adam delved and Eve span
> Who cleaned out the lavatory pan?

Or is it, rather, that women are already primarily polluted by menstruation and childbirth, and hence the more obvious candidates for further pollution? And how is it that in many British households (most?)

men are responsible for 'putting out the rubbish' but not for controlling any other 'matter out of place'? (Douglas, 1970.)

These are important questions which are, so far, unasked, let alone answered. The issues they raise are highly pertinent to the question of women and the 'caring capacity of the community', for if we are dealing here with a system of taboos rather than norms, then it is extremely unlikely that men can become responsible for tending incontinent people. Should they do so they would threaten their own sense of personal order and that of the people they care for; they may also create for themselves a publicly outcast position. In other words, one might be forced to argue that, given the existence of this taboo, the caring capacity of the community for large numbers of the incapacitated who are incontinent is irretrievably confined to women. But if we accept that argument, then the fact that women in our society are the managers of this area of human life also has serious consequences for the cared for. For, as already suggested, most women experience motherhood and child-rearing, and there are clear spillover effects into tending. The management and control of human excreta has a central place in the image of successful mothering, since mothers are responsible for introducing the order of 'toilet training' into the babies' lives. The successful imposition of that order is of enormous symbolic as well as practical importance – it is, like the development of speech, a most significant indicator that the baby is human and can impose his or her own control on himself and his or her environment, and enjoy social interaction with other humans. The further implication is that the breakdown at any age of this particular order is also of enormous significance. It immediately sets the incontinent person apart as not properly human – or, at the very least, not properly adult; the temptation for the carer, particularly a woman who has struggled in the past to impose this order on her children, is to categorise the *whole* incontinent person as a child or a failed human being, with possibly disastrous consequences for the whole caring relationship between carer and cared for.

Another system of taboos relevant to tending is much more widely recognised and, indeed, is subject to public legal sanction. These are the incest taboos. A great deal of tending necessarily and, in cases of incontinence, inevitably involves touching genitalia. Where the tending is carried out by kin, the system of incest taboos is, I am sure, of enormous importance. An article by Annis Flew in *New Society* on 'Looking after Granny' gave a graphic account of the relationship between her and her very old and senile mother-in-law. A great deal of her time is taken up with keeping 'Granny' clean. I invite all readers to imagine Mrs Flew to be her husband (whose mother 'Granny' is) or to imagine themselves caring for their own parent or parent-in-law of opposite sex to themselves, in equivalent ways. To me, such a prospect is horrifying, although I am also sure many carers do, under force of circumstance, break down the powerful taboo system to which we are all subject and carry out such cross-sex tending. However, I suspect that beliefs about incest are a powerful 'background noise' in determining the success or otherwise of such tending at home. In the particular case of women carers looking after male relatives other than their husbands, there is clearly a conflict between the demands of the taboos about human dirt which I have argued effectively act to exclude men carers, and the taboos about incest. Hence such women may find themselves in exceptionally trying circumstances. Having suggested, however, that fears of incest act as a powerful 'background noise' I suspect that the 'noise' is peculiarly silent – in other words, the fears are left unarticulated and largely unrecognised. Thus, while tending relationships may break down as a result of them, the ostensible reason for their breakdown may be some quite different issue, and professionals dealing with the allocation of community resources may completely misunderstand the dimensions and seriousness of the breakdown. Alternatively, general practitioners who normally act as the 'gatekeepers' to further resources (Hunt, 1970) may, consciously or unconsciously, give priority to families where the tending relationship is potentially an incestuous one and remove the person in need of care to an institution.

To conclude this section on 'tasks and taboos' and to return to where we began: Wilkin's and Nissel's task orientated research has been very important in developing our knowledge about sex-role stereotyping and particular tending tasks. However, their classification systems, based as they are on the activity of the particular task and the need for the relative to be present, do not, on the whole, unravel the full complexity of the tending relationship. On looking at the sexual division of labour between tasks, it is clear from Wilkin's work that not all 'physical care' tasks are of the same kind: lifting, for example, is conventionally – though not necessarily rationally – regarded as a 'man's job', whereas other physical care tasks are regarded as a woman's preserve. But, more importantly, I have tried to indicate that there are relationships involved, not just between those such as husbands and wives who share the tending task, but also between the carers and the cared for. I have therefore suggested that there may be two taboo systems operating which are applicable to these relationships, and allow us to make general hypotheses about them.

In order to test the existence of these systems and to understand their effects one would have to adopt a rather different classification system. In particular, the chief variables in such a new classification would be the sex of the carer, together with the sex of the cared-for, the kin relationship between them and the particular nature of the physical care tasks involved. Some of this kind of classification, derived as it is from analysis of domestic situations, might also be relevant to the investigation of tending relationships within institutions, more obviously in the case of dealing with human dirt.

Conclusions

It should by now be clear that this paper has been concerned with analysing the dimension of the *relationships* between carers and cared for. It seems to me vital that we develop our understanding in this area, if only to increase the sensitivity and understanding of the professionals who are chiefly responsible for and dependent on the maintenance of good informal caring at home. I have therefore tried to suggest a number of ways in which relationships of this intimate kind are constrained and determined. In particular, I have stressed the problems that might arise when carers adopt a model of tending suitable to one kind of relationship (mother/child) and transfer it, both within institutions and at home, to relationships of quite another kind. I have also suggested that domestic relationships are different from institutional relationships in that they have a *history*, and this again might give rise to particular problems when roles have to be exchanged, particularly between mothers and daughters. Last but not least, I have suggested that the sex of the carers and the cared for is important, partially because it may determine the boundaries of their tending relationship, and partially because the quality of their tending may be related to whether or not they had (and continue to have) an explicitly sexual relationship.

I am, therefore, in fundamental agreement with Margaret Stacey (1981, p. 189) when she writes:

> We must admit the importance of feeling states over a wider range than the recognition of consciousness of the kind which we are familiar with in class formation... It has been a major contribution of the recent women's movement to put feelings, experiences, consciousness on the agenda for political action; to insist that politics cannot be understood without taking account of the politics of the family, of the experiences of women in their relationships with men... a similar point has to be made with regard to sociological theory.

Stacey's main point is that there are analogies between the relationships that hold in the 'public domain' and those that hold in the 'private domain', particularly in the area of what she calls 'people work'. I have argued a similar point, although I would qualify it by suggesting that some of the relationships, particularly those relating to the question of incest, are exclusive to the 'private domain' and have no analogy elsewhere. Moreover I suspect that sociological theory could and should learn not only from feminism, but also from other theoretical perspectives from within anthropology and psychoanalysis. Mary Douglas's work on *Purity and Danger* (1970) could provide a useful basis for an understanding of taboos and beliefs about dirt, while psychoanalytical theory should be similarly helpful when considering the impact of the motherhood model of tending and the boundaries enforced by incest taboos.

However, even if we are beginning to develop better ways of conceptualising the relationships that hold within and between 'private' and 'public' domains, there remain the problems of actually doing the research demanded by these new concepts. Any research that involves the uncovering of largely unarticulated social rules and the recognition of the complexity of hidden and unrecognised feelings is of extreme sensitivity, and some might think it too difficult to handle. This is the policy of defeat; moreover, continued ignorance in this difficult area might well mean that decisions about the allocation of resources, or the institutionalisation of someone in need of care, are being made on mistaken, implicit, or even brutalising assumptions. The two chief principles of any such research, whether it takes place in institutions or in domestic settings, have to be first, that the feelings and attitudes of the cared for as well as the carer are accounted for, and secondly, that the sexual division of labour and its relation to tending tasks has a central place in any analysis of the caring relationship.

Note

1 This paper arises out of work commissioned and funded by the SSRC and submitted to them in a report entitled *Women, Work and the 'caring capacity of the community': a report of a research review*. I am grateful to the SSRC for the grant which enabled me to do this work and for their permission to reproduce some of the report here.

7 'It's a pleasure to cook for him': Food, Mealtimes and Gender in some South Wales Households
Anne Murcott

Introduction

> I think it lets him know that I am thinking about him – as if he knows that I am expecting him. But it's not as if 'oh I haven't got anything ready'... Fair play, he's out all day... he doesn't ask for that much... you know it's not as if he's been very demanding or – he doesn't come home and say 'oh, we've got chops again', it's really a pleasure to cook for him, because whatever you... oh I'll give him something and I think well, he'll like this, he'll like that. And he'll always take his plate out... and he'll wash the dishes without me even asking, if I'm busy with the children. Mind, perhaps his method is not mine.

Every now and then an informant puts precisely into words the results of the researcher's analytic efforts – providing in the process a quotation suitable for the title! The extract reproduced above, explaining the importance of having the meal ready when her husband arrives home, comes from one of a series of interviews on which this paper is based.[1] The discussion starts by remembering that 'everyone knows' that women do the cooking: all the women interviewed – and the few husbands/boyfriends or mothers who came in and out – took it for granted that cooking was women's work. Informants may not enjoy cooking, or claim not to be good at it; they may not like the arrangement that it is women's work, or hanker after modifying it. But all recognise that this is conventional, some volunteer a measure of approval, most appeared automatically to accept it, a few resigned themselves and got on with it.

Studies of the organisation of domestic labour and marital role relationships confirm that cooking continues to be a task done more by women than men; this is also the case cross-culturally (Stephens, 1963; Murdock and Provost, 1973). Emphasis in the literature has shifted from Young and Willmott's (1975) symmetrical view of sharing and marital democracy. Now rather more thoroughgoing empirical study suggests their assessment is little more than unwarranted optimism (Oakley, 1974a and b; Edgell, 1980; Leonard, 1980; Tolson, 1977). This work improves on earlier studies of the domestic division of labour by going beyond behaviourist enquiry about 'who does which tasks' to consider the meanings attached to them by marital partners. The distribution of work turns out not to correlate neatly with assessments of importance or allocation of responsibility. (Oakley, 1974b; Edgell, 1980).

Part of this effort (in particular, Oakley, 1974a and b) has in addition attempted to analyse domestic work as a 'job like any other', considering housewives' work satisfaction, routines, supervision and so on. While this line of enquiry has undoubtedly made visible much of women's lives conventionally rendered invisible, it has perhaps not gone far enough. The study of housework as an occupation needs to attend in addition to features such as quality control, timekeeping, client as well as worker satisfaction, and perhaps further consideration of who, if anyone, is a housewife's boss. As will be seen, each of these is implicated in the discussion that follows.

These occupational aspects of housework provide, moreover, additional means of examining the relationship of the domestic division of labour to the economic structure as a whole. Recent commentary has also proposed that the view of the family as stripped of all but the residual economic function of consumption is ill-conceived and over-simplified. Domestic labourers refresh and sustain the existing labour force and play a key part in reproducing that of the future – as well as providing a reserve of labour themselves. The precise manner in which the political economy is to be accounted continues to be debated (West, 1980; Fox, 1980; Wajcman, 1981). For the moment, however, the general drift of that discussion can be borne in mind by recalling the everyday terminology of eating; food is consumed, meals have to be produced. The language favoured in cookbooks echoes that of industry and the factory (Murcott, 1983a). Home-cooking may nicely embody the terms in which the family and household's place in the division of labour has to be seen. It may also provide a convenient arena for the further exploration of the economic and labour relations in the family and the relation of the marital partners to the means of production of domestic labour (Middleton, 1974).

Examination of the household provision of meals in these terms is, however, some way in the future. This paper does no more than offer some empirical foundation on which such study might build. It brings together informants' ideas about the importance of cooking, their notions of propriety of household eating and indicates their relation to gender. It starts with views of the significance of good cooking for home life, and goes on to deal with the place of cooking in the domestic division of labour. The familiar presumption that women are the cooks is extended to show that their responsibility in this sphere is tempered with reference to their husband's, not their own, choice. The paper concludes with brief comment on possible ways these data may illuminate some of the questions already raised.

Home cooking

> Aside from love, good food is the cornerstone of a happy household... (Opening lines of a 1957 cookbook called *The Well Fed Bridegroom*).

Right through the series of interviews three topics kept cropping up; the idea of a proper meal, reference to what informants call a 'cooked dinner' and the notion that somehow home is where proper eating is ensured. Moreover, mention of one like as not involved mention of another, sometimes all three. The composite picture that emerges from the whole series suggests that these are not merely related to one another in some way, but virtually equated.

It first needs to be said that informants seemed quite comfortable with a conception of a proper meal – indeed the very phrase was used spontaneously – and were able to talk about what it meant to them. Effectively a proper meal is a cooked dinner. This is one which women feel is necessary to their family's health, welfare and, indeed, happiness. It is a meal to come home to, a meal which should figure two, three or four times in the week, and especially on Sundays. A cooked dinner is easily identified – meat, potatoes, vegetables and gravy. It turns out that informants displayed considerable unanimity as to what defines such a dinner, contrasting it to, say, a 'snack' or 'fried'. In so doing they made apparent remarkably clear rules not only for its composition but also its preparation and taking. I have dealt with their detail and discussed their implications in full elsewhere (Murcott, 1982). But in essence these rules can be understood as forming part of the equation between proper eating and home cooking. And, as will be noted in the next section, they also provide for the symbolic expression of the relationship between husband and wife and for each partner's obligation to their home.

The meal for a return home is, in any case, given particular emphasis – a matter which cropped up in various contexts during the interviews. Thus, for some the very importance of cooking itself is to be expressed in terms of homecoming. Or it can provide the rationale for turning to and making a meal, one to be well cooked and substantial – not just 'beans on toast... thrown in front of you'.

The actual expression 'home cooking' – as distinct from 'cooking for homecoming' – received less insistent reference. Informants were straightforward, regarding it as self-evident that people preferred the food that they had at home, liked what they were used to and enjoyed what they were brought up on. Perhaps untypically nostalgic, one sums up the point:

> When my husband comes home... there's nothing more he likes I think than coming in the door and smelling a nice meal cooking. I think it's awful when someone doesn't make the effort... I think well if I was a man I'd think I'd get really fed up if my wife never bothered...

What was prepared at home could be trusted – one or two regarded the hygiene of restaurant kitchens with suspicion, most simply knew their chips were better than those from the local Chinese take-away or chippy. Convenience foods had their place, but were firmly outlawed when it came to a cooked dinner. In the ideal, commercially prepared items were ranged alongside snacks, and light, quick meals: lunches and suppers in contrast to proper dinners. Informants talked about home cooking, but used this or some such phrase infrequently; the following is an exception:

> I'd like to be able to make home-made soups and things, it's just finding the time and getting organised, but at the moment I'm just not organised... I think it would probably be more good for us than buying... I suppose it's only – I'd like to be – the image of the ideal housewife is somebody who cooks her own food and keeps the household clean and tidy.

The sentiments surrounding her valuation of home-made food are not, however, an exception. Time and again informants linked not only a view of a proper meal for homecoming, but a view of the proper parts husband and wife are to play on this occasion. So cooking is important when you are married.

> you must think of your husband... it's a long day for him at work, usually,... even if they have got a canteen at work, their cooking is not the same as coming home to your wife's cooking... I think every working man should have a cooked meal when he comes in from work...

Cooking is important – though not perhaps for everybody 'like men who don't cook' – for women whose 'place [it is] to see the family are well fed'.

In this section, I have indicated that informants virtually treat notions of proper meals, home-based eating and a cooked dinner, as equivalents. The stress laid on the homecoming not only underlines the symbolic significance attached to both the meal and the return home. It simultaneously serves as a reminder of the world beyond the home being left behind for that day. Put another way, the cooked dinner marks the threshold between the public domains of school or work and the private sphere behind the closed front door. In the process of describing these notions of the importance of cooking in the home, it becomes apparent that the familiar division of labour is assumed.

Cooking in the domestic division of labour

As noted in an earlier section, all those interviewed took it for granted that it is the women who cook. What they had to say refers both to conventions in general, and themselves and their circumstances in particular.[2] There are two important features of their general presumption that women are the cooks; one indicates the terms in which it is modifiable, the other locates it firmly as a matter of marital justice and obligation. The upshot of each of these is to underline the manner in which the domestic preparation of meals is securely anchored to complementary concepts of conduct proper to wife and husband.

To say that women cook is not to say that it is only women who ever do so. It is, however, to say that it is always women who daily, routinely, and as a matter of course are to do the cooking. Men neither in the conventional stereotype nor in informants' experience ever cook on a regular basis in the way women do.[3] Husband/boyfriends/fathers are 'very good really'; they help informants/their mothers with carrying the heavy shopping, preparing the vegetables, switching the oven on when told, doing the dishes afterwards (cf. Leonard, 1980). Such help may be offered on a regular enough basis, notably it is available when the women are pregnant, dealing with a very young infant, unwell or unusually tired. But none of this is regarded as men doing the cooking.

More significantly, it is not the case that men do not cook – in the strict sense of taking charge of the transformation of foodstuffs to some version of a meal. They may make breakfast on a Sunday, cook only 'bacon-y' things, can do chips or 'his' curries: all examples, incidentally, of foods that do *not* figure in the proper cooked dinner (Murcott, 1983c).

For some, however, competence in the kitchen (and at the shops) is suspect: he'll 'turn the potatoes on at such and such a time... but leave him he's hopeless' and another just 'bungs everything in'. For others, it is men who make better domestic cooks than women, are more methodical, less moody. Another couple jokingly disagree: she 'not taken in' by Robert Carrier on TV, he claiming that 'the best chefs are men'. The point is that either way, of course, informants do regard gender as relevant to the question of who is to cook.

It is not even the case that all men cannot cook the proper, homecoming meal. One or two, when out of work for a while, but his wife still earning (this only applied to those having a first baby) might start the meal or even have it ready for her return. But once he is employed again he does not continue to take this degree of responsibility, reverting either to 'helping' or waiting for her to do it. Now and again, wives have learned to cook not at school or from their mothers, but from their husbands. But it was still assumed that it was for the woman to learn. This was even so in one instance where the informant made a 'confession... my husband does the cooking'. But now that she was pregnant and had quit paid work she would take over; 'it would be a bit lazy not to'. Like others for whom the cooking may have been shared while both were employed, cooking once again became the home-based wife's task (cf. Bott, 1957, p. 225; Oakley, 1980, p. 132).

The issue is, however, more subtle than an account of who does what, or who takes over doing what. Men and women's place involve mutual obligation. 'I think a woman from the time she can remember is brought up to cook... Whereas most men are brought up to be the breadwinner.' The question of who does the cooking is explicitly a matter of justice and marital responsibility. A woman talks of the guilt she feels if she does not, despite the greater tiredness of late pregnancy, get up to make her husband's breakfast and something for lunch – 'he's working all day'. Another insists that her husband come shopping with her so he knows the price of things – he's 'hopeless' on his own – but she has a clear idea of the limits of each person's responsibility: each should cook only if the wife *has* to earn rather than chooses to do so.

Here, then, I have sought to show that informants subscribed in one way or another to the convention that it is women who cook. In the process it transpired that it is certain sorts of cooking, i.e. routine, homecoming cooking, which are perennially women's work. The meal that typically represents 'proper' cooking is, of course, the cooked dinner. Its composition and prescribed cooking techniques involve prolonged work and attention; its timing, for homecoming, prescribes when that work shall be done. To do so demands the cook be working at it, doing wifely work, in time that corresponds to time spent by her husband earning for the family (Murcott, 1982). This is mirrored in Eric Batstone's (1983) account of the way a car worker's lunch box prepared by his wife the evening before is symbolic of the domestic relationship which constitutes the rationale for his presence in the workplace; he endures the tedium of the line in order to provide for his wife and family. It transpired also that men do cook in certain circumstances, but such modification seems to reveal more clearly the basis for accounting cooking as part of a wife's responsibility (to the family) at home corresponding to the husband's obligation (to the family) at work, i.e. their mutual responsibilities to each other as marriage partners.

Who cooks for whom?

At this point I introduce additional data which bear on cooking's relation to the question of marital responsibility. Repeatedly informants indicated that people do not cook for themselves; evidently it is not worth the time and effort.[4] But the data suggest implications beyond such matters of economy. Two interrelated features are involved: one is the distinction already alluded to in the previous section, between cooking in the strict sense of the word and cooking as preparation of a particular sort of meal. The other enlarges on the following nicety. To observe that people do not cook for themselves can mean two things. First it can imply that a solitary person does not prepare something for themselves to eat while on their own. But it can also imply that someone does not do the cooking on their own behalf, but in the service of some other(s). Examination of the transcripts to date suggests that not only could informants mean either or both of these, but also that each becomes elided in a way that underlines the nuances and connotations of the term cooking.

The question of a lone person not cooking themselves a meal unsurprisingly cropped up most frequently with reference to women themselves, but men, or the elderly were also thought not to bother.

Informants are clear, however, that not cooking when alone does not necessarily mean going without. Women 'pick' at something that happens to be in the house, have a bar of chocolate or packet of crisps later in the evening or a 'snack'. Men will fry something, an egg or make chips. No one said that a man would go without altogether (though they may not know), whereas for themselves – and women and girls in general – skipping a meal was thought common enough. Men – and occasionally women – on their own also go back to their mother's or over to their sister's for a meal. One informant was (the day of my interview with her) due to go to her mother's for the evening meal, but fearful of being alone in the house at night, she was also due to stay there for the next few days while her husband was away on business.

The suggestion is, then, that if a person is by themselves, but is to have a proper meal, as distinct from 'fried' or a 'snack' then they join a (close) relation's household. The point that it is women who cook such meals receives further emphasis. Indeed, when women cook this particular meal, it is expressly *for* others. In addition to the temporary lone adults just noted who return to mothers or sisters, women in turn may cook for the older generation, as well as routinely cooking for children or for men home at 'unusual' times if unemployed or temporarily of a different shift.

This conventional requirement that women cook for others is not always straightforward in practice. At certain stages in an infant's life the logistics of producing meals for husband *and* child(ren) there as well meant the woman felt difficulties in adequately meeting the obligations involved. And not all informants enjoyed cooking; most just accepted that it needed doing, though there were also those who took positive, creative pleasure in it (cf. Oakley, 1974b). Part of this is expressed in the very satisfaction of providing for others something they should be getting, and in turn will enjoy.

More generally cooking can become tiresome simply because it has to be done day-in, day-out. The pleasure in having a meal prepared for you becomes all the more pointed if routinely you are cooking for others[5]. In the absence of any data for men, it can only be a guess that going out for a meal is thus specially enjoyable for women. But for those who on occasion did eat out this clearly figures in their pleasure. Even if it rarely happened, just the idea of having it put in front of you meant a treat: 'it's nice being spoiled'.

The question 'who cooks for whom?' can now begin to be answered. Apparently it is women who cook for others – effectively, husbands and children. If husbands and children are absent, women alone will not 'cook', indeed many may not even eat. It is the others' presence which provides the rationale for women's turning to and making a proper meal – that is what the family should have and to provide it is her obligation. Men – and children – have meals made for them as a matter of routine: but for women it is a treat. That solitary men do not 'cook' for themselves either, and may go to a relative's for meals (cf. Rosser and Harris, 1965; Barker, 1972), or that a woman on her own may also do so does not detract from the main proposal that it is women who cook for others. For it is not only that informants or their husbands will go temporarily back to their mother's, not their father's, home-cooking. It is also that both men and women revert to the status of a child for whom a woman, a mother, cooks. The mother may actually be the adult's parent, but they – and I with them – may stretch the point and see that she may be mother to the adult's nieces or nephews or indeed, as in the case of cooking for the elderly, she may be mother to the adult's grandchildren.

The appreciation that it is women who cook for others elaborates the more familiar convention, discussed above, that in the domestic division of labour cooking is women's work. First of all it indicates that this work is service work. Cooking looks increasingly like a task quite particularly done for others. Second, when cooking for others women are performing a service to those who are specifically related (sic) rather than for a more generalised clientele known only by virtue of their becoming customers. The marital – and parental – relationship defines who is server, who served.

That said, there remains the question of deciding what the server shall serve. As already discussed in an earlier section, the conventional expectation shared, it seems, by both woman and man, is that meals shall be of a certain sort – a cooked dinner for a certain occasion, most commonly the return home from work, or the celebration of Sunday, a work-free day. The 'rules' involved are not entirely hard and fast, or precisely detailed. Cooked dinners are neither daily nor invariable affairs (Murcott, 1982). And the cooked dinner itself can properly comprise a number of alternative meats (and cuts) and range of different vegetables.

What, then, determines the choice of meat and vegetables served on any particular day? Some of the factors involved, as will be seen in the next section, once again echo ideas of responsibility and mutual obligation.

Deciding what to have
A number of factors feature in deciding what to have for a particular day's meal.[6] First, a question of cost was taken for granted. This does not necessarily mean keeping expenditure to a minimum – eating in the customary manner despite hard times was highly and expressly valued by some. Second, the conventional provision of proper dinners itself contributed to the determination of choice. These two factors present themselves as marking the limits within which the finer decisions about what the precise components of the day's dinner are to be. Here reference to their husband's – and, to a lesser extent, children's – preferences was prominent in informants' discussion of such detailed choices.

It was indicated earlier that in an important sense women's cooking is service work. This sort of work has two notable and interrelated aspects affecting decisions and choice: is it the server or served who decides what the recipient is to want? Exploring the mandate for professionals' work, Everett Hughes (1971, p. 424) highlights a key question: 'professionals do not merely serve: they define the very wants they serve'. Servants, and service workers such as waitresses (Whyte, 1948; Spradley and Mann, 1975) compliantly provide for the wants identified by the served. On the face of it, then, the professional has total and the waitress nil autonomy. Examples reflecting this sort of range occurred among informants varying from one woman apparently always deciding, through to another always making what he wants for tea. But in the same way that the maximum autonomy of the professional is continually, to a certain degree, a matter of negotiation and renegotiation with clients, and that, similarly, the apparent absence of autonomy is modified by a variety of more or less effective devices waitresses use to exert some control over customers, so a simple report of how meal decisions are reached can, I propose, either conceal negotiations already complete, or reveal their workings.

Thus informants interested in trying new recipes still ended up sticking to what they usually made because their husbands were not keen. Others reported that 'he's very good' or 'never complains' while some always asked what he wanted. A non-committal reply however did not necessarily settle the matter, for some discovered that being presented with a meal she had then decided on could provoke adverse and discouraging remarks. But it was clear that even those who claimed not to give their husbands a choice were still concerned to ensure that he agreed to her suggestion. It is almost as if they already knew what he would like, needed to check out a specific possibility every now and then but otherwise continued to prepare meals within known limits. Deciding what to have already implicitly took account of his preferences so that the day-to-day decision *seemed* to be hers. The material presented in this section provides only a glimpse of this area of domestic decision-making. Other aspects need consideration in future work. For instance, what degree of importance do people attach to the matter (cf. Edgell, 1980, pp. 58–9)? Attention also needs to be paid to wider views of the legitimacy of choice in what one eats. In what sense do restaurant customers choose and mentally subnormal patients not? Does a child that spits out what it is fed succeed in claiming a choice or not? And in apparently acquiescing to their husband's choice, are wives circumscribing their own? But it looks as if deciding what to have is of a piece with a shared view of marital responsibility whereby he works and so deserves, somehow, the right to choose what she is to cook for him.

Gender and the production of meals

> I know a cousin of mine eats nothing but chips, in fact his mother-in-law had to cook him chips for his Christmas dinner and she went berserk...

This 'atrocity story' recapitulates various elements of the preceding discussion. Such unreasonableness is, no doubt, unusual but its artless reporting emphasises a number of points already made. Not only do chips break the rules of what should properly figure in a Christmas meal, superior even to the Sunday variant of a cooked dinner, but it remains, however irksome, up to the woman to prepare what a man wants. The burden of this paper, then, may be summarised as revealing allegiance to the propriety of occasion such that a certain sort of meal is to mark home (male) leisure versus (male) work-time, and that such meals are cooked by women for others, notably husbands, in deference, not to the woman's own, but to men's taste.

This examination of cooking, mealtimes and gender within the household has implications for the continuing analysis of domestic work as work. While it does not shed light on why such work is women's, only reasserting that conventionally this is so, it clearly casts the work of meal provision as service work.

The everyday way of describing dishing up a meal as serving food is embedded in a set of practices that prescribe the associated social relationships as of server and served. As already observed this involves two interrelated matters: control over the work, and decisions as to what are the 'wants' the worker shall serve, what the work shall be. Each is considered in turn.

Oakley (1974a and b) reports that one of the features of housewifery that women value is the feeling of autonomy. Care is needed, though, not to treat such attitudes as tantamount to their analysis. Just because housewives express their experiences in terms of enjoying being their own boss does not mean that their conditions of work can be analysed in terms of a high degree of autonomy. The material presented in this paper suggests that doing the cooking is not directed by the woman herself, but is subject to various sorts of control.

First of these is the prescription for certain kinds of food for certain occasions. The idea of the cooked dinner for a homecoming is just such an example of cultural propriety. Related to this is a second control, namely that the food is to be ready for a specific time. Mealtimes construed in this way may exert just the same sort of pressure on the cook as any other production deadline in industry. Third, control is also exerted via the shared understanding that it is the preferences of the consumer which are to dictate the exact variant of the dinner to be served. What he fancies for tea constrains the cook to provide it. These kinds of control in the domestic provision of meals find their counterpart in the industrial concerns of quality control, timekeeping and market satisfaction. A woman cooking at home may not have a chargehand 'breathing down her neck' which is understandably a source of relief to her. But this does not mean to say that she enjoys autonomy – simply perhaps that other controls make this sort of oversight redundant. Evidence either way is extremely sparse, but Ellis (1983) suggests that failing to cook according to her husband's wishes can contribute to a wife's battering.

Linked to the issue of control of domestic cooking is the question of decision-making. Edgell (1980) has drawn attention to the degree of importance couples attach to different aspects of family living about which decisions have to be made. He distinguishes assessments of importance from, first, whether the decision is mainly the wife's or husband's responsibility and second, from the frequency with which the decision has to be made. So, for instance, moving is the husband's decision, perceived to be very important and infrequent, a contrast to the matter of spending on food. What Edgell does not make clear, however, is quite what either his informants or he mean by 'importance'. As an analytic device, the idea does not distinguish between family matters which partners may identify as both important and somehow major or permanent such as moving, and those identified as mundane, or fleeting but important nonetheless, such as daily eating. Like refuse collection or sewage work which is regarded as vital but low status, the importance attached to meals may not be remarked in the general run of things, though noticed particularly if absent. But that does not necessarily mean that both husband and wife regard it as unimportant. And, harking back to the question of autonomy in decision-making, reports such as Edgell's that food spending, cooking or whatever is regarded as the wife's responsibility, cannot, of itself, be seen as evidence of her power and freedom from control in those areas. For as Jan Pahl (1982, p. 24) has so cogently observed, 'being able to offload certain decisions and certain money-handling chores on to the other spouse can itself be a sign of power'. The delegate may be responsible for execution of tasks, but they are answerable to the person in whom the power to delegate is originally vested.

The preliminary analysis offered in this paper has theoretical and political implications concerning power and authority in marriage and the relation between domestic and paid work. The exploration of ideas about cooking and mealtimes starts to provide additional approach to detailing the means of domestic production. And the sort of work women are to do to ensure the homecoming meal provides a critical instance of the juncture between the control of a worker and the (his) control of his wife. The meal provides one illustration not only of a point where the public world of employment and the private world of the home meet one another; it also shows how features of the public take precedence within the private. For the stress informants lay on this mealtime offers an interesting way of understanding how the industrial rhythms which circumscribe workers are linked to the rhythms which limit women's domestic work (cf. Rotenberg, 1981). And women's continual accommodation to men's taste can also be seen as a literal expression of wives' deference to husbands' authority (Bell and Newby, 1976; Edgell, 1980, p. 70). This acquiescence to his choice provides the cultural gloss to the underlying economic relationship whereby industry produces amongst other things both the wage, and the raw materials it buys, for the domestic to produce what is needed to keep the industrial worker going. Part of the conjugal contract that each in their own way provide for the other, it does indeed become 'a pleasure to cook for him'.

Acknowledgements

I am very grateful to all those necessarily anonymous people who made the research possible and who generously gave their time to answer my questions. I should like to record my appreciation of conversations with Tony Coxon, Sara Delamont, Robert Dingwall, Rhian Ellis, Bill Hudson and Phil Strong at various stages during the preparation of this paper and of the computing help and advice Martin Read provided. Only I and not they are to blame for its deficiencies. And I must thank Lindsey Nicholas, Joan Ryan, Sheila Pickard, Myrtle Robins and Margaret Simpson very much, despite flu all round, and an unusually scrawly manuscript, for their help in typing both drafts.

Notes

1 In order to begin remedying sociology's neglect (Murcott, 1983b) of food beliefs and of the social organisation of eating, I conducted a single-handed exploratory study (supported by a grant from the SSRC) holding unstructured tape-recorded interviews with a group of 37 expectant mothers attending a health centre in a South Wales valley for antenatal care (22 pregnant for the first time), 20 of whom were interviewed again after the baby's birth. No claim is made for their representativeness in any hard and fast sense, though they represent a cross-section of socio-economic groups. For present purposes the data are treated as providing a composite picture. The prime concern here is to indicate the range and variety of evidence gathered. An instance that occurs once only thus becomes as interesting as one occurring 30 times. This is reflected in the discussion by the deliberate use of phrases such as 'some informants' rather than '6 out of 37'. In any case reference to numbers of instances is no more exact, and risks implying a spurious representativeness.

These qualifications are most important. But for the sake of a tolerably readable account I do not hedge every other sentence with reminder of these limitations. Yet they do actively have to be taken as read.

2 Informants referred not only to themselves but also to mothers, sisters, sisters-in-law and women friends doing cooking.

3 No informant who had children old enough to cook currently shared the household with them.

4 Market researchers know how to trade on such reports. During the period of interviewing a TV commercial was running which sought to persuade busy housewives not to neglect themselves but have a frozen ready-cooked meal at lunchtime.

5 Interestingly, no one talked of hospital meals put in front of them as a treat. (None had a home delivery.) Rather it was the quality of the food provided which informants concentrated on. Institution cooking could not be home cooking.

6 It might have been expected that nutritional criteria would figure in these decisions. Analysis so far suggests that cultural prescriptions for proper eating at home override what is known about healthy eating. (Murcott, 1983d).

8 'Women and Old Boats': the Sexual Division of Labour in a Newfoundland Outport[1]
Marilyn Porter

Introduction

In this paper I want to explore the nature of the sexual division of labour and its relation to the subordination of women by examining how it operates in one, particularly clear, context. By the sexual division of labour I mean something altogether broader than 'men's jobs' and 'women's jobs', or how a married couple split the household chores. I mean all those things we say and do, how we say and do them and what social consequences they have that are conditioned by our gender. We need, I think, to return to our initial astonishment that so much human activity is gender specific.

Feminist attention has been focused on societies, or groups within a society, which have demonstrated a more flexible sexual division of labour, or where women have constructed areas of autonomy or even power: where the mould of inevitability has been broken (e.g. Rowbotham, 1972; Caplan and Bujra, 1978; Croll, 1978).[2] Behind this search lies the hope that such exceptions, like the swallow, will herald the summer.

We have long since exposed the myth of the 'tokenism' at the individual level, but at the societal level we still cling to it – a habit which prevents our understanding how the struggles of the few can become the common sense of the many. In this paper, however, I want to take the opposite approach, and turn my attention to a situation in which the sexual division of labour appears to be especially rigid and intense. In this way I hope to get some purchase on the interlocking and overriding structures of male domination and capitalist exploitation. My focus is *labour*, rather than sexual divisions rooted in religion, forms of marriage or other ideological structures. It therefore seemed appropriate to examine a society or community that was characterised by an entirely male occupation.

Maritime communities

There are many occupations that are pursued principally by men, but fishing was isolated by Murdock and Provost (1973), along with hunting and herding large animals, as a task most often reserved entirely for men in most known human societies. Stereo-typically, fishing is dangerous, requires great strength and stamina and long absences from home. Even so, there is, as Andersen (1979) says, 'no clearly natural sexually based division of labour in fishing'. Despite a number of women actively engaged in fishing around the world, e.g. in Japanese oyster fishing or in Russian freezer-trawlers,[3] it continues to be identified as something that only men can or should engage in. Very occasionally, intrepid women have fished in Newfoundland,[4] but, by and large, the stereotype holds there too. From the time of the earliest settlements in the sixteenth century, the principal and very nearly the only occupation on the island was fishing. Eschewing the barren interior, the colonists set up tiny communities all along the 6000 miles of rugged coastline to exploit the bountiful supplies of cod offshore. Thus, each little 'outport' is a microcosm of a wider community devoted to fishing. And only men fish. James Faris (1972, p. 12), like many of the anthropologists who have described outport culture, economy and social structure, took it for granted that 'in a fishing community one could reasonably expect a sharp division of labour along sexual lines'. The title of this paper is taken from one of his informants in Cat Harbour who, accounting for why they called new boats 'he' but old boats 'she', said 'You can't count on women and old boats; they'll both leak after a few years.' Indeed, Faris describes a sexual division bordering on hostility.[5] Women, if not witches, are certainly strangers and 'jinkers' who pollute the fishing so that they might not set foot in the boat or go near the nets. Here we are not talking simply about 'men's work', but about entire communities that are identified in terms of an activity that is, by definition, gender specific. In such communities women do not simply have unequal access to the means of production, as in pastoral communities; they are specifically excluded from fishing. But, as Andersen and Wadel (1972) point out, in Newfoundland women are (or were) undisputably part of the *fishery*. In the production of the traditional sun-dried cod, they made up most of the 'shore-crowd', who split, salted, washed and dried the fish on the 'flakes', a process that was both skilled and added considerably to the value of the catch (Brox, 1969; Antler, 1976).[6]

Thus, in the traditional inshore fishery in Newfoundland, the sexual division of labour was drawn between the harvesting and processing sectors. With the changes in the inshore fishery to produce deep frozen cod products, this division has had to be renegotiated with crucial consequences for the sexual division of labour.

There were many technological changes in the Newfoundland fisheries from the 1960s to the early 1970s. However, the vast majority of the smaller outports are still characterised by the traditional inshore fishery, heavily concentrated on cod, using small (under 30 foot) open skiffs, operated by family-based crews, and employing a variety of strategies, e.g. jigging, gillnets, trolling and lines – but with the cod-trap predominating. In contrast, the women's lives have been directly affected and fundamentally changed by the virtual elimination of the dried-salt cod industry and its replacement by frozen products. From the 1950s, the sun-dried lightly salted cod trade declined as frozen fish processing plants began to be established round the island until now the frozen fish products are dominant.[7] There are fish-plants, or at least holding depots, in virtually all communities. Instead of going to the family stages and flakes for processing, fish now go directly from the boats to the fish-plants. These plants employ a substantially female workforce, and any involvement the women have in the fishery is now as individual wage labourers in these local fish-plants. Thus, while the catching sector remains virtually untouched, both the technical means and the social relations of production have been transformed in the *processing* sector. Under the old system, the men who 'owned' the fish could appropriate women's surplus in accordance with the amount of fish caught. As this no longer happens women are free to redistribute their own labour and to control the wage they earn, by 'choosing' to work in the plants.

The men are fishermen, but are the women fishermen's wives?

Women in Newfoundland

There is very little specific material on any aspect of women's lives in the Newfoundland outports, apart from a few descriptive accounts of 'life in the old days' (Murray, 1979) and a scatter of papers dealing with different aspects of outport life. But even among these there is evidence of an unexpectedly positive economic role for women (Antler, 1976; Szala, 1952; Davis, 1979 and 1980; Bradbrook, 1980).

For the rest, there is some implicit and covert material hidden in 'general' studies, but a more important source are the anthropological monographs published by ISER.[8] These are, coincidentally, all written by men who tend to be preoccupied with fishing, the composition of crews, land inheritance and other androcentric concerns. Women only appear momentarily as they scuttle round doing odd chores and not being very interesting, or as the 'O's in kinship diagrams. They are, as Loftland (1975, pp. 144–5) has said 'essential to the set, but largely irrelevant to the action. They are, simply, there.' More importantly for the purposes of the present paper, male anthropologists usually talk to men, and their information is, therefore, often skewed.

Aquaforte

Aquaforte is a small maritime community dominated by traditional inshore fishery described above.[9] The sun-dried fish gradually gave way to frozen fish after the Fermeuse plant was opened in 1952 and the smaller owner-managed plant at Aquaforte opened in 1972.[10] The flakes and stages, which used to stand at the water's edge below each house, fell into disrepair and boats now gravitate to the community wharf by the fish plant. Forty men in 14 crews are involved in fishing on a regular basis.

Aquaforte lies some 60 miles south of St. Johns on the southern shore, with a total population of 203 in 56 households (1981). All the houses have electricity, and all but one have a telephone. Many of the younger couples have built large modern bungalows with help from the Newfoundland & Labrador Housing Corporation. Most families have at least one car or truck. There are three general stores, two garages, and the old school is used as a community hall. The (Catholic) parish church, three schools, doctor, clinic, post office and government agents are situated in Ferryland, a larger community lying on the adjacent bay to the north. Ferryland and Fermeuse also provide a few jobs, some slightly larger general stores and the bars and other social meeting points. Branch meetings of most of the voluntary associations, the bingo evenings and other social events take place in Ferryland, often in the Legion Hall. There is no bank anywhere on the shore, and for larger shops, hospitals and most government offfices, they must go to 'town', St. Johns, 60 miles away.

One of the important changes in recent years is the ease and frequency with which they can do this. The road was 'made' in 1965, and paved in 1972. It is no longer an all day trek in a 4-wheel drive vehicle, but an easy $1\frac{1}{2}$ hour trip. Five women and one man commute daily, during the summer, and some through the winter as well.

In this respect, too, Aquaforte is typical of many small communities that were linked up by road in the last 15 years, thus vastly increasing both mobility and a tendency to depend more heavily for jobs, goods and services on the larger towns.[11] This opportunity for employment outside the narrow confines of Aquaforte is especially important for the younger women, as we shall see later.

Aquaforte provided the context I needed – a small maritime community, with a traditional inshore fishery. Here I should be able to observe a clear and visible sexual division of labour.

The method I used was ethnographically based. I went to live in Aquaforte, and though the stay was too brief for a real ethnography, I was able to collect most of the usual demographic, economic and kinship data as well as conducting 39 formal interviews. But most of the time I spent where the women were – visiting, shopping, in church, at the Darts Club, Bingo and the Women's Institute – watching to see what the sexual division of labour was, how it operated and how it was interpreted. Most of the material that follows derives from this 'watching'. Let us first take, for example, two women – a widow, whose three sons fished together in their father's boat, and one of her young daughters-in-law.

Two women: Lizzie and Cheryl

Cheryl was 22 years old. A few months before I met her she had married Russell (aged 23 years) whom she had dated since she was 15. When she left school she took a secretarial course at the Trades College in St. Johns and then worked as a secretary in the College of Fisheries. All her six sisters are – or were – in clerical work and all six brothers fish in her home community of Renews.

Russell fishes with his two brothers, and Russell and Cheryl live in a modern bungalow he built with their help, a few hundred yards from his widowed mother's house. Lizzie (aged 59 years) was widowed six years ago. Her three daughters are all in St. Johns – one married with two children and the other two in clerical jobs. One of her sons, Steve, still lives with her and the other two are close by.

Cheryl 'called by' as many as six times a day to see to her mother-in-law because 'I get bored up there by myself.' It didn't take long to clean their newly built bungalow (with a vacuum cleaner) or to cook for the two of them (in a modern oven). In the afternoon, like all the younger women and most of the older ones, she watched 'The Story' on TV.[12] When the truck was free, she drove across to visit her mother and about once a month she took her to St. Johns.

When I first met her, Cheryl said she didn't want a job at the plant, 'I wasn't trained for that', and she didn't fancy standing ankle deep in water all day for less money than she got as a secretary. But when a job did come up, she snatched it. At least it was something to do, and someone to talk to. She didn't belong to any association or club, but she was pressing Russell to join the Kinsmen so she would be eligible to join Kinettes and, as Lizzie said, 'if she leans long enough, she'll get there'.

Lizzie was always aware of Steve's departure at 4.30 a.m. though she didn't get up until it was time to cook his breakfast at 9.00 a.m. After that, her days were a whirl of activity. Both her other sons and daughters-in-law visited several times a day, and Steve wandered in and out constantly, all of which kept Lizzie supplied with information, which was traded to the stream of visitors, or on the 'phone' 'up and down the road'. Lizzie knew all the ways with cod, salmon, herring and caplin. There was frozen moose in the freezer and fresh eggs from her hens. But her real pride was her knitting and her bedspreads, some of which she had sold through craft outlets. A devout Catholic, she went to mass some weekday evenings, as well as on Sundays, and she took her part in the church cleaning, flower arranging and other Women's Auxiliary activities. The church ran a bingo evening once a week which she rarely missed, sitting with her friends at the same table. A recent past president of the local WI, she not only attended the meetings but was active in the works projects, craft displays and fund raising, to say nothing of the outings they arranged. She had just triumphantly passed her post to a much younger woman, 'it's so difficult to get the young ones in...'. With showers, weddings and funerals and going along to 'support' the guides dinner, the 4H Achievement Day and other gatherings, she was rarely at home in the evenings.

At weekends the two younger daughters came down from St. Johns and Lizzie prepared even more enormous meals to sustain them through their hectic evenings at the bars and dances in Ferryland and Fermeuse.

Although Lizzie had never been in a boat and knew little of the technology, she could store the figures of the catches in her head and watched her sons' progress intently and with pride. For her, it was part of a long and valuable tradition epitomised by her life with her husband. She liked talking about 'the old days' and much of her effort in the WI was spent preserving the old 'women's culture', and trying to pass it on to the relatively few young women members.

Lizzie was well aware of Cheryl's predicament, and worried about what would happen to her own younger daughters. One was courting a draggerman from Portugal Cove South, an even more remote outport beyond 'the barrens'. She could see clearly that for Selene to live there, away from her job, her friends, her svelte jeans and her holidays, was a recipe for disaster, but Selene was impervious to her warnings. All Lizzie could hope for was that when they married, Paul could get a job on the St. John's draggers and they would live there.

Lizzie's position of helpless concern typified the older women's desire to preserve what was left of their identity of 'fishermen's wives' in an active present, coupled with the realisation that the structural basis for that life no longer existed for her daughters.

Past and present

The past is a powerful influence in Aquaforte – less the historical past, than a collective, constructed memory, hypostatised to protect them from an unpredictable and wicked present day world.

For the men, this past is bound up less with the occupation of fishing than with the identity of 'being fishermen'. Even the 23 out of the 73 adult males who had other occupations (including 4 in fish-plants) still acknowledged the primacy of fishing. Many of them fished in their spare time or intended to return to fishing when they could afford to. For the Aquaforte fishermen (in common with most of the other inshore fleets) could not live from what they caught. They, in the disparaging words of the local rural coordinator 'fish for stamps'. In other words, their catches during the summer[13] are chiefly valuable because they qualify them to claim Unemployment Insurance Compensation for the rest of the year. Far from detracting from their status as fishermen, they, and everyone else, saw it as an advantage to have time to 'go to the woods', 'to be free', 'to be your own man'. In fact, on the basis of a relatively short season, the men won time to build and maintain their houses, their boats and their gear, cut timber and hunt moose, caribou, turrs and rabbits and pursue any number of more individual activities. This combination of cash and subsistence ensured, for most of them, a reasonable standard of living, with comfortable houses, TVs and cars. Their winter identity was just as much that of a fisherman as the actual fishing they did in the summer. 'Fisherman' means that set of plural adaptations which enabled them to continue the traditional *lifestyle*.

Life in the outports has always demanded this kind of flexible response in order to survive in a harsh physical environment at the end of a harshly exploitative capitalist chain. What distinguishes the present set of adaptations is the way in which they have negotiated a space between capital, state and subsistence that ensures both a much improved material standard of living *and* a degree of autonomy.

There is very little distinction in either ideas or practice between the older and younger men. The younger ones are slightly more inclined to try new methods, and they certainly drink more alcohol, but their sense of identity is the same.

Not so among the women, for whom there is a definite generation gap between the women of about 50 years and over who can remember life before Confederation in 1949, and the women of 45 years and younger. The older women are guided by the past in much the same way as the men, and they too defer to the identity of 'fishermen'. The younger women have no such allegiance and most of them frankly dislike their husbands' role. Everyone agrees that 'fishing is a gamble', but younger women are not prepared to tolerate such insecurity, and, believing that there are alternatives, they maintain only a reluctant loyalty to the *status quo*.

None of the women can actually live the traditional lifestyle the way the men do. Their role as fishermen's wives has vanished. Not only are there no fish to be dried on the flakes, but virtually all other aspects of their past lives have gone as well. In particular, women have stopped having large families. None of the younger women had more than three children, while the women in their sixties had brought up eight or nine or ten children – one had seventeen. Furthermore, they had done this before labour saving devices, convenience foods or easy access to St. Johns. Many of them had reared children before Confederation in 1949 had eased the crushing poverty in the outports. All the women over 50 could remember life as Hilda Murray described it: they could tell you where the fish flakes were, the variety of animals and poultry they kept, about the constant baking, cooking and washing, the wood chopping and water drawing, the gardens and the berry picking, the bottling, pickling and preserving – and the 'times', the festivals and ceremonies. Now they were left with faint echoes. The older women still baked bread two or three times a week, used traditional recipes and ingredients, knitted, kept hens, grew potatoes and cabbage and went berry picking and trouting. But it was not like it was. The women under 40 who couldn't remember pre-Confederation days showed little inclination to keep it alive. So whereas the past is still an active part of the young men's lives, for the younger women it has become mere idle tales.

This tension between older and younger women is intensified by exogamy. Men (aged about 25) marry women (aged about 23) from the other villages up and down the shore. Initially, they bring their wives into their parents' house and then, when means allow (fairly soon these days), they build a house close by.[14] Thus, women are separated from their own mothers and thrust into a very close proximity with their mothers-in-law. This they resist by keeping in close contact with their own mothers, greatly aided by the telephone. Mothers and daughters in neighbouring outports ring each other at least once a day, and as local calls are free, the conversations can be lengthy. As most of the younger women also have access to a car, they can expect to visit their mothers at least once a week.

The older women's criticisms of their daughters' 'modern' lifestyle were muted by their acute sense that they themselves have lost their own place as 'fishermen's wives', and this was expressed in a grudging admission that, materially speaking, life was a lot better for the younger women. The women in their sixties admitted that 'there was a lot of fate in those days'. It was hard work, they were poor and there were no luxuries. This remembered reality meant that they didn't really expect their daughters to wash nappies by hand when they could get Pampers, or to use the local midwife when hospitals were available and so good, or have too large families when it would threaten their new (relative) affluence. How can they deny a 'better' life for their daughters, when they can't assert, positively, as their husbands can, the benefits of the traditional lifestyle?

Ironically, the older women's eroded identity as fishermen's wives is reflected in their interest in the fishery and their fervent avowal of the fishermen's cause. Many provided details of the fish, the traps, the problems and the politics. Many of the details were wrong because the older women had rarely been out in the boats and had no direct connection with the fishing. Nor did they go to the many meetings called to decide the trap-berths, to vote on the price of fish or to protest at the depradations of the inshore draggers. But they were keenly interested and listened carefully when the men discussed such things in the kitchen. Some of them handled all the paperwork, most worried about getting the men up in the morning at 4.30 to go off. When the fishing season starts, the 'phones buzz with an efficient information network, so that within minutes of the boats returning, every house will have the details of sizes of catch and who caught how much and where.

Whenever I returned after a few days away, my landlady's opening remarks all had to do with the fishing, how many pounds her son had that morning, what it was like in Renews, or, if it was bad, 'it's so quiet it's like a place in mourning'. The younger women took part in the information network – especially in terms of relaying details of catches from other outports via their mothers – but they usually disclaimed all knowledge of the fishery and even resisted being drawn into the white hot debates of the day, for example, whether someone should lose his trap-berth when he went to work on the oil rigs or how to stop the inshore draggers from trespassing inshore. On the other hand, they were less inhibited about actually going in boats and quite a few enjoyed a Sunday's jigging, though this was never equated with fishing proper.

Let us now look more closely at these younger women.

And this little piggy went to market...
More girls than boys continue in post high school education. A few boys and girls go straight to work in the fish plants. A few boys go fishing, and a few girls babysat for the women working in the plants. A majority of girls who go to university become teachers and nurses, and they, like the male graduates from this town, will not return to Aquaforte, but will marry and settle elsewhere on the island, Labrador or the Mainland. However, the boys who go to Trades School will return as soon as they finish their courses, and will go directly into fishing if they can. If not, they will work on the roads, the forestry or in garages, until they find a berth. For the girls, it is different. Usually, after a Trades School secretarial or clerical course, they will get jobs in St. Johns, for there are no jobs in Aquaforte and precious few (e.g. as doctor's receptionist) in Fermeuse or Ferryland. Some of these girls may well commute up to St. Johns daily, at least during the summer. The rest 'come down on week-ends' specifically to go to the bars and the dances – to have a good time and look for husbands. In this they are usually successful. Very few of the young Aquaforte secretaries will marry 'off the shore'.

So within a few years of leaving school, men and women have opted for two contrasting worlds. The young men have returned to the ways of their fathers, but the young women are wholly absorbed in the modern, urban, sophisticated and materialist life of the big city. In dress, manners, assumptions and ambitions they are indistinguishable from millions of young North American women. They enjoy their financial and social independence. They dress smartly and travel afar – to Florida for holidays or to Alberta to visit emigrant relatives. Yet unlike their sisters who are teachers and nurses, they remain firmly attached to the shore, and, above all, they marry on the shore. When I talked to them at weekends, they accepted that they would, one day, have to give up their jobs, independence and lively social life because 'there's no work down here'.

And this little piggy cried 'wee wee' all the way home
When it actually happens, it comes as an acute shock. Even if, at first, the young couple live in St. Johns, they will be unable to afford a house there. And, inexorably, when the babies come, they return to their husband's outport. This is the point of maximum disillusionment. The young married women in Aquaforte were, of course, from neighbouring outports. They confessed openly that they were bored, lonely and frustrated.

Why, then, do they do it? Marriage and return to the shore are not inevitable, as the experience of their more qualified sisters shows. Yet, it had not occurred to any of the young women I spoke to that they would do otherwise. A combination of very expensive housing, acute unemployment and low wages force the issue once the young couple marry, but it does not answer the question as to why the girls did not move to the mainland, or marry boys with good St. John's jobs or even marry boys from one of the other towns with more clerical jobs.

It is not, of course, seen as choice. Such 'choices' rarely appear as obvious as they do to watching sociologists.

In the social determinations of the young St. John's typists the option not to marry is not appealing; nor, indeed, are the wages and prospects good enough to offer a long-term career. And through the rosy spectacles of romance there were clear prospects that offered some trade-off beyond the immediate disillusionment. They would secure a modern house, a car and a decent material standard of living. They would all insist on acquiring all the material accessories they knew to be vital – the electrical gadgets, the luxurious furnishings, the large picture window. Nor were they blind to all the real advantages of outport life. They enjoyed the lack of traffic and the healthy environment for their children.

As the babies come the young mothers see more of each other, and dedicate themselves to building a reproduction Canadian suburban lifestyle. Soon, too, they are drawn into the energetic activities of the voluntary associations[15] – Women's Institute, Kinettes, Darts Club and the Legion, to name but a few.

Most of the Voluntary Association activity was dominated by older women who saw in it not only some outlet for their own energies but also a way to involve younger women in the activities of the community.

Indeed, after the initial singles 'hunting' sessions in the bars, the two sexes draw apart for the bulk of their social life, only coming together for the big banquets and garden parties and certain Church and Legion events. Apart from meeting about the fishing, men go out very little, especially during the fishing season. Thus, in the evenings, you find the men in each other's kitchens, visiting and babysitting, while the women are more frequently out than not. In this, the older women's frustration at being deprived of their traditional role combines with the younger women's frustration at being deprived of their suburban Canadian role to create a defensive but effective 'women's culture'.

Men, women and power

The ideology of male dominance is strong in Newfoundland culture. A combination of the male culture of fishing (as exemplified in Faris, 1972), a strong Church presence,[16] a kinship system which separates women from their own community, seems to ensure an ideological domination which reflects the male control of the technical means of production. But we have already noted that while men controlled the gathering sector of the fishery, it was women who commanded the *processing* sector. They also showed other signs of economic self-reliance and female solidarity, e.g. selling berries, taking jobs as telegraphists, selling bait to schooners, etc. Ideological domination, indeed, did not seem to reflect the much more complex economic reality. If we look more carefully at the material on traditional outport life, it is clear that both sexes accepted the sexual division of labour; both men and women worked unremittingly hard and everybody was poor. Nobody had any *real* power, being helpless in the hands of the merchants and the 'truck system'. Family cooperation was a matter of necessity, and beyond that emerges an equality of respect. 'Outport men can turn their hands to anything'. 'The woman was more than 50%'. While a certain ideological authority was invested in the man by the outside world (Church and merchant), it had less reality in the practice of the family. For without the women, the men could not operate. They were manifestly dependent on the women not only for the usual 'servicing' of cooking and caring, but to realise the value of their catch.

Returning to contemporary Aquaforte, we find evidence of some ideological skewing (though not as much as Faris reports). The Church was still powerful and both men and women accepted the place of fishing and fishermen at the apex of community esteem. But what does this mean in practice? Is ideological dominance reflected in real power? What, in other words, do the women lose by not fishing?

It is women who, by tradition, run the post office. They also run all three shops. Few women are active on the public political stage, but two who are have gained places at the provincial level. Marriages are long-lasting and, in conditions where the couple are in close physical proximity, there is little overt tension. Nor is there much deference. On the contrary, women speak their minds, come to decisions jointly with their husbands and lead independent social lives.

The sexual division of labour is strong, but while to an outsider (and to the men) fishing is valuable, exciting and skilful and men's activity is, therefore, evaluated as more significant than women's, it is hard to see that this assumption is justified by the correlation of economic with ideological dominance.

Conclusion

The mutuality of the relationship between men and women based on the traditional division of labour between fishermen and fishermen's wives has been broken. Men no longer depend on women to 'make the fish'. Yet the economic independence shown by women has been transferred to their new position as wage labourers in the fish plants. In many households, their wage is not just crucial to the family's economic survival, it may even be more than the men's contribution from fishing. What has altered, then, is that the women now have a direct relation with capital as individual workers.

Ever since Joseph Smallwood took Newfoundland into the Confederation in 1949, there have been disputes about how to support the scattered outports of the island, and the outcome has been a conflict within the capitalist structure that the inshore fishermen have been able to exploit. Fluent in the complex vagaries of UIC, licensing and quotas, they have carved a niche that is an amalgam of welfare state and subsistence. Despite the obvious disadvantages and drawbacks of outport life – high unemployment, low wages – the outport men have retained dignity and independence. Their time is their own, and few would swap it for the dehumanised existence of a Hamilton assembly line or an Alberta oil rig. And, at the moment, they don't have to. But the younger women have rejected this package of plural adaption. Deprived of their substantive share in outport economic life, they now want the suburban lifestyle, and that means more money. They, therefore, put pressure on their husbands to 'go to the rigs' or at least to get a job on one of the big draggers working out of St. Johns or Trepassey. They also demand more services on the shore, not only for their convenience as consumers but also to provide them with the jobs they so desperately want. Yet would a transformation of the shore in this direction enable capital to redirect the fishermen into waged jobs and to withdraw the substantial subsidy to the inshore fishery and thus force the men into the waged jobs they so desperately *don't* want?

In other words, the thrust of the younger women's initiatives may be to sabotage the delicate accommodation the men have come to. The sexual division of labour in Aquaforte has been transformed by the intervention of the capitalist means of production in the processing sector. The men and women occupy wholly different positions in the relations of production. The sexual division of labour cannot be understood simply or even primarily as a matter of subordination; and without clarification of the role of the sexual division of labour, we are unable to understand this complex social formation. In this paper, I can only raise certain questions and indicate some possible consequences.

While the existence of the generation gap among the women and the consequent fracturing of the 'women's culture' seem clear enough, it is by no means certain that the combination of a reasonable material standard of living and increased involvement in the culture of the voluntary associations will not, in time, erode the younger women's resentment. There is nothing inherently antagonistic about the new sexual division of labour.

Nor is it clear what would be the consequences of the pressure from the younger women for clerical jobs resulting in, for example, the establishment of a bank on the shore. On the one hand, clerical work pays better wages than the fish plants and could result in both a greater discrepancy between the women's economic contribution and the men's from fishing, and also between families with a wife so employed. On the other hand, a bank would certainly make life easier for the fishermen. Would it, at the same time, intensify the encroachments of capitalistic 'rationality' on one of the last outposts of petty commodity production? There is no doubt that most of the women, if they had the choice, would take any clerical or service job in preference to work in the plants. Would they be replaced by male labour for which the companies have an undisguised preference, and would that drive the women even further from any involvement in the fishery?

Such questions point the way to further research. But such questions cannot even be raised until we take seriously the concept, and the complex reality, of the sexual division of labour. There is no inevitability about capitalist development. Class struggle can intervene in the process – but classes consist of men *and* women. The Aquaforte men cannot either resist or redirect the forces of capitalism without the active help of the women. They are still dependent on them: women are still 'more than 50%'. Nor can the women retain their economic independence and social autonomy without that space that the men have guarded so carefully. The fractured sexual division of labour has to be renegotiated to enable men and women to construct their own lives in conditions of their own choosing.

Notes

1 The research on which this paper is based was carried out in Aquaforte, Newfoundland, February–July, 1981, with the help of a grant from ISER. I am grateful for help and comments from Bob Hill, Rick Johnstone, Peter Sinclair, George Storey and Marion Glastonbury on the original draft.
2 The obverse strategy, of course, is to focus on particular horrific examples or defeats, e.g. witches, genital mutilation or women in particularly degrading jobs.
3 For other examples, see Hornell (1980).
4 Before the war, the youngest daughter frequently went as a cook aboard her father's boat for the Labrador 'floater' fishery. In addition, women have always jigged for squid for bait for their husbands and, as Szala points out, in offshore ports where the men are away for long periods, the women must catch enough for their own subsistence, and there are occasional references to women fishing with hook and line either with their husbands or on their own. I also found three women who had fished in their own right around the island in the recent past.
5 There have been similar accounts which stress rigid and hostile sexual divisions; for example Wadel on Norway; Tunstall on Hull; Cohen (n.d.) on Whalsey Island and Clarke (n.d.) on Peerie Island.
6 On the Labrador Banks' 'voyages' where the catch of several months was brought back 'saltbulk', the women's task was even more important. There are also indications of women organising to negotiate conditions (G. Storey, personal communication).
7 Although the frozen fish division of the industry is clearly dominant, it should be noted that between 14 and 35% of fish caught is still salted, mainly by or through the Canadian salt fish corporation.
8 E.g. Faris (1972); Firestone (1967); Wadel (1973).
9 There is no such thing as a truly 'typical' outport. The variety among the 6000 or so outports resists oversimplified categories. For my purposes, Aquaforte's 'typicality' serves. However, I should note some obvious peculiarities. Firstly, it was the only largely Protestant community on the Catholic dominated southern shore. This may have rendered the church less powerful in the community. Secondly, it was relatively close to St. Johns. Some communities were nearly 500 miles away, some still only have communication by sea. Thirdly, the Aquaforte fishery was a poor one, and incomes from the fishery were below those of neighbouring outports, e.g. Fermeuse. One consequence of this was that it was one of the few outports to have no longliners. This discrepancy mattered less in 1981 when all the incomes from the inshore fishery were low because of the poor season.

10 The plant at Fermeuse was opened in 1952 under NE Fisheries. It was then bought by Bird's Eye and then by Bonavista Cold Storage which became a part of the vast US based Lake Group. It is a year round plant with two offshore draggers based on it. Aquafisheries was opened in 1965 by a local man, Don Graham and a partner. It is now a substantial operation employing 65 people.
11 A tendency that will increase if the Economic Council of Canada's (1980) report is any indication.
12 This horrendous institution, 'The Story', runs from about 2.30 p.m. to about 5.30, usually consisting of three Dallas type epic soaps and is an occupational hazard of all research work among women in Newfoundland. (cf. Davis, 1979). A nodding acquaintance with the main characters is essential, and a quick check on the plot means that other conversations can go on simultaneously.
13 The fishing seasons vary around the island. In Aquaforte, it begins with the herrring in March/April and proceeds through salmon to cod. These are caught in cod traps in the early part of the season (the summer voyage) till August and then by jigging and hand lining until October/November.
14 The men learn in Trades College how to read blueprints. With the aid of prefab parts, they still build their own houses with a little help from friends.
15 See Davis (1979) and Porter (1983) for further discussion of the importance of female voluntary associations in the creation of a specific 'women's culture'.
16 Religion is strong all over the island but different denominations predominate in different areas. Especially noticeable are the Catholic and Salvationist areas.

9 Dividing the Rough and the Respectable: Working-class Women and Pre-school Playgroups
Janet Finch

Introduction

This chapter considers some aspects of the debate on women and class, using empirical material taken from a small-scale study of pre-school playgroups. Analyses of 'class' position that simply treat women as appendages of men are now widely regarded as unsatisfactory, and some important advances have been made by women scholars towards developing alternative theoretical accounts (Delphy, 1977; Acker, 1973; Garnsey, 1978; Beechey, 1979; Eichler, 1980). But empirical studies are also necessary: to explore the ways in which women experience the cross-cutting of gender and other social divisions in their own lives, how they make sense of those experiences, and how far they try to modify them. Using empirical studies in this way can significantly advance our analysis of class and gender by both complementing and informing theoretical analyses (cf. Porter, 1978). In the process, however, it can expose some powerful, indeed painful, contradictions in women's lives.

My study of five voluntary playgroups in Lancashire, based on a two-year observational period followed by interviews, took place between 1978 and 1981.[1] I focused specifically on 'working-class' playgroups, which I defined as groups located in inner urban areas or on council estates and run by local women with minimal formal education or qualifications. One suburban group was added for purposes of comparison. This chapter draws principally on data from the two working-class playgroups which remained open throughout the observational period.

The reason for my interest in working-class playgroups was that they seemed to represent a rather interesting anomaly. Playgroups began in Britain as a middle-class response to the lack of nursery school places and they flourished initially in suburban and similar areas, although by the mid-1970s, people associated with the playgroup movement were claiming that they had moved well beyond their middle-class origins (Plowden, 1973; Edwards, 1977; Finch, 1983a). Nevertheless, it seems to me that the voluntary, non-profit-making playgroup remains fundamentally a middle-class solution for several reasons. Firstly, there are class divisions in the use of playgroups, with a clear reluctance on the part of the poorest families to use them at all. These are usually referred to as the 'problem' of 'hard to reach' families (Shinman, 1981). Secondly, there can be little doubt that the typical two-mornings-a-week playgroup cannot cater for the child-care needs of most working women, even part-time workers, since it implicitly assumes the presence of a full-time mother in the home (Hughes *et al.*, 1980). Thirdly, setting up and running a voluntary organisation historically is an activity strongly associated with the middle classes, including middle-class wives (Stacey, 1960; Bruner, 1980; Hatch, 1981). Thus it seemed to me that, if working-class women were indeed engaged in setting up and running their own playgroups, they were undertaking an activity culturally alien to their own experience. This gives rise, *inter alia*, to the question: what meaning does their participation in the playgroup have for the women involved?

Boundaries in the playgroup

Playgroups – perhaps in common with other voluntary bodies – are places where boundaries get drawn between categories of individuals, and tasks and privileges are assigned on that basis. The most obvious of these boundaries concern the actual running of the groups, and divide participants into 'mothers' who use the groups, 'staff' who run them, and sometimes 'committees' who make the decisions.

As my study progressed, I became aware that these boundaries had a significance which went well beyond the practical issues of how to organise the playgroup. In essence they seemed to be both an expression of and the means of reinforcing social divisions between the women, by creating 'in' and 'out' groups. Further, those divisions seemed to bear some relationship to perceptions of the placement of individuals within hierarchies of class or status.

At Skyways – a playgroup situated in an inner urban area of mainly terraced housing – the significance of the boundaries between 'in' and 'out' individuals became apparent in the playgroup sessions themselves, especially towards the end. A number of mothers began to stay on the premises during sessions, but were not 'properly' integrated to the leaders' satisfaction. Barbara, one of the leaders who had been in the playgroup from the beginning, gave me this account,

> We got a new group of ladies with their children and we found that these were congregating in a circle and smoking and drinking tea and weren't interested in helping the kiddies... they made themselves a nice circle of chairs and they had a table in the middle and all they wanted was their two cups of tea and their cigarettes, and a good talk.

The presence of this group of women was felt by the leaders to be highly problematic. At the same time, they were quite prepared to tolerate, and even to welcome, the presence of other mothers in the group. The boundaries were being drawn therefore *between* different mothers, as well as between leaders and mothers. The different groups could be distinguished quite clearly by their territorial location in the hall where they met, by the activities in which they engaged, and by the facilities to which they had access. This is clear in the following account which I recorded after one observational visit, before actually I had fully grasped the significance of what I was seeing,

> There were 14 children and 11 adults in the hall, all more or less 'with' the playgroup. Barbara, Marjorie and two others inhabited the kitchen area and were more or less 'in charge'. Two older women, one of whom was referred to as 'Grandma', were sitting at a table with a couple of children. They were smoking and chatting but more or less playing with the children... The rest of the women were sitting round one table, smoking and talking but taking no part with the children... Barbara and Marjorie greeted me warmly but felt that they needed to apologise for aspects of the group. Barbara began and ended this way. At first, she said that I was just in time for a cup of coffee which she was making 'for us', indicating the other women, 'these ladies' round the table, had already had some... I thought immediately that making an extra cup of coffee for approved people only was a very clear way of marking boundaries.

On this occasion, it was very apparent that the leadership group inhabited the kitchen area, which enabled them to keep control of the coffee-making facilities, the 'excluded' group of mothers created their own territory around one table and well away from the children, whilst the more acceptable mothers occupied a different table with the children and, whilst they were not offered an extra cup of coffee, neither were they subject to the active hostility of the leaders.

At Manchester Avenue – a playgroup located on a council estate on the outskirts of a mill town – the boundaries did not get drawn within the playgroup itself, since this was always maintained as the exclusive territory of the staff. Mothers only penetrated the marginal regions, such as the cloakrooms and the doorway to the main hall, at the beginning and end of sessions. That was an extremely effective way of marking the leader–mother boundary, but did not of itself lead to distinctions being made between 'in' and 'out' mothers. The particular characteristic of Manchester Avenue was the use of the playgroup committee for drawing significant boundaries[2]. The membership of the committee comprised mainly women who had been associated with the playgroup from the beginning and it was chaired by Mrs Gordon, the local councillor for the estate. The committee itself very much constituted the 'in' group for the playgroup with a core of longstanding members, and thus it provided a means for distinguishing between included and excluded helpers, as well as mothers.

The latter were invited to become committee members, and perhaps also helpers, if they seemed suitable and 'interested'; thus the core group were able to express approval of certain mothers by offering selective invitations to join the committee and indeed to participate in other social events. I recorded the following note after attending one committee meeting,

> They expressed frustration at the 'lack of interest' on the part of the mothers who would not really get involved. Two particular mothers were mentioned as being the only ones prepared to throw themselves in, e.g. by volunteering items for the Christmas Fair. These two had in fact been invited to the committee meeting but were not able to attend, and they are also going to be invited to the planned 'girls' night out'.

These very effective mechanisms for drawing in certain approved individuals left the core group with an image of the rest of the mothers as an apathetic mass whose only contact with the playgroup was to hand over their children and pay their money. In comments made by the core group, these mothers often merged with another, even more apathetic mass, namely the women who did not send their children to playgroup at all. This is clear from the notes that I made after a conversation with one of the core group,

> She spoke with some fervour on the subject of women who wouldn't send their children to the group... They have tried all sorts of ways to advertise the group and encourage more people to use it, but it's very difficult to do that. When I asked her why did she think people did not want to use the group, she replied that it was the kind of people who now live on the estate... It's now being used as a dumping ground, there are lots of people coming down here now who are problem families – women who don't seem to know really how to run a home properly or to bring up children, and men who are out of work.

It seems clear that the kinds of social boundaries which are being drawn through the playgroup form part of the total experience of these women's lives in a particular locality. Whilst the boundaries do coincide to some extent with the organisational aspects of the playgroup, they do not do so straightforwardly, because they provide the means of distinguishing included and excluded individuals *within* the organisational categories of 'leaders' and 'mothers'. Nevertheless, the organisation of the playgroup itself does not provide the means by which such boundaries can be drawn fairly clearly, and a core 'included' group can be identified: in Skyways, this was the leadership group, in Manchester Avenue, the committee. The possibility of drawing new people into the core group makes the boundaries very effective, since it enables them to be maintained despite the changing clientele of the playgroup.

If social boundaries are being drawn in the playgroup, are they in any sense accounted for by the 'objective' class placement of the women? That is, are the core group the élite of the area on the basis of their husband's occupational status or their own? So far as their own personal educational and occupational histories were concerned, virtually none of the women would be able to lay claim to the label 'middle class'; and leaders and mothers seemed broadly similar to each other in terms of their own occupational and educational histories. Equally, the use of a conventional placement which accords the women their husband's status in the occupational hierarchy reveals no significant variations between the core groups and the rest.

So in terms of occupational hierarchies, the boundaries in the playgroup were not to do with 'class'. However, I want to argue that they were fundamentally to do with what I shall, for the moment, call an aspect of 'class'. It seems to me that the real significance of these boundaries is that they were dividing the rough from the respectable working classes. Participation in the playgroup offered, *inter alia*, the opportunity for women to draw such boundaries so as to place themselves on the 'correct' side, thus enabling them to construct and reinforce their own position. Far from simply being the passive recipients of their husband's position and status, they were very much in the business of actively constituting their own position in some relevant social hierarchy.

Dividing the rough and the respectable: content and method

The distinction between the rough and the respectable working classes is well established in theoretical and empirical writings, although there is not always a single, clear dividing line. As Bell and Newby (1971, p. 202) note, the rough and respectable may represent the two extreme ends of the spectrum, with the mass of the 'ordinary' working class in between. Margaret Stacey's (1960, pp. 105–6) first study of Banbury distinguishes categories of 'rough', 'ordinary' and 'respectable' working class, with features which prove similar to those which I identified in Lancashire two decades later, as will become apparent.

Historically, there are strong links with the Victorian 'respectable artisan', whose superior economic position was expressed in a 'distinctive style of life within the working class which marked off a separate upper stratum' (Gray, 1974, p. 23). In this stratum the classic bourgeois Victorian virtues of thrift, independence and respectability were paramount, in contrast to the assumed characteristics of the idle, feckless and, above all, underserving poor. In Banbury in the 1950s, the characteristics associated with the respectable working classes were decency, cleanliness and thrift (Stacey, 1960, p. 181). So respectability among the working classes seems partly to be associated with a superior economic position, but not to follow directly from that: it needs to be worked at. As a lifestyle, respectability has to be established and maintained, and has to be recognised and acknowledged with a particular social setting. Traditionally women are central to this task (Delamont, 1980, p. 146).

What kind of images of roughness and respectability were being operationalised in the working-class playgroups in my study? It seems to me that the 'excluded' women, who were being constituted as rough working class, were identified by the 'respectables' on four types of overlapping criteria, to do with personal conduct, lifestyle, housekeeping and mothering. Firstly, there are matters of personal conduct. Marjorie, one of the Skyways leaders who talked in some detail about these issues, described the unwelcome group of mothers as 'a harder type of person, their whole attitude was on a lower plane'. One particular feature of their conduct to which the leaders objected was bad language,

> Their language was pretty awful. Sometimes we used to have to ask them to tone it down a bit. Just in the normal course of conversation they were saying things that the kiddies shouldn't really hear.

In both groups, smoking cigarettes seemed to be an important identifying feature of the rough working-class women. Smoking in the playgroup was regarded as particularly inappropriate, but the excluded women were also said to prefer to spend money on cigarettes for themselves rather than on things for their children.

This links with the second identifying feature: aspects of lifestyle. The main features of this seemed to be inappropriate priorities and lack of foresight. The 'roughs' were variously described as: being unable to get up in the mornings; being unable to plan their lives in advance; leaving young children in the charge of older ones while they go to the pub; not being prepared to spend money on sending their child to playgroup; preferring just to push them out onto the streets instead. This last item of course applies *par excellence* to those women *not* involved in the playgroup. This did not prevent the playgroup being used to place them on the wrong side of the rough/respectable boundary, since the very fact of their non-use was seen as a 'rough' characteristic. Examples of the kind of comments made about lifestyle are

> I used to live next door to a woman who had a free place in a nursery and couldn't be bothered to get up and take the children. (Manchester Avenue)

[On the difficulties of organising a mothers' rota]:
Perhaps it was just that they weren't organised, you know. Perhaps they just couldn't organise their life. They'd go out shopping – say they had to go to town. Instead of thinking ahead, well, I've got playgroup so I won't go to town today. (Skyways)

Thirdly, the rough working-class women are seen as having lower standards of housekeeping, especially in tidiness and cleanliness. The historical continuities are obvious here. Davidoff (1976, p. 129) has noted that cleanliness has always been the hallmark of respectability for the working classes, and in Banbury, standards of housekeeping were an important distinguishing mark between rough and respectable (Stacey, 1960, p. 106). This was clearly expressed to me by one of the Skyways leaders, a graduate teacher who had been involved for a short time only, who both recognised and disliked the divisions being created in the playgroup,

[The other leaders] are very critical of the other people who come from this area and won't join in. They make remarks about the way they keep their house you know, and they take it as a sign that they're not quite – to me they divide into these two groups who are not very tolerant of each other. I mean they've been brought up with very strict standards of how often you dust and so on.

Finally, respectability and roughness were related to styles of mothering, which was of considerable importance, because the interaction between the women primarily concerned preschool children. Again, there are historical continuities. Michael Anderson (1971, pp 68–9), in his study of families in nineteenth century Lancashire, shows that middle-class writers regarded the working classes as uncaring parents, inclined to neglect and ill-treat their children. Similar imagery of the rough working classes was apparent in my study. Apart from those 'roughs' who couldn't be bothered to send their children to the playgroup but put them out on the streets instead, the ones who did use the group were said not to control their children properly, and to wish simply to offload responsibility for them onto someone else. The following quotes illustrate something of this – the first (Skyways) is taken from fieldnotes, the second (Manchester Avenue) from the interview transcript,

They didn't want to get rid of their children exactly, but they didn't want to take responsibility for them either. The playgroup was more or less acting as a café for them. They could come there and have a cup of tea, but the difference was that they didn't have the responsibility of having their child with them. They were the kind of mothers who wanted to get out of the house, they wanted to release themselves from the responsibility for their child, and they wanted something for themselves as well.

> I would say that this area is – how, not a poor area, but the majority of people who live here are – sort of you know. We was just talking today about the number of children that are sort of neglected really, and they are... there's a lot of little ones that play on the street all day long and on the front there. They are poorer families intellectually I would say, not sort of poor – materially. They just don't care or they don't know any better.

Given the defining characteristics of 'rough' women which were being employed, the playgroup can now be seen as very suitable setting for drawing the boundaries. It is suitable for at least two rather different reasons. Firstly, because it involves interactions about child-care, it gives opportunities for assessments of mothering and of lifestyle which are so crucial in drawing the dividing lines. Mothers can, as it were, be judged by their children's practice in the playgroup. Their own handling of their children is visible at least when they leave and collect them, and, in turn, the playgroup is a setting in which one effectively gives a public display of mothering. If mothers stay in the playgroup, the opportunities are further increased. Sandra, the graduate who had been a Skyways leader, gave a very clear instance of this process,

> I think there is a very subtle way of discouraging people... We had one little girl who hardly spoke at all, and her mother was often severely criticised because she used bad language. And she brought a little baby who misbehaved and she didn't control him so the baby disrupted the playgroup. And it used to upset me so – they all used to talk about her.

Just as it gives opportunities to exclude people because of their own practice, so also the playgroup provides opportunities for women to 'prove' themselves. I noted that much of the casual conversation between leaders during playgroup sessions concerned matters of housekeeping and children, and this in a sense was the routine business of maintaining the rough/respectable divide by reinforcing each others' own (implicitly superior) standards. In an important sense, playgroup sessions at Skyways, and committee meetings at Manchester Avenue, offered the settings in which women could provide an audience for each other's efforts to constitute and consolidate their own position as 'respectable'.

Secondly, the voluntary, self-help playgroup provides a suitable setting for this activity precisely because it is a form of child care, and a form of voluntary provision, characteristically associated with the middle classes. What better means, therefore, by which to lay claim to being at least at the respectable end of the working classes?

Important though the playgroup seems in drawing significant boundaries in the lives of these women, it has to be seen as only a part of the picture, as part of a wider task of constructing and maintaining one's position as 'respectable' within a given locality. On the basis of the playgroup study, it is only possible to make suggestions about this wider picture. Firstly, it seems clear that claims to respectability must align quite closely with the reality of one's lifestyle in order to make those claims appear credible. Certainly I observed that most of the 'respectables' did have very clean and tidy houses and to plan their lives in advance, neither of which was necessarily true of the 'roughs'. Furthermore, the homes of the 'respectables' seemed organised to demonstrate symbolically the respectability which they claimed. This was especially notable at Manchester Avenue, where the council houses in which both roughs and respectables lived were identical structurally, but the way in which furniture was arranged seemed to have symbolic significance. Whereas most of the 'roughs' had their furniture pulled as close to the fire as possible, the 'respectables' seemed to favour an arrangement where it was pushed back round the edges of the room, symbolising perhaps a greater degree of comfort, where it is not necessary to huddle over the fire.

It also became clear that the use of the playgroup to create and maintain social divisions was only one of several forums in which this activity took place. Marjorie noted that at Skyways, it was always the same people who were involved in the playgroup, and activities at the school.

> In this community we seem to be – we're on all the committees... I think it's the place where we live really; It's not like a big town. And like there's people that will and there's people that won't, and if there weren't these people that would do these things, nothing – I mean the same people organised the street parties for the [royal] wedding.

At Manchester Avenue, the core committee group were the women on the estate who, in the words of one of them, were the 'initiators' and the ones who 'kept everything going'.

Being the respectables was part of a total lifestyle for these women. Perhaps establishing their position was an especially necessary activity in areas which were undergoing population change, and therefore where they were unlikely to have access to long-established reputations by which they and their families could be placed (cf. Elias and Scotson, 1965).

This wider context raises some fascinating questions which could only be fully addressed through further empirical work in settings other than playgroups. These include: In what circumstances does it become especially important for women to take action to construct and maintain their position as 'respectables'? What range of methods and settings is available for this activity? How far is an individual limited in establishing such claims by the material conditions of her life?

Hierarchies among women: some observations about class and gender

The picture which emerges from this playgroup study is of women actively creating and sustaining hierarchically arranged social divisions. Far from being simply the passive recipients of a social position based on their husband's occupation, the 'respectables' in my study were engaged (individually and collectively) in constructing their *own* position, and also that of their family. Neither conventional sociological nor indeed feminist analyses of class can easily make sense of this. In terms of conventional analyses, these women almost all share a common class position as working class, whether one assigns that on the basis of their own occupational status or on their husbands'. Such analyses, by taking the public sphere of economic production as their focus, do not easily take account of women, whose productive activity takes place in the domestic sphere. Feminist analyses again would tend to emphasise their common position as married women, as economically dependent on the male wage and as full-time mothers. Neither an analysis of their position as working class nor as economically dependent women easily suggest why the creation of the rough/respectable boundary should be so significant.

Equally, it seems inadequate to designate these divisions as merely 'status', not linked in any sense to the material world in which 'class' is located. Such a response would dismiss the creation of hierarchies among women as simply games which women play in their private domain, and leaves unasked questions about what benefits women *do* derive from their positions in such hierarchies. Conventional concepts of both class and status have been derived from the perspective of the public domain of men, and cannot easily be stretched to take account of the reality of many women's lives.

It seems to me that the most important point at which to begin making sense of these hierarchies among women is to ask: what are the potential benefits that make these distinctions worth creating and maintaining? What do women get out of being 'respectable' rather than 'rough'? Are there any material benefits? Or do they 'merely'derive prestige and status? The material benefits of being regarded as 'respectable' are difficult to identify, especially in the short term. In the case of the women in my study, they gained control over the playgroup, but that brought no direct material gain. In the longer term, the total task of producing a 'respectable' household could be seen as an investment in future material rewards via one's children and husband (Finch, 1983b), but this still does not explain why it seems so important to be *acknowledged* as respectable by other people.

The evidence of this study seems to me to suggest that the *reputation* of respectability in itself was regarded as a valuable commodity, whether or not it brings direct material gains. If one takes seriously the experience of the women themselves, then the very status of acknowledged respectability was in itself a real gain. The real significance of this can probably only be established on the basis of empirical data from different settings, but I can suggest three possible perspectives which may begin to make sense of it. Firstly an individual woman's experience of her own placement within any significant social hierarchy is probably very complex, since she is located within cross-cutting hierarchies of gender, class and perhaps status groupings mediated, as Morgan (1975, pp. 164–5) has argued, through her position in a particular community. A 'respectable' reputation may provide, as it were, a summarising label, which subsumes several elements and gives a woman some comprehensible basis on which to handle daily relationships. Secondly, the creation of hierarchies among young mothers may be part of a wider pattern of such hierarchies which a woman experiences at different stages in her life. Certainly, recent studies of adolescent, working-class girls have documented rather similar divisions between respectable girls and 'slags' or 'tarts' (McRobbie, 1978; Cowie and Lees, 1981). In this instance the distinctions are based primarily on sexual reputation rather than domestic reputation as appears to be the case for older women. Thirdly, an identity as 'respectable' should perhaps be seen as offering a way of being accorded status which distinguishes a working-class woman from her neighbours when no other means are available, since she shares both their economic position and their sex. On both counts – as an economically dependent woman and as the wife of a wage-labourer – her status is inferior, with little prospect of individual improvement. Small wonder, then, that women regard the gains of being 'respectable' as very real, especially when they can establish their position in the context of an activity such as a playgroup, which at least give a toe-hold in the public domain, in contrast to the private domain of women to which they are otherwise consigned.

As indicated earlier, I found this exercise of linking a discussion of women and class with an empirical study had revealed some contradictions which I find both powerful and painful. These contradictions arise from recognising that whilst the women in my study shared many common experiences and a common position as the wives of wage-labourers and as full-time mothers, they were profoundly divided against each other and some of them were actively increasing those divisions. The contradictions here are that the 'respectables' could only establish their own position at the expense of other women, thus undermining any potential basis for solidarity between them, whilst the 'roughs' could only improve their position individually, not collectively; that is, by starting to play the same game.

All this of course is an entirely comprehensible response to being precisely in the material position which they all shared: accorded inferior status on many counts, with the only real possibility of scrambling off the bottom of the pile being to establish a superior position *vis-à-vis* other women. Successfully achieving such superiority, however, has the consequence of obscuring the real commonality of interests between 'rough' and 'respectable'. It also leaves unrecognised the processes whereby the care and education of young children is constituted as a women's problem (in the interests of men) and as a private problem rather than a public issue (in the interests of keeping state funding to a minimum). The process of dividing the rough from the respectable really does *divide*: it divides not only rough from respectable, but woman from woman.[3]

Notes
1 Forty-eight interviews, covering both playgroup leaders and mothers who simply used the groups, were conducted in the three playgroups which remained open at the end of the observational period. The SSRC funded this stage of the project, and Felicity Harrison assisted in transcribing the tapes and indexing the interview data.
2 Skyways, by contrast, had no formally constituted committee.
3 I would like to thank participants in the Women's Research Seminar at Lancaster University for discussion and constructive criticism of a draft of this paper; and especially Felicity Harrison, Sue Scott and Sylvia Walby.

# 10 Purification or Social Control? Ideologies of Reproduction and the Churching of Women after Childbirth
Peter Rushton

The enduring popularity of religious *rites de passage* in modern Britain has attracted considerable attention from sociologists, many of whom contrast this enthusiasm with the general indifference to regular church attendance (Pickering, 1974). One ritual that is still performed is that of the churching of women after childbirth, officially a thanksgiving but popularly regarded as a form of purification or 'coming-out' ceremony, after which normal social life is again permitted. This ritual, whose performance has been intermittently noticed by fieldworkers since the 1950s, presents a number of analytical problems both for the sociologists of religious ceremonies and female sexuality, and for the historians of church authority and moral control. It is the purpose here to explore two aspects of this rite: the conflict over its meaning and purpose in the present era, and the way that these have changed since early modern times. It will become evident that neither a view of the ceremony as a quaint 'survival' nor the assumption of a single social meaning will provide an adequate explanation. In addition, the historical and sociological evidence on the social contexts of churching has implications for the study of the rituals of female pollution and their differential definition by men and women, officials and populace. Above all, the equations between male and official, female and popular, have a unique significance here because churching is the one ceremony provided by the male clergy of the Church of England for women alone. There is no male equivalent. The dangers of adopting an official, male model of the meaning of the rite, so common in anthropology according to Ardener, are obviously heightened by this polarisation (Ardener, 1975; Needham, 1979, pp. 17–18). Indeed, the potential for conflict is probably enhanced by this structure in which women require men to perform their key rituals for them.

The cultural definition of women's nature

Before beginning the case study of churching, it might be fruitful to ask why natural events such as childbirth attract what might be termed 'ritual attention'. This is not found only in the Judaeo-Christian cultures, but occurs in many disparate societies which mark childbirth with religious and social rites. Usually a whole range of physical changes such as puberty and menstruation are also marked in some way. The conventional explanation for such rituals has stressed the way they function as rites of passage to aid both the individual and society to adjust to the transition to a new physical and social status. On the principle that a physical or social transition is analogous to crossing a boundary, Van Gennep, in his classic formulation, proposed a general structure for rites of passage, in which separation from ordinary society for the purposes of transition is followed by reincorporation once the change is complete. This pattern permits the transformation of the individual away from everyday life and the reorganisation of social attitudes and expectations concerning him or her. Thus both personal change and the reshaping of social relations take place: childbirth and the move to the status of mother are a good example of this process, in many ways. Religion is involved in this pattern because, says Van Gennep, 'among semi-civilised peoples such acts are enveloped in ceremonies, since to the semi-civilised mind no act is entirely free from the sacred' (Van Gennep, 1960; see also La Fontaine, 1972).

The tendency in this kind of perspective is to show how the social organisation of personal change is eased through the use of rituals. In more modern terminology, the aim is to show how the public domain has to contain and handle the difficulties thrown up by the private process of personal change. In this way any personal change of status is irrevocably social. It also becomes difficult to distinguish between the natural and the social changes affecting the individual. As Van Gennep's analysis demonstrates, these rites deal with both physical and social events, together or separately. Thus childbirth is distinguished from baptism (physical arrival from social welcome), just as physical death is to be distinguished from the social farewell of the funeral. There is a great temptation to regard the *natural* as posing an inherent social problem, that is, to see natural events as posing an inevitable difficulty of social organisation. But this would be to see natural, biological events as somehow extra-social, affecting individuals from the outside. So the ritual attention paid to personal biology could be explained in terms of the need to deal satisfactorily at the social level with the naturally unavoidable.

But this would be a naive dichotomy between the social and the natural, as Van Gennep shows. It is in many ways hard to distinguish the rituals of birth and death from those such as initiation rites which establish a metaphorical pattern of death and rebirth. Thus 'natural' events are not so easily isolated in the life-cycle of the individual. On the contrary, there is a strong tradition in anthropology of seeing 'nature' as essentially a social construction. Hertz (1973a, p. 120), in particular, in his work on right and left-handedness in different cultures, demonstrated this by pointing to how, while many occupations (surgery, playing numerous musical instruments) actually require people to be ambidextrous, the ideology of asymmetry has produced, through social training, a population which is virtually one-handed. As he says, 'organic asymmetry in man (sic) is at once a fact and ideal'. The fact, however, is socially created and sustained (see also Sudnow, 1967).

If nature is always irrevocably a social product, we need to enquire how women's and men's natures are defined and culturally organised, and what part religious rituals play in that process. This would avoid any simple identification of women with 'pure' nature, leaving society and culture to men. This equation is favoured by Ardener and Ortner, supported mostly on biological grounds. Callaway (1978, p. 164), for example, says, 'to be female is first to be identified with biological reproduction – "the most essentially female function of all" '. But to equate culture with men and nature with women is, as Brown and Jordanova (1981) rightly stress, to accept this kind of conventional biological definitions and explanations of women's domesticity and subordination. Moreover, there is a dangerous tendency to assert this cause as a universal cultural pattern lying behind women's supposedly universal social inferiority. While understandably criticising social anthropologists' naive acceptance of men's views of 'their' society, Ardener in fact stands in danger of reproducing them in the name of social science. As Rogers (1978, p. 137) comments, 'any general theory of sexual differentiation based primarily on the constraints of women's physiological functions and childrearing responsibilities is... a clear reflection of our cultural priorities.'

It would be a misconception, therefore, to see rituals associated with women's biology as some masculine effort to keep them at a distance from society. The point is that both men and women have been defined as possessing a biological nature which supposedly suits them for particular social roles and tasks. Ironically, exponents of biological explanations would see through the nature/culture dichotomy almost immediately: from the eighteenth century savants to the modern sociobiologists there have always been those who assert that women's biology equips them uniquely well for domesticity, and that men's nature is best suited to public affairs such as politics and the economy. The ideology of gender in the western tradition has always consisted of concepts of nature mingled with assertations of appropriate social location (Brown and Jordanova, 1981).

The taboos and fears seemingly associated with women's biology may not, therefore, stem from the social fear of natural forces: rather, they may derive from anxiety caused by a natural event occurring outside its proper place. This indicates that the public/private dichotomy may have more explanatory power than the culture/nature one since it points to the way that the 'natural' is constructed within strictly enforced social boundaries. So supposedly natural events are strictly policed according to the associated setting or occasion for which they are sanctioned. And, of course, these settings create as much as control the events. So a conventional ideology generates self-reinforcing and tautological conceptions: sex is always private, economic work is public and so on. What we need to know is how the two general domains are kept separate when so many things are likely to affect both. The consequences of sex or death, personal change or disappearance have to be negotiated publicly. They are all both private and public, and rituals of various kinds may help police the boundaries between the two areas. Parenthood is a good example: while childbirth is still essentially private, motherhood is public, a key social status for a woman. The results of what occur in private have to be publicly acknowledged and, as Van Gennep suggested, many of the apparent threshold rites make this transformation easier, ensuring social acceptance. At the same time the rituals affirm the fundamental division between the spheres and the genders associated with them: in marriage a woman leaves one household on the arm of her father, and the church on the arm of her husband to enter another household. But because women pass from private to public and back again on so many ritual and social occasions, it is hard to allocate them to one domain on a permanent basis. As Hastrup (1978, p. 57) argues, 'the boundary areas, or the ambiguous classifications are points of danger...they give rise to ambivalence and marginalisation'. Women, therefore, may find themselves not so much mediating between the two domains as standing ambiguously between them.

Both the culture/nature and public/private metaphors have stood in danger of being too crudely formalised or utilised too mechanically. While favouring the latter over the former, I would want to stress the way that the social reality of attitudes and ritual actions may not be neat or coherent. The boundary areas between the two domains might well generate confusion rather than precise methods of resolving the contradictions. Certainly some of the contemptuous imagery of women in previous centuries suggests that it has proved impossible to mould social reality to the ideal: as De Bruyn (1979) points out, the good woman in the sixteenth century was contrasted with the witch, the wanton and the shrew, but so much anxiety would not have been aroused if women were well confined to the domestic role. Similarly, the attitudes of official performers of rituals may well vary from sympathy with the laity to critical hostility.

Women differ from men in their self-definition, and the social fabric may be split on class and denominational grounds. One of the problems in the analysis that follows is the difficulty in using essentially anthropological insights from simpler societies in the context of diverse western cultures. Nevertheless, the aim here is to explore the rites of childbirth as they affect women in the history of our more complicated Christian society.

The origins of the rite

'Churching' is the popular name for the ancient Christian ritual performed a few weeks after a woman has given birth (in the medieval church, *ordo ad purificandam mulierem post partum, ante ostium ecclesiae* – 'the rite for the purification of a woman after childbirth, before the church door'). It probably derived originally from the Jewish rites of purification specified in Leviticus 12 (Blunt, 1905, p. 160; New English Bible, 1970, pp. 120–1). The threshold location of the rite and the unusual dress (women usually wore veils and carried candles) indicate that it was a symbolic form of reincorporation into the congregation after separation because of pollution. The fear of women, and the association of their bodily changes with pollution and danger, were present in other early Christian customs, such as the banning of menstruating women from church (see Douglas, 1970, p. 76), or a general prohibition on women beyond certain areas of churches (Raine, 1850, p. 18).

At the Reformation there was a sustained attack against official 'magic', and churching lost its status as a purification rite (for the fullest historical account, see Staton, 1980). Yet it is clear from Puritan criticisms that purificatory elements remained despite Anglican attempts at rationalisation. Henry Barrow (1962, pp. 462–5), for example, in the 1590s mocked this part of the 'priest's trade', designed to make women holy again after they had come through a hazard (childbirth) that he saw as essentially natural, ordinary and common. 'Is not all this absolutely Jewish?', he asked acutely. There seems to have been confusion among the clergy as to the suitable timing and dress for the rite, and the Church of England took no steps to clarify its exact purpose within a reformed church (Thomas, 1973, pp. 68ff.).

Churching and the bawdy courts

Churching was not only the subject of theological disputes: it became a vital source of conflict between clergy and laity in the enforcement of ecclesiastical law. The church courts were responsible for the prosecution of moral and religious deviants, concentrating particularly on sexual offences (hence the popular name 'bawdy court'). But they also pursued those who avoided, or contradicted, the religious rites of the Church of England. These included some witches (Rushton, 1982), and many women who had offended the authorities in the matter of churching. The church courts had two primary apparent aims: to enforce a uniformity of practice (against Catholics and Protestant dissenters), and to provide the rites of the Church only on its own terms. The latter involved the withholding of rites until previous offences had been duly presented before the courts and penances performed (for a full range of cases before the courts, see Hair, 1972). So on the one hand the Anglican authorities were trying to force churching on their religious opponents, and on the other refusing to church immoral women.

The moral aspect of this sanction should have been straightforwardly applied, since instructions to the clergy not to church mothers of illegitimate children were standard in most dioceses from the 1570s (Frere, 1910, p. 278).

It is clear, though, that the local clergy were the weakest link in the chain: they could easily be persuaded to church women (and baptise their children) without presenting them before the courts or exacting any prior penance. This was quite common in Northumberland in the early seventeenth century, where the vicars themselves were occasionally prosecuted for allowing this. In other cases, the churching was performed if the woman promised to marry ('upon their wordes to marie' as a case in Corbridge in 1603 recorded). The clergy were obviously nervous of the social disruption that refusing churching would produce.[1]

More typical were those cases where women's inability to prove that they had been churched was taken as evidence of dubious moral character or of religious dissent. The first is related to notions of community, and the importance of demonstrating membership through observance of religious rites. Hence to be a 'maide unchurched', or to be unable to show that churching had been properly performed, were likely indications of a transient habit and probable avoidance of communal moral obligations. Consequently, for both husbands and wives as well as single mothers, proof of correct religious observance allayed the local anxiety about vagrancy among a people who were increasingly mobile in the seventeenth century.[2] In other cases this kind of evidence was taken as reflecting religious dissent. This was so where women had flouted the Anglican monopoly by being churched in private by Catholic priests. These recusants (significantly meaning those who *refuse*) were taking great risks, given the official hunt for the illegal priesthood. For example, a Warkworth woman in 1606 was allegedly 'churched by a seminarie priest' in her husband's house, and her child baptised. On other occasions the husband was prosecuted for recusancy, and his wife's private churching used as corroboration; sometimes they were prosecuted together.[3] Most opposition to official churching, though, came from Puritans who, as Thomas (1973, p. 69) notes, opposed the whole magical business in the century before the Civil War. Afterwards, from the 1660s on, there was a steady stream of men and women, Quakers, Independents, Anabaptists and other 'separatists', flowing through the Durham and other courts accused of refusing churching.[4]

It is uncertain how long churching remained an issue in ecclesiastical law. By the mid-eighteenth century there are signs of uncertainty among the local clergy, who seem to have carried on churching without any moral sanctions (Hair, 1972, p. 130; Woodforde, 1935). Moreover, as has been noted in the case of Devon, the church courts as a whole seem to have lost their power, leaving the policing of morals to the civil magistrates and Poor Law authorities (Warne, 1969, pp.84–5). What is evident throughout the period after the Reformation, though, is the general determination of women to be churched, whatever their moral character or denomination. It was only among the minority of fundamentalist Protestants that the rite was rejected altogether. Because of the value they placed on it, churching was an ideal issue in the social control of women.

Folk versus official religion

By the nineteenth century the custom of churching had vanished from the legal framework of ecclesiastical law enforcement along with the power of the church courts. However, the subject was reconstituted as folklore. As folk customs are regarded as inevitably moribund, the rediscovery and the imminent death of churching have been frequently reported in the last 150 years. When nineteenth century observers saw fit to comment on churching, they made it clear that there had been some changes compared with earlier periods. For one thing, the idea had gained currency among dissenting communities. Richardson (1842, p. 180), for example, reports of the Scottish Borders in 1842:

> the mother made it a point of observance to enter no friend's house until she attended divine service at either church or chapel, and on her way thither she was generally accompanied by her husband who took with him a portion of bread and cheese, and bestowed it on the first person who they met on the road. On this occasion it was and is still deemed unlucky to go forth empty-handed.

Although Richardson was regretful that these customs were supposedly dying out, it is clear from subsequent accounts and modern memories that most have survived, even down to the gift-giving on the way to church at christenings and weddings. But the mention of 'chapel' should not surprise us, since there is much evidence of deliberate syncretism among dissenting communities in the first half of the nineteenth century. Clarke (1978), for example, in his study of Staithes, shows that Methodism had to make compromises with local taboos and superstitions, despite their formal rejection by ministers. More recently, Staton (1980) has noted that among Methodists, although there is no separate rite, the first attendance at church after childbirth serves as the point of resuming a normal social life of a woman.

This dichotomy between official and folk beliefs, though rarely breaking into open disputes, was a constant feature of the time. Obelkevich (1976, p. 273), for example, reports the healthy state of popular underground 'superstitions' in Lincolnshire in the middle of the nineteenth century. Of churching, he says:

> Its popularity, which was great, was due not to the pious desire to render thanks to God, but almost entirely to two superstitions: that it removed the impurity which was thought to taint women after childbirth – 'clean' in local dialect referred to 'a woman after being churched' – and that a mother who left her house to go visiting before being churched would give birth to another child within the year.

The notion of pollution or uncleanness was certainly influential, for a woman who avoided churching was generally thought to invite misfortune upon herself or any she met. If she visited a house, the woman of the house would become pregnant within the year, it was believed. More sinister was the belief in the North of England that any unchurched woman could be insulted or attacked without any legal penalities (E. and M.A. Radford, 1978, p. 38; Henderson, 1979, p. 8). The social separation of a woman after childbirth (which rarely seems to have existed during pregnancy) is clearly indicated in these forceful sanctions. Popular Christianity, therefore, remained very distinct from the official versions. As Obelkevich (1976, p. 273) notes, 'Christianity provided the ritual, but paganism gave it its meaning.'

The Anglican authorities in the nineteenth century seem to have come under greater popular pressure, with the result that the rite of churching was made available to any woman who requested it. This resulted from a legal case in 1856, and from then on 'there was much uncertainty, indeed, whether or not the service is intended for all women who have born children or only for those who have born them in lawful matrimony'. Playing safe, legal handbooks for churchwardens stated – 'this rite is intended for all women safely delivered in childbirth, and therefore it cannot be refused because the child is illegitimate or the mother is a dissenter' (Blunt, 1905, p. 160; Whitehead, 1911, p.81). There remained confusion, however, about the time and the dress suitable for the ceremony, although all agreed that a veil could not be enforced. Commentators regarded the rite with some misgivings, reflected in the different terms to describe it. Although officially known as the 'Thanksgiving of Women after Childbirth', it was common to add 'formerly Purification of Women' or 'the Churching of Women'. The official view was forced to acknowledge the popular undercurrents of belief. Another (female) commentator on the Book of Common Prayer regarded the rite as signifying the 'restoration of the woman to the privileges of the Lord's House', which is tantamount to admitting that the abnormal state of pregnancy and childbirth should isolate a woman from the congregation and everyday social and religious life (Phillimore, 1873, p. 834).

Twentieth century fieldwork indicates a considerable degree of continuity with these nineteenth century customs and beliefs, although most of the accounts come from long-established urban communities rather than the classic folklorists' territory of the countryside. All references are to the working classes, too, which suggests that the rite is no longer popular among the middle class. There is a remarkable consistency in the pictures of the social context of churching. Everyone – particularly the men interviewed – agrees that churching is women's business, and that it is only pressure from other women which ensures its survival. Most of the women referred to by Young and Willmott (1962, p. 52) excused their churching by blaming it on maternal pressure, and this was also a common reason given to Staton in Newcastle eighteen years later.

This may be partly because of the greater religiosity of women which has been an obsession of sociologists since Durkheim. Certainly communities in the nineteenth century witnessed an increasing dominance of women in churchgoing, as Obelkevich (1976) reports. It may explain the complete absence of men from the rite in the twentieth century accounts, in contrast to those nineteenth century reports quoted above. But there is also evidence that men have developed considerable hostility to churching – especially in the Bethnal Green study. 'It's your religion, isn't it?', one husband is reported to have said of his wife's churching, while simultaneously blaming it on undue pressure from his mother-in-law (Young and Willmott, 1962, p. 52). It looks as though this kind of use of religious rituals constitutes a specifically female tradition, autonomous from the male beliefs.

The problem of pressure, reflected in the somewhat shamefaced motives expressed by women to fieldworkers, is one which has not usually been raised with regard to either female religiosity or the rites of passage. For one thing, it militates against the recorded responses being entirely genuine; the diversity of motives expressed may simply reflect the women's estimate of what the investigators would find acceptable or plausible (Wright Mills, 1971; Taylor, 1972). On the other hand, the diversity may also reflect an underlying uncertainty among younger women concerning a tradition that has been forced on them. The tradition may continue to be powerful precisely because of the uncertainty and fears that pregnancy and childbirth generate, perpetuated by the professionalisation of the whole process (Hubert, 1974). The motives seem to vary from the desire to give thanks (the official interpretation), to have sins forgiven, to acquire luck, or just to be blessed. This confusion is well expressed by one of Staton's (1980, p. 217) respondents:

> It is a sin to have a baby. It is unlucky not to be churched. You don't have any luck if you don't get churched. My mother would shut the door on you.

This notion of sin and luck runs through attitudes to other rites of passage, especially baptism. Unbaptised babies are frequently avoided as unlucky, and liable to go to hell if they die: despite official rejection of this by Protestant churches, the idea still lingers on. Luck seems to govern the attitudes to most rites of passage, as Pickering (1974) suggests. The power of the 'superstition' is always likely to be strong when the incentive is offered that it cannot do any actual *harm* to go through the ceremony. But as we have seen, the unusual thing about churching is the extent of public pressure brought by other women to enforce obedience to the custom.

Official attitudes to these beliefs are more than hostile: all other churches except the Church of England have rejected them. The Catholic Church, for example, abolished churching after Vatican II and merged the thanksgiving ceremony with baptism. Even in the Anglican church, there is individual evidence of hostility by local clergy, some of whom are now refusing to perform the rite. It may be that where the communal sanctions of the popular belief are no longer possible, the churches will win converts to the more 'rational' view of churching. Certainly Staton found that some women from outside his tightknit community were able to avoid the ceremony without adverse social reactions. But it would be premature to conclude, as Douglas (1970, p. 76) does, that 'now it is difficult to find instances of ritual uncleanness in Christian practice'. Popular beliefs about sin and purification still survive, not as quaint local customs, but as a living force in many communities where churching is still performed.

Churching and the images of reproduction

The most extraordinary feature of this albeit brief and fragmentary history of churching is the continuity of women's determination to have the ceremony performed, whatever the degree of official opposition, and the maintenance of a set of beliefs, virtually unchanged since medieval times, associating it with purification. Consequently, it would be unwise to pronounce on the imminent death of this undercurrent of belief and practice. Although churching may at first glance be similar to the other rites of passage on offer to the public by any Christian church, it is unique in at least two respects: it is only performed for women, and it is alone in being associated with popular sentiments of pollution and cleansing. In Van Gennep's (1960, pp 10–1) terms, it is less a rite of transition to a new social status than one of cleansing and reincorporation after separation from society. So, although motherhood is a prerequisite for churching, entry into that status does not depend on churching. If that were so, there would be no need to repeat the rite after each child, as is still done in Newcastle. So churching does not so much signal a permanent change in social status as help to resolve the ambiguities of pregnancy and childbirth. As Van Gennep (1960, pp. 46–7) himself observes,

> although its character is more mundane than magico-religious, it is easy to see what it must have been during the Middle Ages – the woman's reintegration into her family, her sex group and her society.

As we have seen, this is still a vital part of the popular culture. A woman after churching, like the newly purified Brahmin woman Van Gennep describes, passes back from an abnormal state to resume her appropriate place in society.

The key element of belief is clearly the implicit notion of pregnancy and childbirth as abnormal, a feature of popular, if not official, culture. There is, of course, a medical and legal tradition of regarding childbirth at least as psychologically disorienting. As Edwards (1981, p.94) point outs, this has been incorporated in the law of infanticide, and this legal logic may be broadened to include other physiological changes such as menstruation. But while providing scientific explanations for unusual (non-masculine) behaviour, this official expertise, so closely guarded, denies women the right to establish their own understanding of physical changes in their own bodies. As a result, alongside the technical knowledge, monopolised by the medical and legal professions, there is a wide undercurrent of popular beliefs about the nature of pregnancy and childbirth and their effects on women and their children. This culture, as Hubert (1974) and Graham (1976) have shown, flourishes despite all attempts to 're-educate' women. The culture tends to stress two aspects of pregnancy: it is seen as a time of enhanced vulnerability, requiring special precautions, and of loss of personal control. The pregnant woman is thus supposedly in a more dangerously vulnerable state than others, and less able to behave in a conventional manner. At the same time, as Graham (1976, p. 293) points out, this anomalous state is not socially destructive: it is usually regarded as a 'demonstration of an indisputable claim to womanhood'. It is therefore fundamental to the fulfilment of feminine identity.

The transitional state, though, requires careful and circumspect handling because of the dangers involved. The *vulnerability* of pregnancy derives from its two-in-one nature, and it is an old idea that special precautions need to be taken because more than one 'person' is involved. Traditionally this took the form of many avoidance rules or taboos, because many characteristics of small children's development were explained by events during the pregnancy. To take an early seventeenth century source, almost at random, Robert Burton drew on this theory of pre-natal influences to explain the pattern of inheritance of melancholy and other features from parents. Because 'the strange imagination of a woman works effectually upon her infant', he says, and leaves a mark on it, many physical and psychological characteristics of people stem from their mothers' experiences during pregnancy. Harelips, birthmarks, drunkenness and other things could be explained in this way (Burton, 1972, p. 215). That this is not a moribund tradition is demonstrated by modern folklorists, who have found that people still explain harelips by the mother's sight of a hare during her pregnancy, and features such as speech difficulties or oddities in eye colouring are explained similarly. Pregnant women have also been regarded as dangerous as well as vulnerable, and were frequently forbidden to work in certain agricultural areas at tasks such as food preparation because they were thought to make it turn bad (E. and M.A. Radford, 1978, p. 87; Edwards, 1981, p. 77). The theory of prenatal influence on the child provided (and probably still provides) a sanction for the special precautions that a woman has to take, and which automatically separate her from the rest of the population. Today, the precautions may have been medicalised, so a pregnant woman is distinguished from all others by her avoidance of normal nasty habits such as smoking and drinking.

Pregnancy is also thought to affect the mother in ways that she cannot control. Graham's (1976) work is almost alone in exploring this aspect of popular culture, demonstrating that pregnancy is thought to affect the woman in a uniquely abnormal way that produces behaviour that would not normally be sanctioned. Secondly, pregnancy is a role that requires assistance, since it is recognised that to a significant extent a woman is helpless in the face of her own condition. So, as Graham points out, a woman may be blamed for getting pregnant but not for *being* pregnant. While in that condition she may demand special treatment or particular goods (food for example) not otherwise given her. On the other hand her condition is subject to expert handling over which she can exercise little influence. Thus special needs and desires are recognised, granting a kind of elevation to the pregnant woman, but at the same time there is increased reliance on others to satisfy those demands and carry pregnancy through to its successful conclusion. Graham understandably draws a comparison with the victim of spirit possession in other cultures studied by Lewis. As she concludes, 'pregnancy provides the actor with a ritual licence, a token equality, thereby enhancing her reproductive status, but ultimately acting not to undermine, but rather to underline and perpetuate, the nature of sexual divisions' (p. 305).

Pregnancy is thus a difficult, anomalous, state, as viewed by popular – and in part, perhaps by scientific – culture. It is something *special*, and consequently distinguishes women in their transitional state from the rest of the population, even other women. Childbirth, as we have seen from the beliefs associated with churching, has a similar effect in that its perceived abnormality produces social separation. At the same time there is a difference between the two states: pregnancy involves special precautions and licensed unconventionality, while childbirth apparently requires a kind of social exclusion. Only the physically sick or the mad could be expected to behave or be treated in the latter way. The whole image of childbearing, of which the rite of churching is the final part, is a combination of elements of abnormality, unique to women, and of dependence during a period of social isolation. The informal culture thus reinforces what Ettore (1980, p. 8) calls the 'reproductive ideology', according to which 'women appear falsely as more reproductive than men'. Reproduction is thus thought to affect mainly the female rather than the male. In addition, Ettore suggests, the ideology is sustained through an artificial dichotomy between subjective experience and the objective interpretation of it by which, 'ironically, women are alienated from the experience of their own bodies, while being totally defined by their bodies'. As this outline of some aspects of the feminine folk culture demonstrates, there is a surprisingly similar emphasis in both popular and scientific views on the predominance of women in reproduction.

The culture of churching, sustained by women over the centuries, has contributed to this ideology of reproduction. Women have actively embraced this by practising a kind of pollution taboo that has kept them apart after childbirth. It is difficult to know exactly what this notion of pollution constitutes. It might be the masculine view, familiar to anthropologists, of a danger to men which must be avoided. On the other hand, because men seem to regard churching with a kind of baffled hostility, it may be that women, as a means of celebrating their own uniqueness in reproduction, of marking out their identity, see themselves as 'contaminated with holiness', in Leach's (1976, p. 78) phrase. It may be a means of expressing their own femininity, in their own eyes, and, unwittingly reinforcing their subordination. The effect of the ideological definition of reproductive states as publicly abnormal or anomalous is to confine women – literally and metaphorically – during their childbearing. This is both restricting and enabling, as we have seen. While it is assumed that women should be kept within the domestic sphere till their 'time' comes, the abnormal state may be an acceptable excuse for deviant public actions. The boundary between the public and private domains, however, is carefully reaffirmed, and normality is restored when the mother is churched and 'returns' to society.

It is difficult to know how common this subculture is in Christian societies today, if there *are* any societies that could be called so. There is evidence from Greece (Hirshon, 1978) and Brittany (Hélias, 1978) that many of the same elements have been present in the twentieth century. Both seem to share the spatial control of women that is present in many Mediterranean societies – as evinced, or example by Reiter's (1975) work in southern France. But the crucial factor throughout is the self-enforcement of these boundaries by women themselves. Such apparently self-defeating actions are not new in western societies, of course. In earlier centuries patriarchal ideologies of sexual morality and witchcraft were frequently applied by women against each other. These traditions, like that of churching, suggest that a crucial element in the maintenance and reproduction of ideologies is their active practice by their victims as much as the willingness of official organisations to countenance them. Unlike witchcraft, however, churching has survived because of the skill of a folk culture in enlisting the cooperation of an official church, however reluctant. The rite has become a part of the culture of femininity despite, rather than because of, the male church which would no doubt agree with Dr Johnson in this instance that 'an age of ignorance is an age of ceremony' (Hill, 1974, p. 101). To paraphrase a judgement quoted earlier, the church still provides the rite, but today it is women alone who give it its meaning and popular force. Without this force, churching would die along with the ideology of reproduction it supports.

Acknowledgements

Firstly, I must thank Reverend Maurice Staton for his permission to quote from his unpublished M.A. thesis on churching, and for his help and encouragement. Secondly, many thanks to my Sunderland students, churched and unchurched, who speedily disabused me of the idea that churching was long-dead, and who regaled me with items of local folklore rather than discuss my seminar topics.

Notes

1 Church court records for the Diocese of Durham, in the Department of Palaeography and Diplomatic, Durham: Visitations, Vol. 5, ff. 125a, 163 and 178a; Vol. 7, f. 155b; Archdeacons' Act Books, Vol. 2, f.6a.
2 Hair, 1972, p. 169; Archdeacons' Act Books, Vol. 1, f. 83b; Visitations, Vol. 5, f. 139b; Vol. 6, f.33b. There are some similar cases in the York records – see Purvis, 1948.
3 Visitations, Vol. 5, f.157a, and Archdeacons' Act Books, Vol. 1, f.61b (1621), and Vol. 2, f.67b (1620).
4 Visitations, Vol. 3, ff.114b, 147 and 167b.

11 Do Her Answers Fit His Questions? Women and the Survey Method
Hilary Graham

Introduction
This paper aims to extend the boundaries of the feminist critique of social research. This critique has pointed to a ubiquitous male bias within sociology, a male bias which has structured the knowledge base of the discipline (Smith, 1974, 1979; Stacey, 1981) and the social relations of its production (Stanley and Wise, 1979; Morgan, 1981). What has been left unexplored is the status of the research methods through which both the knowledge base and the social relations of sociology are constructed. We have yet seriously to consider the possibility that the ideological forces at work within our discipline penetrate to the heart of the data generation process itself, with gender bias introduced through the methods by which we do our empirical investigation.

Neutrality and bias, of course, are well-worked themes within the world of social research. It may be that to incorporate them within a specifically feminist critique is to labour the obvious. But, as Morgan (1981, p. 88) has observed, 'the obvious deserves at least as much attention from the sociologist as the extraordinary. It is also more difficult to recognise.' Recognising the obvious is all the more urgent because so much of our recently discovered knowledge about the position of women is derived from the research technique that has come to dominate and typify mainstream sociology: namely, the survey method. The survey method occupies a unique and a highly ambiguous position, as the basis on which both the reputation of 'masculinist sociology' and the new-found credibility of social research on women has been built.

The survey method reflects the ideology of the nineteenth-century world in which it was developed. While its principles of individualism, equivalence and rationality may accord with those which govern the operation of the state and the economy, it is, as we will see, more difficult to apply them to women's work in and for the family. Recognising these difficulties means confronting a potentially serious contradiction in the endeavours of those (like myself) who have attempted to contribute to a 'sociology for women' (Smith, 1979) by documenting the experiences of women through the medium of the social survey. For it appears that the survey may well frustrate, from its inception, a feminist programme committed to understanding 'how the female subject in our time sees herself, or would, were she given the opportunity to provide a spoken account of her existence' (Elshtain, 1981, p. 304), introducing into the data base of feminist theory the very limitations that the new body of theory seeks to overcome.

Elshtain, in *Public Man, Private Woman* (1981), spells out what this new body of theory should contain, and by implication, highlights the dilemma which may face the survey researcher who seeks to contribute to it. She argues that we need a theoretical framework:

> which can incorporate the self-understanding of the female subject as an essential feature of its overall logic of explanation. We need to be able, cogently, to articulate the bases and steps in the creation of female identity, public and private. We need a way to explore female speech and language... The search for the female subject is simultaneously a quest for a form of inquiry that serves the ends of explanation, understanding, and critique along public and private vectors. This means that the theorist must reject out of hand any mode of explanation which requires or sanctions the imposition upon the female subject of the theorist's own views as to who she is, what she wants and what she should have in advance of any attempt to probe that subject's self-understanding. (pp. 302-3).

The feminist critique of social research

Over the last decade, sociologists have become increasingly aware of the extent to which the sexual divisions which scar western society are reflected and reproduced within western science (Okin, 1980; Elshtain, 1981; Brighton Women and Science Group, 1980). Sociology itself has not escaped criticism, with a pervasive male bias identified within its research programme and its mode of analysis.

In the early 1970s, the feminist critique of sociology was linked to the phenomenological critiques advanced, among others, by Cicourel (1964) and Filmer *et al.* (1972). While phenomenologists sought to expose the distorted model of science and the social world embedded within positivism, writers such as Bart (1971), Smith (1974) and Oakley (1974b) pointed to the way in which this model related to a wider system of sexual stratification. Their analyses opened up two avenues of enquiry: the problems of doing research on women and the problems of women doing research. Firstly, the points at which sexism surfaces within the conceptual apparatus of sociology have been more accurately located. Smith (1978), Ardener (1978) and Stacey (1981) have described the intellectual barriers against feminist research, arguing that the dominant modes of analysis inhibit a sociological understanding of women's experiences. Other writers have focused on a second and related set of issues. While noting the limitations imposed by the theories and methods of sociology, their attention has been drawn to the way in which ideologies of gender have structured the social relations of research. They have described the pervasive effects of gender on the process of research: on the pattern of interaction between researcher and researched, between researcher and researcher, between researcher and publisher (Roberts, 1981; Stanley and Wise, 1979). For example, Oakley (1981) discusses the masculine imagery which pervades textbook descriptions of the interview process, where the interviewer is expected to remain detached, distant and in control. Morgan identifies an equivalent process of 'academic machismo' at work in the research community. He suggests that the social relations among academics encourage 'the competitive display of masculine skills, more redolent of gladiatorial combat than scholarly debate (Morgan, 1981, p. 101). Spender too, identifies 'a problem of male dominance' within publishing, with men acting as the gatekeepers 'who are in a position to decide what gets published and what does not' (1981, pp. 187-8).

The two areas of feminist concern – the impact of gender on the means of sociological production and upon the social relations in which it is embedded – are clearly interrelated. In fact, fundamental to the studies described above is the recognition that the social relations of sociology (and society) are etched indelibly into the discipline's theories and methods. Separating one from the other is possible only as a heuristic exercise; and it is for this purpose that the two are distinguished here. The remainder of the section describes the feminist critique of the theories and methods of sociology, while the second and third sections focus the spotlight more narrowly still, by examining the nature of the survey method.

The feminist critique of sociology has addressed itself primarily to the misogynic nature of sociological theory. Sociological theory, it is argued, has been built upon and from man's relation to his social world. Smith illustrates the discipline's male orientation with the example of housework:

> how sociology is thought – its methods, conceptual schemes and theories – has been based upon and built up within the male social universe... [this] conceptual apparatus... rests uneasily upon the actual experience of women... If we started with housework as a basis, the categories of 'work' and 'leisure' would never emerge .... The social organisation of the role of housewife, mother and wife does not conform to the divisions between being at work and not being at work. Even the concept of housework as work leaves what we do as mothers without a conceptual home. (1974, p. 7; 1979, p. 137.)

Recent analyses have drawn attention to the way in which sociology's concern with 'the male social universe' has both a sexual and a socio-spatial dimension. Sociology is oriented not simply to men, but to the social arenas to which men have privileged access. Sociology, Stacey (1981) argues, focuses on the activities and relationships in these 'public domains' which form the governing apparatus of our society: management, government, the police and the military, health and educational institutions, the media. As traditionally 'private' areas of life – such as health care – became incorporated within the boundaries of the public domain, the subject matter of sociology has shifted also. As Shirley Ardener (1978) notes, it is the presence of men which typically defines a space as 'public' and the province of sociology. 'Private' and 'public' do not therefore have an exact and tangible location: places remain constant while definitions of their social space change.

The coincidence between sexual and spatial divisions has other dimensions. Edwin Ardener (1975), Rich (1980) and Spender (1980), for example, argue that these divisions have their equivalent within language. Ardener suggests that there are 'dominant' and 'muted' modes of expression reflecting, and generated by, the wider power divisions within the society. Since the dominant mode expresses the relation of the dominant group to the social world, it fails to capture the relations through which the experiences of the muted group are mediated. It is a 'man-made language' (Spender, 1980) in which, according to Rich (1980, p. 199) significant aspects of women's lives become 'not merely unspoken but unspeakable'.

Shattering the silence of women remains a major commitment of the women's movement both within and beyond the academic world. It is a commitment which raises crucial questions about the way sociologists collect as well as analyse social data. However, while the critique of sociological theory has gone on apace, with notable exceptions (Acker and Esseveld, 1981; Roberts, 1981), women's position within the traditional methods of social research has remained relatively unexplored. We shall know little about how the social survey (or participant observation or the experiment) transforms individuals, with gender and class identities, into 'respondents', and how women's experiences are represented, or misrepresented, in this process.

One area that has received attention, however, is the congruence between the theoretical tendencies which characterise sociology and the division between 'quantitative' and 'qualitative' research. Bernard (1973) argued that this division mirrored the theoretical divisions between public and private, instrumental and expressive, *Gemeinschaft* and *Gesellschaft* – and the wider structure of social divisions between men and women. Other writers have explored the link between gender and methodology in more detail (Millman and Kanter, 1975; Roberts, 1978; Reinharz, 1979; Morgan, 1981). Quantitative research is seen to represent the male 'style of knowing' (Reinharz, 1979, p. 7) – adopting an active but impersonal stance compatible with the masculine ethos of the public domain in which it is typically employed. Qualitative research is seen to operate within a different paradigm, representing a female style of knowing. Researchers adopt a more personal approach, seeking out 'soft' data about the private world through categories unlikely to lend themselves to quantification and statistical analysis.

This critique points to the way in which ideology permeates the apparently neutral techniques of data collection. It suggests that the two paradigms – the quantitative and the qualitative – express in methodological terms the gender divisions apparent within sociological theory. Questions nonetheless remain. Two issues in particular need to be addressed: one political, the other practical.

Firstly, the logic of the critique suggests that qualitative methods are better suited to the structure of women's lives, while quantitative methods are reserved for the study of (and by) men. Such a sexual division may yield useful data, but only at the same time, by reinforcing the tendency to analyse women and men's lives separately. In so doing, it underlines the notion that women are locked into a 'women's world', marginal to mainstream culture and integrated into society only through the mediation of men. Rather than building a methodological ghetto for women, we need to design research strategies that take account of their complex and overlapping interrelationships with the public and private domains. As Berk argues

> the substance of women's lives is shaped by two worlds of work: the home and the labour market. Thus, to treat such realms as independent or to imagine that the 'public' has no connection to the 'private' is to ultimately evade or distort the relation women have to the social world (1980, pp. 25–6).

The wholesale adoption of qualitative research by and for women may thus reinforce the very divisions that feminists are seeking to destroy. If the existence of two research strategies reflects the operation of a sexual bias within the social sciences, then a programme of qualitative research may not guarantee its elimination.

This raises a second and more immediate problem: what research methods should sociologists use to study women's experiences? The categories of 'quantitative' and 'qualitative' are notoriously difficult to define and operationalise, indicating tendencies within a research design rather than a rigid set of procedures. Further, the knowledge that these tendencies reflect the existence of a gender bias within social research provides few firm guidelines for those stationed 'in the field'. In the absence of clear directives (and in the search for the cash and career opportunities to do research on women), field-workers have turned to the social survey: the method which provides the empirical base for mainstream masculinist sociology. The method fits uneasily at the intersection of the qualitative and quantitative paradigms, and feminist researchers have typically preferred its more qualitative variants. Thus, for example, Hunt (1980) used in-depth and informal interviews in her study of gender and class consciousness, while Oakley (1981, p. 47) sought to temper the exploitative tendencies of the formal interview by establishing 'a relatively intimate and non-hierarchical relationship' with her respondents in which she came to be regarded as 'friend rather than purely as a data-gatherer'.

Although a hallmark of recent empirical work on women (for example, Barrett and Roberts, 1978; Graham and McKee, 1980; Pollert, 1981) the value of these modifications remains unclear. If distortion is not introduced at the moment of data-collection (through the interview structure or questionnaire design) but springs from the principles which underlie survey research, then modifications to the data-collecting instrument may be unable to compensate for it. This is not to suggest that such measures are unimportant; as Oakley argues, they have both a practical and a political significance. The crucial issue here, however, is whether these refinements are sufficient to ensure a research method – and ultimately a sociology – sensitive to the structure of women's lives. What we need to confront is whether, however informal the questionnaire and however friendly the interviewer, the survey method itself eclipses what Elshtain calls 'the self-understanding of the female subject' (1981, p. 302).

Principles of survey research

Sociology's methods, like its theories, are seen to have their origin in the social changes precipitated by the development of capitalism (McGregor, 1957; Kent, 1981). Easthope, in his *History of Research Methods*, notes how these changes 'led men to realise that they did not understand the social world around them'. He continues:

> the same changes can be related not only to the rise of a science of society but to the rise of the methods used by that science (1974, pp. 10–11).

The changes that 'men' sought to understand had their origins in the process and place of production. Changes here were seen to have altered the character of work, transforming it into an object separate from the individual who performed it. 'Work' became regulated by the external discipline of clock and machine and rewarded by measured quantities of money. Traditional labour patterns became increasingly relegated to the home, where an orientation to task rather than time meant that a multiplicity of tasks could still be accomplished by each worker and each family. Outside the shrinking boundaries of the home and community lay what E. P. Thompson (1967, p. 82) describes as 'the familiar landscape of disciplined industrial capitalism, with the time-sheet, the time-keeper, the informer and the fines'.

Time-sheet, time-keepers, informers and fines. Each, interestingly, has its place within the methods that Easthope's men designed to measure their social landscape. Like economic production, the disciplined production of empirical data demands data-sheets and data-collectors; it relies upon a network of informers and a system of rewards (material and psychological) to encourage cooperation. The capitalistic ethos is perhaps most clearly embodied in the survey method, the method which came to exemplify the emerging science of society. The method, as Ackroyd and Hughes (1981) note, has its historical roots in the public domain, as an instrument in the administration of the state; and the exercise of political control. While these were the early censuses instigated by Augustus Caesar and by William I, the crucial phase of survey development was in the late nineteenth century when the method was used to measure the impact of the new mode of production upon the employment and well-being of the population. 'The father of scientific social surveys' (Moser and Kalton, 1971, p. 6) was Charles Booth, whose survey of the *Life and Labour of the People of London* was published in 1889. His method was later refined by Bowley and Rowntree. Arthur Bowley pioneered the idea of sampling, as a refinement to Booth's method of surveying all those within the research population, and, in his study of *Livelihood and Poverty*, published in 1915, introduced the technique of random sampling. Seebohm Rowntree improved upon Booth's method of asking questions through the intermediary of school board visitors by employing interviewers to collect the data direct from households (which, in practice, meant housewives). These modifications, however, left unchanged the basic principles of Booth's methodology which continue to inform the practice of modern survey research.

Contemporary methods textbooks identify these principles in different ways. Typically, however, a social survey is seen to include some or all of the following:

1 Surveys deal with social units;
2 These units are equivalent;
3 Units and their products have an object-form which:
 is external to the individual;
 can be verbalised;
 is stable;
4 Units and their outputs are measurable.

These principles appear to accord well with those embodied in the ideology of nineteenth century capitalism. If this is so, if the survey method is modelled on the form of labour relations prescribed for capitalist production, are they compatible with the social relations which determine women's lives? How do these principles relate to those placed at the interface of the public and private world, whose experiences are shaped by the cross-cutting forces of social class and gender? A brief consideration of the four principles points to significant areas of tension.

1 Surveys deal with social units

People enter into social surveys as the items which make up the research population: as individuals, households (Rowntree, 1901; Bowley and Burnett-Hurst, 1915) and streets (Booth, 1889). These items are treated as units, assumed to be for the purposes of the survey, single and complete.

Household and street surveys are regarded as unsatisfactory sources of data on women's lives because they tend 'to assume that the household is an entity in itself and to forget that it is made up of individuals with varying characteristics' (Nissel, 1980, p. 8). In particular, they tend to treat households as bundles of equivalent individuals and not as men and women occupying different and unequal positions within both the home and the wider society (Nissel, 1980; Land, 1977; Pahl, 1980). As Hartmann (1981a) has argued, family and household-based data obscure the fact that individuals, although family members, are also members of gender and generational groupings. As a result, they tend to conceal inequalities in the distribution of resources and responsibilities between individuals, inequalities which are known to be closely related to the patterns of women's participation in the private and public domain (Land, 1981).

Because household-based surveys highlight differences between rather than within families, most empirical research into the attitudes and experiences of women (and men) has taken the individual as the unit of analysis. However, the basic problem still remains. Individuals, like the households into which they are aggregated, are still treated as autonomous and self-functioning entities. As Galtung observed (1967, p. 28), 'Characteristic of the traditional survey is the tendency to treat the individual as a social unit.' This characteristic is exaggerated when the survey is based upon a sample and not a census of the population under study, since samples have a greater tendency to exclude the groups and processes of which individuals are a part. Here, according to Galtung (1967, p. 150), 'the individual is literally torn out of his social context and made to appear in a sample of one person to be compared with other samples of one person'.

This process of excision applies to social phenomena, too. The logic of the survey method demands, for example, that social class or race or gender are treated not as dimensions of social structure, but as properties of individuals. It requires that patterns of attitudes and behaviour are similarly treated as personal characteristics, as things people have and hold rather than ways individuals define their relationship to their social situation. Such restrictions can seriously inhibit our understanding of contemporary social problems like depression, as Davies and Roche (1980) argue. It also raises problems for those who continue the nineteenth century tradition of Booth and Rowntree, and use the social survey to study poverty. In *Poverty in the United Kingdom*, Townsend hints at the way his methodology de-politicised the nature of poverty. His survey method, he found, prevented him from reaching the very social structures of work and community through which poverty is mediated:

> the survey method... is highly individualistic. The network of contacts in community and at work is played down and the overlapping nature of 'group' consumption is ignored... The individual [is] an island of income and spending (1979, p. 114).

The 'excessive individualism' (Ackroyd and Hughes, 1981, p. 64) of the survey method is clearly a problematic issue for all those engaged in social scientific research. But the problems appear to be particularly acute when women are the focus of study. Two specific problems should be noted. Firstly, women's welfare and women's identity appear to be particularly closely locked into the social processes which the survey method closes off from analysis. Women's experiences of health, of housework and childcare are governed by precisely those patterns of group consumption and social contact which the survey method obscures. Data on women's lives can still be collected, as recent surveys amply testify (Oakley, 1974b; Graham and McKee, 1980; EOC, 1981). The data, rich in textural detail, record the reality of women's subordination as played out in their experiences of housework and childbearing, paid work and voluntary service. But do they tap the *impact* of gender relations, as etched into individual experience, rather than the *structure* of these relations? Can surveys of women reach into the political economy of family life, where the patterns of who-controls-what and who-does-what are determined? Or must we again agree with Becker, that 'while sociologists like to speak of ongoing processes and the like, ... their methods usually prevent them from seeing the processes they talk so glibly about' (Becker, 1966, p. xiii, also quoted in Armstrong, 1982).

This possibility brings with it a second and related problem. In obscuring the relationships that mould women's lives, the survey method masks the nature and patterns of power which derive from these social relationships. A method which blurs the political dimensions of gender and class is clearly a problematic base on which to construct an analysis of women's position. For as Saunders observes:

> Power is a quality of social relationships rather than an attribute of individuals. Attempts to measure power on an individual basis violate the very concept of power by assuming that it is an individual attribute which can be decontextualised form the social relationships in which it is embedded (1979, p. 337).

2 Individuals can be treated as equivalent units

According to Hughes:

> the logic of the survey implies that every unit is equal to every other unit. Thus, when counting and then asserting that X per cent of a sample have property Y, we are treating each unit as equal to each other unit (1976, p. 183).

Such a principle provides the basis for measurement, ensuring that individuals within the sample have 'approximately equal rights to representation in the analysis and description of results' (Townsend, 1979, p. 114). However, this principle, based as Galtung (1967, p. 157) notes, on 'the practices of democracy, examinations in schools and hearings in court', has a major flaw; namely that individuals, and groups of individuals, occupy different and unequal positions and interact in the context of these differences and inequalities. As Galtung puts it:

> The democratic principle... may be valid in systems where individuals count about equally much or equally little, but not in systems with tremendous differences in the degree to which people count (1967, p. 157).

Since both patriarchy and capitalism qualify as 'systems in which there are tremendous differences in the degree to which people count', this principle again appears to present problems for our understanding of women's experiences.

Firstly, there is an analytic problem, best expressed perhaps, in its most extreme form. Is there a fundamental contradiction at the core of feminist survey research; namely that survey researchers who seek to explore systems of social stratification, whether that of gender or class or race, employ a method which operates as if the phenomenon under study does not exist? Although theoretically committed to understanding the structures of inequality, survey researchers find themselves nailed by their methodology to an egalitarian model of society. This does not mean that survey researchers can not measure the effects of social inequality: Townsend's study of poverty clearly indicates that they can. The problem comes when they wish to move from the description to analysis, when they seek to understand causes as well as consequences.

Although not blind to social structure, the survey method has strong myopic tendencies: its commitment to studying individuals as equivalent units, as Galtung puts it, 'torn from their social context' severs the link between individual and society. To bind individual differences to social divisions, researchers have to relocate their findings within a broader theoretical framework. Without such a framework, survey data can generate micro theories to explain macro problems – a criticism which Davies and Roche (1980) level against the *Social Origins of Depression* (Brown and Harris, 1978).

Secondly, the principle of equivalence raises problems for the collection as well as the analysis of survey data on women's lives. Galtung's cautionary comments assume a special significance in the context of sexual stratification and conflict, where men and women occupy socially and spatially separate domains:

> *The survey methodology works across relatively narrow social distances.* The survey method is for the ingroup, not for the outgroup; for your friend not for your enemy.... It presupposes verbal interaction that is friendly, or at least not hostile.... A social science based on surveys will tend, at present, to be a science where society is presented in a less discordant state than might be considered realistic. The method thus has ideological implications in distorting the total image of society. (1967, pp. 158–9, emphasis original.)

All empirical research, to the extent that it relies on cooperation and not coercion, is likely to prove problematic when it is your enemies which you wish to study. The important point to consider here, however, is whether women's participation in social surveys contributes to an image of society, and an image of women, at odds with the reality of life in a patriarchal social order. This seems to be the case when women are the investigators: McKee and O'Brien (in this volume), Stanley and Wise (1979) and Pollert (1981) have all noted how the relationship between the researcher and researched was coloured, and sometimes dominated, by sexual politics and class antagonism. Yet, they found that the etiquette of social research denied them the means of adequately expressing and handling these conflicts. Until we have more studies like Oakley's (1979, pp. 309–17) and Acker and Esseveld (1981) which record the experience of being surveyed, we are unlikely to know whether female respondents find themselves similarly constrained by the unwritten code of survey research. Until we do, we must surely question the extent to which the social survey does indeed have 'ideological implications in distorting the total image of society'.

3 Units and their outputs have an object form
Built into the principles of individualism and equivalence is the

assumption that social phenomena have an existence separate from the social relations in which they are embedded. This assumption, again, raises questions for the study of women. Three issues are identified here.

Firstly, the principle implies that social phenomena have an ontological status external to the individual. This means, for example, that 'depression' can be abstracted from the individuals whose feelings are captured by the concept and from the social relationships in which these feelings occur (Davies and Roche, 1980). Depression is transformed into an entity separated from its social context by getting individuals to talk about their experiences. Through talk, the phenomenon assumes a form which can be defined, labelled, and measured.

Secondly, therefore, the principle implies that experiences can be verbalised. What can't be put into words in an interview or on a questionnaire can't be recorded and can't be studied. The social survey assumes a society in which actions are rational and, in Rich's (1980) sense, 'speakable'. Galtung concludes that the method is unsuitable for cultures in which significant areas of experience remain unverbalised, since the society of the survey is one which prescribed that 'people shall express what they feel and feel what they express; they shall act in accordance to what they say and report what they have done' (Galtung, 1967, p. 152).

Such prescriptions are difficult to reconcile with Rowbotham's advice that those concerned with the women's experiences 'must listen carefully to the language of silence' (1973, p. 30). It is difficult, too, to square these prescriptions with the evidence that silence masks a female speech community, a 'way of talking between women in their roles as women' (Jones, 1980, p. 174). While participating in the man-made language of the public domain, Jones (1980) and Spender (1980) argue that women communicate their personal experiences through an oral culture untapped by social scientists.

Thirdly, the principle that social phenomena can be objectified assumes not only that phenomena have an external and verbalisable form, but a stable one. As Denzin (1970) has observed, surveys provide snapshot pictures of reality which are assumed to be sufficiently ordered and permanent to enable generalisations to be made across social contexts and across time. Social surveys, for example, assume that material elicited in one social context – an interview – is representative of the range of responses an individual makes in others. Galtung (1967, p. 157) notes that such an assumption is inappropriate in cultures characterised by 'sudden and rapid changes' where social forces outside the compass of the survey result in unpredictable changes in individual attitudes and behaviour. While Galtung is talking about political instability in the Third World, a similar point could be made in relation to groups within Western society whose lives are characterised by discontinuity and uncertainty. We know that discontinuity and uncertainty are ubiquitous features of women's experiences, as they mediate the demands of the private and public domain. Within the home, women's responsibility for reconciling the demands of the family commits them to a life structured around 'small chores, errands, work that others constantly undo, and small children's constant needs' (Rich, 1980, p. 43). Women's labour in the public domain is similarly fragmented and other-directed, where, in their roles as clerical workers, cleaners, nurses and social workers, women perform housekeeping tasks on behalf of society (Adams, 1971).

4 Units and their outputs can be measured

Measurement is a fundamental process in social research. It is also a highly problematic one. As Hughes notes (1976, p. 78), while measurement presumes the precise definition of social phenomena, the social world is inherently ambiguous. Cicourel (1976) argued that social researchers have obscured this problem by developing classification procedures which have an assumed but never proven relationship to the real world. Interviewers employ these procedures by relying on their 'implicit commonsense assumptions about the actor, concrete persons and the observer's own views about everyday life' (Cicourel, 1964, p. 21). This technique presents obvious problems when women are the object of study. For the introduction of 'common-sense' assumptions into survey research does not occur in a social void, but arises out of the particular (male) perspectives which dominate the social sciences. Measurement may be a process which captures, in a reasonably adequate way, the activities and social relationships of men. Women's lives, however, lying 'hidden from history', may conform to different configurations than those assumed in measurement. Their activities and pattern of relationships may thus defy – or be lost within – the process of measurement.

Perhaps the problem can be pinpointed more precisely. Measurement is closely tied to the marketplace, where activities are quantified and regulated through the medium of money. As Weber argued, 'rational capital accounting' is the basis on which commodities are produced and bureaucracies are created. Measurement and the recording of statistical information thus became the hallmark of rational organisations (Shaw and Miles, 1979, p. 34). Like capitalists, social scientists identify their endeavours as rational: they, too, measure activities in numerical units – of output, of time, of money. It is thus possible for social researchers to understand women's attitudes and experiences when they fit within the established classification and scaling systems. However, a recent series of critiques suggests that this is not the case with the traditional measures of social class, political commitment, psychological stability and economic activity (Broverman *et al.*, 1970; Nissel, 1980; Stacey and Price, 1981).

Thus, for example, it is possible for social researchers to study women's labour – of cooking and caring, washing and cleaning, teaching and healing – when it is sold through the marketplace. However, the same services performed within the private domain do not 'count'; their value can not so easily be calculated within the reckoning systems of time and money. These services are regulated by different rhythms, not wholly attuned to the measurement of the clock (Thompson, 1967, p. 61). Women, positioned at the intersection of two social worlds, appear to have an ambiguous relation to the systems of measurement which characterise capitalism and the social science which developed within it. They are attuned simultaneously to the task-oriented rhythms of housework and childcare and the time-oriented rhythms of the workplace and the school. As Nelson (1980) argues in her study of household time, this dual orientation cannot be captured by methods built on the time-frameworks of the public world. It appears that alternative methods are required if the measurement systems of survey research are not to remain, like the overarching apparatus of sociology, 'a forced set of categories into which women must stuff the awkward and resistant actualities of their lives' (Smith, 1979, p. 141).

Conclusion: rethinking survey research

Charles Booth developed the survey method to make public, and make political, the reality of poverty (although prior to his investigations he was sceptical about the severity of the problem). As he stated later:

> The lives of the poor lay hidden from view behind a curtain on which were painted terrible pictures... did these pictures truly represent what lay behind, or did they bear to the facts a similar relation to that which the pictures outside a booth at some country fair bear to the performance of the show within? (Quoted in Bulmer, 1982, p. 11.)

A century later, social scientists concerned with the patriarchal nature of contemporary society have similarly turned to the social survey to draw back the curtains on women's lives. While other aspects of the research process have been opened up for critical scrutiny, it has been generally accepted that the survey method itself is not a significant source of gender bias. This may well be so, but the sociological imagination, whether or not it is one informed by feminism, demands that we reflect sceptically upon the taken-for-granted aspects of our scientific practice. It is this space for reflection that the chapter has sought to provide, by problematising the nature of survey research and its place in the rewriting of sociology as a non-sexist discipline.

The chapter has suggested that survey research is constructed on a model of society consistent with the ideology of Western capitalism.

Specifically it has suggested that survey research is premised on the existence of a market-based mass society. In this society, individuals are seen to behave as isolated and equivalent units of labour, sharing in a homogeneous culture which can be accurately and easily articulated in words. Like earlier critiques, this paper has pointed to the ways in which this model seriously distorts the nature of social reality, and particularly the social reality of women. Women do not experience the world from a position of insularity and equality, but from a complex web of asymmetrical social relationships. Their experiences, moreover, are defined through a language which originates from outside these experiences, making 'survey speak' an incomplete and alienating form of communication.

By examining the principles governing the conduct of surveys, the chapter has not launched an all-out offensive against the survey method. Surveys, precisely because they conform to the rules of the public domain, have played an important part in raising the consciousness of those within the scientific and political world. Much of our knowledge about the position and problems of women, knowledge crucial to the promotion (and preservation) of less divisive policies in the field of employment, health and education, derives from survey research. However, the method can not be employed uncritically. We need to be aware that, in seeking to uncover what Elshtain (1981, p. 302) calls 'the self-understanding of the female subject' through the medium of the social survey, we are also in subtle but serious ways, obscuring it.

Acknowledgements

I would like to record my thanks to Celia Davies and Mary Ann Elston for their constructive comments on an earlier version of this paper.

12 Interviewing Men: 'Taking Gender Seriously'
Lorna McKee and Margaret O'Brien

In a book on feminist research David Morgan (1981, p. 94) points out that 'taking gender seriously' has until recently mostly meant taking *women* into account. This was in part a result of the repeated omission of women and women's issues from earlier social enquiry. The realisation that in order to form a fully humanistic and comprehensive theory of gender the researcher has paradoxically now got to bring men back into the picture is, Morgan posits, an even more recent development. The shift in emphasis here is that social researchers now need to study men, not by equating man with human, but instead by recognising the gender content of men's personal experiences and relationships with women, other men, and children. In this paper we question the dominant sociological practice of locating men solely in the public sphere and of equating them with it. Our approach is based instead on investigating men in private and domestic situations where their public persona and status are less conspicuous.

One domain that allows for an exploration of men's experience and provides an occasion to reconceptualise masculinity and gender is the area of fatherhood.[1] In the past few years we have beeen interviewing men at two distinctive periods in the life-cycle – becoming a father and becoming a lone father, after marital separation.[2] Aspects of gender have been heightened in our research experiences both in the collection and analysis of data. From our accounts we hope to show how gender influences the research process and has profound implications both for what is disclosed or withheld, pursued or neglected.

Drawing a sample of fathers
The first problem we encountered in our studies was the recruitment of men as *fathers*. There is no ready-made sampling frame of fathers and as a group they are less accessible and conspicuous than mothers who tend to be more 'captive' to researchers through their involvement in antenatal and child health clinics, maternity hospitals, nurseries and toddler groups.

In the study of 'new fathers', wives were used to enlist the support of husbands/fathers, and it was in the course of interviewing women about motherhood that the topic of fatherhood presented itself. This research dependence on wives/mothers as a point of entry to and contact with fathers can have repercussions. It meant for instance in this study that wives had to be 'won' over to the idea of the research and so give their *permission* for husbands to be approached. Arguably this could have weighted the study towards those with 'good' marriages or highly involved or committed husbands. It also raises potential problems concerning the *'ownership'* of the interview: 'whose interview is it anyway?' The indirect approach to fathers has additional implications both for the *venue* and *structuring* of the interview itself. When the link to the father is through the mother and the home, it seems to be less easy to justify interviewing in the man's workplace or insisting on interviewing the man by himself. For example, when the new fathers were first interviewed five out of the thirteen wives were present, even though they had already had *their* interview and it had been made clear that the focus was on their husbands. The interviewer may further be faced with a clash of allegiances, having some loyalty to the wife/mother who initiated the contact.

In the 'lone fathers' study a sample of married fathers was sought as a comparative group and presented exactly the same recruitment difficulties. This group was to be comprised of fathers with children of primary school age. It was more difficult to locate these men than it was to find lone fathers who do, of course, constitute a minority family form. This discovery reflects the invisibility of fathers. With fathers of school-age children it is possible to use *children* as a way of finding fathers but this brought its own disadvantages. Schools had to be convinced of the validity of the research and heads had to give their *permission* for study to proceed.

An alternative way to conduct research on fathers might be to contact men using 'father-centred' routes of entry where men can themselves give their *own* permission to be studied. The lone fathers study followed this line of enquiry, contacting men at their workplaces and through lone father groups. Going straight to fathers helps to contest the everyday cultural assumption that men are always and only tied to their children through their wives.

Managing interviewer/interviewee interaction

We would like to turn now to the content and dynamics of the interviews to address further the effect of gender on interview relations. Our interview material and related field notes are used not to infer that what emerges in the interview is necessarily a reflection of gender relations more widely, but rather to underscore the complexities inherent in any conceptualisation of gender. The talk and interactions that take place in interview settings have their own degree of autonomy; interviews themselves are social constructs, as are our readings of them.

In analysing the interview transcripts and listening to tapes of interviews with fathers we were alerted to weaknesses of the model which characterises the interviewer/interviewee relationship as being an active/passive or a hierarchical dominant/subordinate relationship. Our fathers, particularly in the lone fathers study, frequently actively 'used' and manipulated or 'controlled' the interview in diverse ways and for diverse ends.[3] Fathers seemed to 'use' the interview to 'get things off their chest'; to meet problems of loneliness and an absence of female companionship; to affirm their experiences *vis-à-vis* other new and lone fathers; to express their grievances against ex-wives and women more generally; to promote the cause of lone fathers or to gain wider social recognition as fathers and to obtain advice and guidance about family problems. Fathers in both studies reported that talking and sharing their feelings was often therapeutic although this was significantly less true of the new fathers as compared with lone fathers or new mothers. These themes are aptly illustrated in the following case examples.

One interview with Mr Raymond, a lone father, ended with him entering into a bitter diatribe about how badly society treated lone fathers in relation to lone mothers, during which he lapsed into phrases such as 'you women' which obviously included the female interviewer as well.

> There are very many lone fathers but one hardly ever hears about them because they just get on and get on with it. They get on with their jobs and go back and deal with their families and do the washing up and do the cooking the same as women do.... I don't think single mothers are a more poverty stricken group now, for the simple reason that you women have your so-called equality, you do have the opportunities for jobs, you do have the opportunity of equal pay and the rest of it and the single parent family male has just the same problems as you women. In fact more so because (voice raising) it is considered OK socially that a woman can have a part-time job, because she must go home and see the kids afterwards, but how funny it is if a man has a part-time job... people think what a funny character, he must be lazy or something.

Some lone fathers seemed to want a *woman* to talk to, emphasising that they were lonely, wifeless and deprived of female company. These interviews often resembled a wooing process whereby they attempted to attract the interviewer's sympathy and concern. This led to some emotional encounters where men bared their souls and became close to tears. The meaning and importance of the interview was underlined by the offering of food, drinks and invitations out: one respondent, John Phillip, even prepared a meal of cheese soufflé and salad plus wine.

From time to time new and lone fathers mentioned their sense of peripherality and isolation and hoped the interview might help to overcome this sense of exclusion. Derek Morris, a new father, perceived the research as redressing the balance, giving fathers some of the limelight too. It was almost certainly the reason why he and his wife, who were very opposed to 'mother-centred' antenatal care and literature, agreed to cooperate.

Much of this interviewee 'use' of the interview has been generally benign and could be accommodated into the interaction. However, there were occasions where the fathers did not readily 'accept' the interview format and seemed to be 'creating trouble'. This was more typical of lone father interviews. A number of lone fathers appeared very 'controlling' and took over the interview once the tape recorder was switched on.[4] In a semi-structured interview these reactions create difficulties for the interviewer, raise anxiety about whether all the question areas will be covered and expose the issue of authority in allegedly hierarchical dominant/subordinate research relationships. Are these issues of control and interviewee-manipulation more likely to occur in cross-gender interviewing? Other researchers who have conducted joint husband–wife interviews (Kadushin, 1972; Burley, 1982) have also reported men taking the lead, questioning the questions and interrupting the interview. One lone father actually made a bargain with the interviewer after she arrived at his home, before consenting to the interview. Mr Highgate, interested in palmistry, astrology and the occult, asked the interviewer if he could read her stars at the end of the interview. When the interview was finished, he took out his charts and materials and began to ask the interviewer about her life.[5] Consequently, the interviewer learnt much more about him as a person and how he explained and organised his own life. It appeared, for example, that he had predicted, using astrology, future problems in his marriage.

> Well this may sound ridiculous to you. Well, being an astrologer, in January 1976 I looked at my chart and it was predictable that April 1978 would be my divorce period and also I have a friend who reads the Tarot cards, who also said divorce. So I looked at my wife's chart and I knew that there would be vast, emotional pressures brought to bear.

It is interesting to speculate whether a woman in a similar situation would have set the same conditions for the interview.

Even within individual interviews men's style of talk reflected these tensions between active and passive relationships and between dominance and subordination; for instance some lone fathers seemed to move between a confiding type of talk and 'speechifying'.

Men and self-disclosure

When comparing the experience of interviewing new fathers with that of interviewing their partners about pregnancy and child-rearing a number of essential and remarkable differences emerged. Firstly, fathers almost uniformly had less to say and took less time to say it. While the average interview with mothers lasted from two to two-and-a-half hours, similarly structured interviews with fathers averaged from one to one-and-a-half hours. Secondly, the initial interview with men was more formal and less 'conversational', although this style altered over time and became more relaxed. Thirdly, the interviewer was far less engaged in and far less likely to be made aware of men's social and familial problems and the context of fatherhood, whereas the social contours of motherhood and 'wifehood' were omnipresent.[6]

Here we try to untangle what might lie behind these differences. Some of the explanations might refer to the *investigator*: her gender, professional status, age, marital and reproductive status, interviewing style, adequacy of the research instrument, competence at interviewing men, and research relationship to their wives. Some might relate to the *researched*: their gender, point of entry into the study through wives, presence of others, especially wives, during the interview orientation to being interviewed, experience as fathers, and familiarity with talking about feelings. Some might be related to *external conditions*: the character of wider social relations between men and women; prescriptions of masculinity and femininity; and qualitative differences between being a mother and being a father.

Firstly, in trying to make sense of why fathers' interviews, especially first interviews, were shorter and less 'conversational' than those with mothers, we raise the concept of 'legitimacy of the topic'. A number of fathers were unused to or unfamiliar with talking about pregnancy and babies – particularly to a non-family member. This emerged in their early comments, where they mentioned an inability to rehearse or anticipate what the interviewer *might want to know* or *what they might want to tell*. Methodologically this is an acute problem, for it is a case of a researcher labelling a research phenomenon and expecting her respondents both to recognise the label and to be able to talk about it out loud. Men's difficulties in talking about pregnancy and/or babies may be a clue to wider cultural prescriptions of masculinity and suggest some boundaries of male preoccupations and orientations. At the end of each interview men were asked how they felt about talking to the interviewer. Their replies capture and clarify this issue of masculine inhibition in connection with pregnancy and birth.

Mm. I must be frank, fairly difficult you know but yet I wanted to.

> But I didn't quite know what there was to talk about. There was one or two things that I didn't realise you can talk about. I can't remember what they are but there was one or two. (Len Kerr, farm manager).

> I was just trying to visualise the things you would ask but I couldn't say I could do that even, you know, what sort of questions can you ask on it, you know? You've surprised me! (Tim Streetly, maintenance fitter).

Men *are* at one remove from the active processes and drama. Expectant fathers' experiences have to be related to those of the expectant mother. Hence in drawing up a research instrument for expectant fathers there always has to be some cross-reference to the expectant mother or the unborn child. Researchers investigating pregnant women do not face a symmetrical problem. Expectant fatherhood therefore is both 'inferential' and 'distant', while expectant motherhood is 'actual' and 'close'. This might explain why later interviews with the *same* fathers were longer. The following comments capture men's perceived distance from pregnancy and birth:

> Let's be honest about it, the father doesn't do a lot does he? I mean he doesn't have any, he doesn't have the aches and pains and all the trouble 'n doesn't have to go through with childbirth. I mean he goes out 'n has a good time while t'poor mother's in hospital having to look after t'baby and having to give birth and what have you so we can't say we're badly done to cos we're not? (Pete Mitchell, policeman, CID).

> It's a subject (pregnancy) men never really talk about, isn't it? I mean women, it's always in a woman's mind but never in a man's mind, so I mean, I talk about *anything but* (Tommy Hooper, milkman).

Another reason for the comparative brevity of men's interviews is again contained in their own accounts, where several men mention being unaccustomed to talking about family matters or personal feelings to an outsider. This issue of self-disclosure recurred in a number of interviews and men suggested that they exchanged 'personal/marital' feelings with wives as *only* or *main* confidants. Such exchanges were likely to take place in the home. On the other hand, close and confiding relationships with men were more often built around '*non-family*' affairs, more likely to be related to work or leisure concerns, and took place away from home. Consequently, a female interviewer who talks to men about their feelings and family details in their own homes contravenes both the rules of domestic/familial *privacy* and of '*marital primacy*' and becomes more *like* a wife in what she wants to know/discuss. This was complicated in the cases of men who talked to *nobody* about feelings or found self-revelation difficult in all circumstances, even with their wives. Men's inability to share feelings has been variously labelled as 'trained incapacity to share' or 'male inexpressiveness' (Komarovsky, 1962; Balswick and Peek, 1971) and this masculine tendency did seem to be operative in some interviews where men themselves remarked on their repeated failure to find the right words saying:

> I find it hard to put my feelings into words;
>
> It's not usual that I can be interviewed, you know, I usually just blank off and I can't think of what to say.

Wives also noted this 'male inexpressiveness', especially the masculine tendency to shy away from 'talk as therapy'. A number of wives described their husbands as 'deep', 'reserved', 'quiet' – indeed as fitting the stereotype of 'the strong, silent male figure' – or the 'sturdy oak ideal'. This gender characteristic has also been commented on by the Men's Movement and writers on men and masculinity.

Some men's strict demarcation between formal and confiding relationships and the tying of the latter to wives and homes has a bearing on the interviewer's gender. Being a woman interviewer may have advantages: some men suggested that cross-gender talk about pregnancy and parenthood was easier, more appropriate and less threatening. The 'girls at work' were perceived as sympathetic while all-male audiences were described not just as disinterested but often as punitive and with a lust for ridicule. Joking and teasing were reported as frequent and essential parts of male dialogue concerning pregnancy and fatherhood. For example, in the pub setting, talk about babies and parenthood could serve to undermine men's masculinity, and conflict with more dominant, public and traditional interests of sport, politics or work.

> I suppose men have other things to talk about other than babies.... I suppose we're all that way inclined – speed-inclined, racing uh, we talk about darts, sport, you know, just a general thing you know, what's happened – work, a lot, we talk about work a lot and mainly just sports and pastimes. I mean all my friends we're all one bunch and we're all interested in cars, motorcycles, planes, ships (Tommy Hooper, milkman).
>
> I get quite a bit of fun taken out of me. I don't mind cos he's my lad as well. 'Aw, you haven't been doing the nappies – aw, again?' And I say 'Aw yeah, I haven't got me gold bracelets out of the bucket all morning.' And it's a standing joke but I don't mind (Sydney Bell, electrician).

Typical reactions by men to the expectant father's news of pregnancy emphasised his foolishness and *naïveté*, 'you silly bugger', 'you silly devil', 'it's a mug's game', 'you must be daft'. Most of the new fathers expected a certain amount of leg-pulling and devised ways of coping with it, namely curtailing any detailed self-disclosure. This reinforced traditional sexual divisions and ensured that male stereotypes went unchallenged. It is possible that these stereotypes could have carried over into the content of the interview with a male interviewer. It can therefore be argued that the woman interviewer was both more 'like' their wives and other women, and by her gender in a 'closer' and less hostile relationship to the topics of pregnancy and babies.

However, while the new fathers may have talked more easily to a female investigator, they still did not talk as openly as wives. Perhaps another reason for this ties in with the interview's focus on men's child-rearing role. For to talk about their working lives and selves, men had to 'overrule' the research brief. The fact that men talk more readily about work and public matters, as opposed to family or marital issues is also raised by Piotrkowski (1978). She speculated that men are *just* much more satisfied with their marriages than women. Certainly, our fathers seemed to confront (or at least, report) fewer problems and changes with parenthood than women. New mothers experienced dramatic changes – loss of job, income, and status; severing of networks and social contacts; and adjustments to being a 'housewife'. None of the new fathers reported similar social dislocations. This alone must influence what there is to 'tell'. Besides, although new fathers varied in their degree of involvement in child-care, mother's involvement was more or less invariant and seldom optional.

The experience of interviewing lone fathers provides some interesting points of convergence and divergence. Interviews with lone fathers were generally lengthy, intimate and often highly-charged. They vividly rehearsed their marital break-up, describing themselves as: 'shattered'; 'mortified'; 'in a dream'; 'suicidal'; 'being all churned up'; 'wanting to dig a hole in the ground and crawl into it'; 'being frightened of being alone' and so on. At the time of the interview some were very upset and grieving the loss of their partner. This may have contributed to more open talk and to breaking down any residual reserve. One married father touched on this theme when asked how he would cope with becoming a lone father; he suggested that men may have hidden reserves of emotional involvement which remain untapped until a situation such as single parenthood arises. A few lone fathers remarked that the experience of their wife leaving made them reassess their past husbandly behaviour, especially not talking enough about feelings or showing enough concern and tenderness in their marriages. For some, losing a wife had also prompted a practical and emotional determination not to keep feelings bottled up. By opening up all the personal issues of marriage, family and children at a time of loss and hurt the researcher frequently found herself addressed as if she were a wife.

More generally, becoming a lone father created significant, and often severe, changes in men's social networks, friendship patterns, and working conditions. They recounted moving into a world 'traditionally' considered the domain of mothers, with the consequence that they needed little encouragement to talk about the everyday details of child-care and general family matters. Unlike some of the new fathers, these lone fathers described a close and continual connectedness to their children and to the 'home'. This was reflected in the fact that only half of the interviews with a 'control' of married fathers were conducted in the home compared to about 80% of the lone father interviews. Many of the lone fathers may have selected to be interviewed at home because they wanted to demonstrate that the home was now their own, their own 'territory', a place they took pride in and where they wanted to be with their family.

The shift from 'male' to 'female' or from public to private concerns is captured in the case of Mr Pattern, a lone unemployed father with four children, who describes his alienation from conventional male friendships, activities, and interests:

> Na, they don't know anything about the price of herrings or whatever you know what I mean. Say you go into somewhere and you come out with remarks quite innocently like 'I wish this bleeding rain would stop, I won't have me washing dry', and everybody looks at you, what's the matter with him the pansy and you're not at all, I mean that's your main concern.

Mr Pattern was acutely aware of the conflicts inherent in being both male and looking after his children and the house full-time. He was very angry at the way adverts only showed women doing the housework and lamented the fact that there was no male equivalent of *Woman* or *Woman's Own*, which seemed in some way to exclude him just because he was a man.

> You haven't got anybody to talk it over as you would if there were two parents. You've got no idea, no contact, like if I was a woman, a wife, I'd be swapping gossip with some of the neighbours and would be able to get my standards of how kids behave etcetera etcetera from other mothers.

Mr Pattern did in fact get involved with home-centred activities in the local community, for example he entered his sausage rolls into a local cooking competition and came third. This pleased him because he had not indicated on the application form that he was a man and remarked to the interviewer: 'I'd stack myself against the average woman in this road at cooking you know, your average plain cooking.' So lone fatherhood appeared to move some men away from their own sex, from what they perceived as the usual activities and concerns of 'the average man in the street' and actively promoted more contact with other women, particularly those with children.

It appears then that men's presentations of becoming a lone father bear some similarities to their accounts of entry into new fatherhood in that the experience can set them apart from other men. Komarovsky (1962) contends that it is marriage that begins the process of separation of men from men – but we would suggest that the arrival of children and close involvement with children can have an even more marked effect. Certainly, at an expressive and public level some men display more ease in relating their feelings about family life to women than to men. But even here inhibitions exist as the new fathers study has shown. This complex area – the communication styles of men and men, and between men and women – has scarcely been researched.

The issue of sex in cross-gender interviewing

In the new fathers project explicit questions were asked about sexual relations as affected by pregnancy and parenthood. Asking these questions sometimes proved straightforward but in some cases was inhibited by the presence of non-respondent wives. Interestingly, the interviewer was more conscious of wives' rather than husbands' feelings and so asked these questions out of earshot where possible for *their* protection. In one case this was not possible and Terry Shapiro's reply about their sex life directly contradicted what Lesley Shapiro had said some weeks before. She had felt their sexual relationship had deteriorated in pregnancy and he felt it had improved. When Terry made this statement Lesley flounced into the adjoining kitchen and started noisily banging pots and pans about. This was a very tense interviewing moment when the research role in stirring up 'marital trouble' surfaced most acutely. These dangers of exposing contradictions, and opening marital sores are exaggerated if the non-respondent partner is present. The importance of the home as a 'locale' shows up in this instance for Lesley was able to exert some control over the interview by withdrawing to the kitchen and in fact she returned later calmed and presented us with tea.[7]

In contrast, the lone fathers study included no direct questions about sex on the recommendation of the research supervisor (a woman), who felt that just talking about sex may in itself be sexually arousing for some men and may cause unnecessary complications for the interviewer. This wariness embodies a cultural stereotype, that a man alone is always on the lookout for a woman and/or sex. Indeed a few respondents came across this attitude once their marriages had ended. One man, an academic, reported that he had had an entire ladies lavatory at the university devoted to him in the early days after his separation. He felt that in academic life the separated man is often thought to be 'predatory and dangerous, a dirty old man going around drooling', and 'unreliable' because no longer a 'family man'. This notion of an uncontrollable male sexual drive was also used by some people to suggest lone fathers should not really care for their young daughters; an attitude which hurt, angered and worried the men who experienced it. One respondent described how his mother-in-law had asked his daughter, 'Does Daddy wash you down there?' (meaning her vagina), and when his daughter replied 'yes', her grandmother had reportedly said, 'Well I think it's disgusting.' Another father described how during a conversation with a group of people he did not know very well, an elderly lady said 'Fathers should never be allowed to bring up girls' to which he retorted:

> Why not? She said because you don't understand the problems. The problems of what? The problems that teenage girls have? What problems? I was trying to get her ... I might not know anything about that (periods), but she don't know anything about boys wanking. You know it's six of one and half a dozen of the other.

Despite the avoidance of overt questions on sex, the topic sometimes spontaneously emerged in the interview. This was strikingly different from interviews either with the new fathers or the 'control' group of married fathers.

Another aspect to cross-gender interviewing is the possibility that any young women who voluntarily enters into a 'strange' man's house alone, may be seen as somehow 'asking for trouble' – a form of 'contributory negligence'? This potential for sexual violation is omnipresent but may or may not present itself in individual interactions. In the new fathers study it was not a dominant concern – counteracted by the frequent presence of wives and/or babies or interviewer's familiarity with wives who had previously been interviewed. Only one new father made the interviewer feel as if she was sexual prey and the interview was loaded with sexual innuendo. He was overtly flirtatious and invited her to drink his home-made beer in the garden. This social gesture, innocuous in itself, coupled with his flippancy and very casual manner made it hard to relax. This was a feeling that never left the researcher and although he never 'pounced' it was always suspected that he might. The fact that he was studying sociology for an Open University qualification also complicated this relationship and he was cynical and derisory of the research exercise. We would suggest that he flaunted his gender and tried to assert dominance both by hanging onto the male symbol – 'the glass of beer' – and by 'eyeing her up'.

Neither of us however experienced physical abuse throughout our research with men, although in two cases in the lone fathers project the interviewer began to feel worried about possible attack and in another two cases was pestered some days after the interview for further contact. In these interviews, the researcher employed a variety of strategies to offset any risk of sexual confrontation: taking conscious decisions about make-up and clothes; and maintaining a 'professional' manner when ambiguities arose. The *props* on these occasions were *things* rather than people: the tape-recorder, the clip-board and interview schedule – although the presence of children and others was also a mediating factor.

Our earlier point about male/female research encounters sometimes mirroring the conjugal relationship and leading to greater male self-disclosure also had its disadvantages when the sexual content of conjugality became especially emphasised. The two occasions in the lone fathers study where real physical danger was keenly sensed make this point more forcibly. One example is detailed to show how the boundaries between women as 'scientific observer', confidant, and sexual being are sometimes finely negotiated and often conflated.[8]

Mr Last was a draughtsman who had looked after his two children for the last ten months. At home, where his parents looked after the children during the interview, he appeared reasonably even-tempered but exploded when driving the interviewer to the railway station afterwards. He claimed that his ex-wife and her new lover were teaching his son to masturbate and that he could not entrust his children to their care. He became more and more angry and bitter, eventually driving *past* the station. When he drove past the next station, the interviewer became very worried, tried to calm him down and neutralise the topic of conversation. At the *third* station she insisted that he stop and let her out there. This was an anxious moment because during the interview he had described his karate skills and drawn attention to his general physical prowess and strength. Although he did not initiate any physical contact, his unpredictable behaviour in the car left the interviewer very relieved to have 'escaped' and at that point glad that the study was not longitudinal in nature!

This railing against ex-partners and against women more generally put the woman interviewer into a difficult moral position. By adopting a non-judgmental interviewing mode she had to listen, and not respond, to offensive and occasionally sexist remarks; the traditional interviewing stance made her powerless. Our silences and failure to confront these issues made us feel uneasy at times (cf. Faraday and Plummer, 1979, p. 793). We had to absorb comments about 'fat' women, 'neurotic' women, unintelligent women, women who were a good 'lay' and so on. This interviewing and specifically gender-related dilemma is rarely discussed in formal method texts.[9]

Conclusion

In this preliminary review of our research experiences we have followed David Morgan's (1981, p. 95) recommendation to take heed of the 'small voice' at our shoulders reminding us at each point in the research process that we are women interviewing men. This self-conscious appraisal of our unique encounters with fathers has demonstrated for us just how underdeveloped are our present concepts of gender and shown the folly of making general statements about male behaviour or self-perceptions, their relations to other men, children and women. The stuff of the interview throws up a much more complicated, contradictory and mixed range of attitudes and behaviour, perhaps mirroring the complexities of real life inherent in the diverse experiences of most men. In both sets of interviews we captured men in some private, familial and traditionally non-masculine or womanly postures: holding babies, putting daughters' curlers in, crying, feeling helpless, being lost for words and talking romantically and mystically about feelings. It is hard to appreciate these experiences under any existing theoretical framework. By 'taking gender seriously' we have exposed some facets of male experience which have had little academic 'airing' and have been largely hidden from history. But also we have uncovered the darker and more disturbing aspect of female/male relationships and encounters: the masculine manipulation and verbal abuse of women and intimate situations, the offensive remarks and statements against women, the fear of and anger against women and wives, the aggression and distance between men. Moreover, the interview highlighted our own contradictory actions as women, as we juggled the assertive, dominant and controlled professional stances with the acquiescent, submissive and assenting subordinate roles. Any new theory of gender relations has of course to incorporate the hierarchical power and control men have in society and the public domain. However, in the end, such a theory will be insufficient if it does not take into account the complex and contradictory ways in which both women and men are contesting the status quo.

Notes

1 Other possibilities lie in examining male friendships, work relationships or by making gender problematic in the reading of fiction, drama, art or social science texts.
2 We will refer to these studies as the 'new fathers' and 'lone fathers' projects respectively.

    New Fathers was conducted by Lorna McKee during 1976–77 and emerged from a larger social survey on mothers' experiences, which was conducted with Hilary Graham. It was kindly supported by the Health Education Council to whom thanks are due. Only first-time parents were interviewed: once during pregnancy, again when the baby was (on average) eleven weeks and again at twelve months. Seven fathers held manual occupations, while five worked in white-collar or professional occupations. One was a student. Their ages ranged from 19 to 31.

    Lone Fathers was conducted by Margaret O'Brien and kindly supported by the SSRC. Fifty-nine London-based men who had main care of their dependent children after marital separation were interviewed once. Twenty-six held or had professional and 'intermediate' occupations and thirty-three had or held skilled non-manual, manual and unskilled occupations. One-fifth were unemployed. A matched comparison group of 'married' fathers were also interviewed. All names in the text are disguised.
3 It was pointed out to us by Colin Bell and Mary Ann Elston that the interview situation has a power and dynamic of its own, being a complex micro-social occasion so that these features of interviewee 'use' and 'control' are not necessarily only features of male/female interaction. For instance, women interviewees may also 'use' interviews with women interviewers for diverse ends. Interviewers of either gender are endowed with powers of control and manipulation which accrue from the nature of the interview itself.
4 Age may be a relevant factor here. The mean age of the lone fathers was 37.6 years, and the interviewer was in her early twenties. It is difficult to separate out influences of age and gender in the analysis, but we of course are aware of the importance of the former.
5 The issue of reciprocity arises in all interviews and is not just a case of interviewee manipulation.
6 In a complementary study of mothers the investigator found that interviewing women sometimes means getting drawn into their problems. She encountered sick babies, depressed women, violent husbands, death and mourning, unemployment, poverty, loneliness and sadness, showing that pregnancy and motherhood cannot always

be bracketed off from real life or placed at the top of the hierarchy of life events.
7 Piotrkowski (1978, p. 295) has noted how many of her interviewees engaged in similar 'domestic' tasks (making tea, putting in the laundry, shaving) to overcome anxiety raised by the interview.
8 The direction of sexual interest cannot always be said to be one way, and the interviewer may also initiate sexual responsiveness.
9 Social researchers typically use a non-directive interviewing style. Our experiences here raise questions about uniformly using this mode. Should a more active style be employed in some research settings? Has the researcher got a role in consciousness-raising? Are research interviews appropriate places in which to challenge gender stereotypes? Should the issue of sex/gender be explicitly considered when research workers are employed?

Notes on Contributors

Eva Gamarnikow studied at LSE and is currently finishing a Ph.D. on the development of nursing and women's entry into the public sphere of employment. She is a temporary part-time lecturer at the University of London Institute of Education, where she works in the areas of education, gender and rights. She is an active member of the BSA and the Women's Caucus.

David H.J. Morgan is senior lecturer in Sociology, University of Manchester. Author of *Social Theory and the Family* (1975) and a paper on masculinity and social research in *Doing Feminist Research* (Ed. by H. Roberts 1981).

June Purvis is a lecturer in the Sociology of Education at the Open University. After studying at the universities of Leeds and Manchester, she taught at Manchester and Portsmouth Polytechnics. Then she took up a SSRC research grant at the OU. She is particularly interested in nineteenth-century sociology, and the development of sexual divisions in the past and in the present. At present she is completing the writing of her thesis on women's education in nineteenth-century England.

Daphne Taylorson lecturer in the Sociology of Education, Department of Education, University of Manchester. Current research on women in higher education.

Patricia Allatt was formerly a teacher, studied sociology at University College, Cardiff and the University of Keele, where she was also employed as a Research Fellow and Lecturer. She has done research on the youth service, crime prevention and family ideology. Her current research is concerned with family structure and youth unemployment.

Janet Finch is a lecturer in Social Administration at the University of Lancaster. She works in the fields of sociology and social policy, with her principal interests in marriage and the family, education, and current welfare policies, especially community care. She has published on aspects of gender in relation to welfare policies for the elderly and handicapped, services for preschool children, and within marriage, in particular, the incorporation of wives in their husbands' work. She is active in the British Sociological Association and its Women's Caucus, and is Vice Chairperson of the Association in 1982–3.

Hilary Graham is a lecturer in Social Policy at the University of Bradford. She is currently working at the Open University as an Honorary Research Fellow on a study financed by the Health Education Council about the division of health responsibilities within the home.

Jalna Hanmer teaches in the Schools of Applied Social Studies at the University of Bradford where she coordinates the new Diploma/M.A. in Women's Studies (Applied). She has published on violence to women and reproductive technology. These two areas are her current research interests.

Linda Imray is 37, unemployed and lives in Sheffield with her son. She graduated from Sheffield City Polytechnic in 1978, and from 1979 till 1982 did postgraduate research into the relevance of class to women's experience of work, marriage and motherhood at Bradford University's School of Studies in Social Analysis. She is active in the BSA Women's Caucus, is a member of the Equality of the Sexes Committee, and edited, with Audrey Middleton, the Women's Caucus Newsletter from 1980 till 1982.

Lorna McKee was born in 1951 in Kilkeel, Co. Down, N. Ireland. She received a B.Sc. from Trinity College, Dublin in Social Studies and an M.A. in Sociology from York University. She has worked in social research on family issues for the past seven years and is joint editor with Margaret O'Brien of *The Father Figure* (Tavistock 1982). Her current work is on a project concerned with the impact of unemployment on marriage and family relations, which is funded by the Social Science Research Council and based at the Department of Sociology and Social History at the University of Aston in Birmingham.

Audrey Middleton is a social anthropologist currently employed as Director of Scunthorpe and District Council for Voluntary Service. She graduated from the Queen's University of Belfast in 1978 and then moved to rural

Yorkshire where her fieldwork focused on the control of women – including herself – by a male clique in the village. She is registered for a Ph.D. at the University of Bradford, and is now working on her thesis as well as exploring alternative ways of disseminating her material. An active member of the British Sociological Association, she is on the Equality of the Sexes Committee, a member of the Women's Caucus, and edited, with Linda Imray, the Women's Caucus Newsletter from 1980 till 1982.

Anne Murcott is lecturer, Department of Sociology, University College Cardiff and Welsh National School of Medicine. Most recently she was editor of a book on 'ideologies' of food and eating and has written various articles on the same topic as well as on the sociology of medicine.

Margaret O'Brien graduated in Psychology at the North-East London Polytechnic in 1975 where she returned as a Lecturer in Psychology in the Department of Applied Social Sciences in 1979. In between time she carried out her Ph.D. research into lone fatherhood at the London School of Economics (Department of Social Psychology), worked as a Research Assistant in the Early Years of Marriage Project at the UK Marriage Research Centre, Central Middlesex Hospital, and lectured in the Department of Sociology at Kingston Polytechnic. She co-edited *The Father Figure* with Lorna McKee in 1982.

Marilyn Porter is currently lecturing part-time at Manchester University, and prior to that taught at Memorial University, Newfoundland, Manchester and Bristol Universities. She is 40 and has two children.

Peter Rushton graduated in Social Anthropology, Cambridge, 1973. This was followed by doctoral research in the family economy and housing conditions in nineteenth century Manchester (Manchester Ph.D., 1977). He is currently Lecturer in Sociology at Sunderland Polytechnic, researching into witchcraft, marriage and other aspects of early modern society in North-East England, based mainly on church and secular court records.

Sheila Saunders works in the Manchester Studies Department of Manchester Polytechnic on the Jewish History Project. While veering between unemployment and temporary posts, she has published research on the feminist response to violence to women in the home in Israel. Her current research interest is problems faced by Jewish women immigrants in Britain 1888–1914 and 1933–9.

Meg Stacey is Professor of Sociology at Warwick University, President of the British Sociological Association 1981–3, and member of its Women's

Caucus. Her main work is in the sociology of health and healing with a special interest in children and the division of labour in health care. This links with her wish to contribute to the revision of malestream sociological theories of the division of labour to include the gender order in ways which will help to take the sexism out of sociology.

Clare Ungerson is a lecturer in Social Policy and Administration at the University of Kent. Her current research and teaching interests focus upon women's studies, and especially women and community care. She has published on this topic, and also on race relations and housing policy.

Bibliography

Acker, J. (1973) 'Women and social stratification: a case of intellectual sexism', *American Journal of Sociology*, **78**(4), 936–945.
Acker, J. and Esseveld, J. with Barry, K. (1981) 'Issues in feminist research', unpublished paper, University of Lund, Sweden.
Ackroyd, S. and Hughes, J.A. (1981) *Data Collection in Context*, Longman.
Adams, M. (1971) 'The compassion trap', in V. Gornick and B. Moran (ed.), *Women in Sexist Society*, Basic Books.
Allatt, P. (1981a) 'The family seen through the Beveridge Report, Forces' Education and popular magazines: a sociological study of the social reproduction of family ideology in World War II', University of Keele, unpublished Ph.D. Thesis.
Allatt, P. (1981b) 'Stereotyping: familism in the law', in B. Fryer, A. Hunt, D. McBarnet and B. Moorhouse (eds), *Law, State and Society*, Croom Helm.
Andersen, R. (ed.) (1979) *North Atlantic Maritime Cultures*, Moulton.
Andersen, R. and Wadel, C. (1972) *North Atlantic Fishermen*, ISER.
Anderson, M. (1971) *Family Structure in Nineteenth Century Lancashire*, Cambridge University Press.
Andrews, R.A. (1973) 'Female participation in the Port de Grave Fishery', unpublished paper in Newfoundland Centre.
Antler, E. (1976) 'Women's work in Newfoundland fishery families', unpublished paper.
Antler, E. (1977) 'Maritime mode of production, domestic mode of production or labour process: an examination of the Newfoundland inshore fishery', paper given to North Eastern Anthropology Association.
Ardener, E. (1975) 'Belief and the problem of women', in S. Ardener (ed.), *Perceiving Women*, Macaby.
Ardener, S. (ed.) (1975) *Perceiving Women*, Macaby.
Ardener, S. (ed.) (1978) *Defining Females: the Nature of Women in Society*, Croom Helm.
Ardener, S. (1981) 'Ground rules and social maps for women: an introduction', in S. Ardener (ed.) (1981).
Ardener, S. (ed.) (1981) *Women and Space: Ground Rules and Social Maps*, Croom Helm.
Armstrong, P.F. (1982) *The Use of the Life History Method in Social and Educational Research*, Newlands Papers no. 7, University of Hull, Department of Adult Education.
Army Bureau of Current Affairs (ABCA)
– Bentley, P. (1943) 'Women after the war', *Current Affairs*, **44**, 22 May.
– Dukes, (Sir) Paul (1943) 'The trouble with Germans', *Current Affairs*, **49**, 14 August
– Ince, G.H. (1942) 'Women at war', *Current Affairs*, **20**, 20 June.
– Williams, W.E. (1943) 'When the lights go on', *Current Affairs*, **48**, 31 July.
– Williams, W.E. (1944) 'Woman's place', *Current Affairs*, **61**, 29 January.
– Williams, W.E. (Mrs) (1943) 'Social security', *Current Affairs*, **45**, 5 June.
– (1941) 'Oil', *Current Affairs*, **3**, 25 October.

Balswick, J. and Peek, C. (1971) 'The inexpressive male: a tragedy of American society', *The Family Coordinator*, **20**, 363-368.
Barker, D.L. (1972) 'Keeping close and spoiling', *Sociological Review*, **20**(4), 569-590.
Barrett, M. and Roberts, H. (1978) 'Doctors and their patients: the social control of women in general practice', in C. Smart and B. Smart (eds.), *Women, Sexuality and Social Control*, Routledge and Kegan Paul.
Barrow, H. (1962) *The Writings of Henry Barrow, 1587-1590*, edited by L.H. Carlson, Allen and Unwin.
Bart, P.E. (1971) 'Sexism and social science: from the gilded cape to the iron cage, or, the perils of Pauline', *Journal of Marriage and the Family*, November, 734-745.
Bateson, G. (1967; original edition, 1936) *Naven*, Stanford University Press.
Batstone, E. (1983) 'The hierarchy of maintenance and the maintenance of hierarchy: notes on food and industry', in A. Murcott (ed.), *The Sociology of Food and Eating*, Gower.
Bayley, M. (1973) *Mental Handicap and Community Care*, Routledge and Kegan Paul.
Becker, H. (1966) 'Introduction' to C.R. Shaw, *The Jack Roller*, University of Chicago Press.
Beechey, V. (1979) 'On patriarchy', *Feminist Review*, **3**, 66-82.
Bell, C. and Newby, H. (1971) *Community Studies*, Allen and Unwin.
Bell, C. and Newby, H. (1976) 'Husbands and wives: the dynamics of deferential dialectic', in D.L. Barker and S. Allen (eds.), *Dependence and Exploitation in Work and Marriage*, Longmans.
Bell, C. and Newby, H. (1977) *Doing Sociological Research*, George Allen and Unwin.
Bell, L. (1976) *The Underpriviledged Underfives*, Ward Lock.
Bentovim, A. (1972) 'Handicapped pre-school children and their families: effects on child's early emotional development', *British Medical Journal*, , 634-637.
Berk, S.F. (1980) *Women and Household Labour*, Sage Books.
Bernard, J. (1973) 'My four revolutions: an autobiographical history of the ASA', *American Journal of Sociology*, **78**(4), 773-791.
Beveridge, W.H. (1942) *Social Insurance and Allied Services*, Cmd 6404, HMSO.
Binney, V., Harkell, G. and Nixon, J. (1981) *Leaving Violent Men*, Women's Aid Federation England.
Blackstone, T. and Fulton O. (1975) 'Sex discrimination among University teachers: a British American Comparison', *British Journal of Sociology* **26**, 261-275.
Blackstone, T. and Fulton O. (1976) 'Discrimination is the villain', *Times Higher Educational Supplement*, 9 July.
Blunt, J.H. (ed.) (1905) *The Book of Church Law*, by Phillimore, (Sir) W.G.F. and Edwardes Jones, G., 10th edn. Longmans.
Booth, C. (1889-1903) *Life and Labour of the People in London*, 17 vols., Macmillan.
Borkowski, M., Murch, M. and Walker, V. (1981) *Community Response to Marital Violence*, Department of Social Administration, University of Bristol, unpublished.
Bott, E. (1957) *Family and Social Network*, Tavistock.
Bowley, F.L. and Burnett-Hurst, A.R. (1915) *Livelihood and Poverty*, Bell.
Bradbrook, P. (1980) 'The telegraph and female telegraphists in Newfoundland', unpublished paper in Newfoundland Centre.
Braverman, H. (1974) *Labor and Monopoly Capital*, Monthly Review Press.
Brighton Women and Science Group (1980) *Alice Through the Microscope*, Virago.
Broverman, I.K. *et al.* (1970) 'Sex role stereotypes and clinical judgements of mental health', *Journal of Consulting and Clinical Psychology*, **34**, 1-7.
Brown, G. and Harris, T. (1978) *The Social Origins of Depression*, Tavistock.
Brown, P. and Jordanova, L.J. (1981) 'Oppressive dichotomies: the nature/culture debate', in The Cambridge Women's Studies Group, *Women in Society: Interdisciplinary Essays*, Virago.
Brox, O. (1969) *The Maintainance of Economic Dualism in Newfoundland*, ISER.
Bruner, J. (1980) *Under Five in Britain*, Grant MacIntyre.
Bullock, A. (1967) *The Life and Times of Ernest Bevin*, Vol. II, Heinemann.

Bulmer, M. (1982) *The Uses of Social Research*, George Allen and Unwin.
Burley, S. (1982) 'A study of grandparents: portraying grandfatherhood in a research interview setting'. Paper presented to the 5th Fatherhood Research Group Meeting at Aston University in Birmingham.
Burton, R. (1972) *The Anatomy of Melancholy*, edited by Holbrook Jackson, Dent and Sons.
BWP. See Directorate of Army Education (The).
Calder, A. (1981, first published 1969) *The People's War, Britain 1939-45*, Jonathan Cape.
Callaway, H. (1978) ' "The most essentially female function of all": giving birth', S. Ardener, (ed.), *Defining Females: The Nature of Women in Society*, Croom Helm.
Callaway, H. (1981) 'Spatial domains and women's mobility in Yorubaland, Nigeria', in S. Ardener (ed.), *Women and Space: Ground Rules and Social Maps*, Croom Helm.
Caplan, P. and Bujra, J. (1978) *Women United: Women Divided*, Tavistock.
The Chartered Society of Physiotherapy (1975) *Handling the Handicapped - a guide to the lifting and movement of disabled people*, Woodhead-Faulkner.
Cicourel, A.V. (1974) *Method and Measurement in Sociology*, Collier-Macmillan.
Clarke, D. (1978) 'Folk religion in a North Yorkshire fishing village', unpublished M.A. Thesis, Newcastle University.
Cowie, C. and Lees, S. (1981) 'Slags or drags', *Feminist Review*, 9, 17-32.
Criminal Statistics, England and Wales, any year, HMSO.
Croll, E. (1978) *Feminism and Socialism in China*, Routledge and Kegan Paul.
Dalla Costa, M. and James, S. (1972) *The Power of Women and the Subversion of the Community*, first published by The Falling Wall Press, Bristol, reprinted in E. Malos (ed.) (1980), *The Politics of Housework*, Allison and Busby.
Daly, M. (1973), *Beyond God the Father*, Beacon Press.
Davidoff, L. (1976) 'The rationalisation of housework' in D.L. Barker and S. Allen (eds.), *Dependence and Exploitation in Work and Marriage* Longmans.
Davies, C. and Roche, S. (1980) 'The place of methodology: a critique of Brown and Harris', *Sociological Review*, 28(3), 641-656.
Davis, D. (1979) 'Social structure, sex roles and female associations in a Newfoundland fishing village', unpublished paper, Newfoundland Centre.
Davis, D. (1980) 'Women's experiences of the menopause in a Newfoundland fishing village', Ph.D. Thesis, University of North Carolina.
De Bruyn, L. (1979) *Woman and the Devil in Sixteenth-Century Literature*, The Compton Press Ltd.
Delamont, S. (1980) *The Sociology of Women: an Introduction*, Allen and Unwin.
Delphy, C. (1977) *The Main Enemy: a materialist analysis of women's oppression*, Explorations in Feminism no. 3., London: Women's Research and Resources Centre.
Denzin, N. (1970) *The Research Act*, Aldine Publishing Company.
Directorate of Army Education (The) (1944) *The British Way and Purpose*, Consolidated Edition of *BWP* Booklets 1-18 with Appendices of Documents of Post-War Reconstruction.
- *BWP* 1 (1942) 'Citizen of Britain', November, 13-44.
- *BWP* 2 (1942) 'Britain in action', December, 45-83.
- *BWP* 6 (1943) 'The setting', April, 186-210.
- *BWP* 8 (1943) 'The citizen at work', June, 237-262.
- *BWP* 11 (1943) 'Education and the citizen', September, 320-357.
- *BWP* 12 (1943) 'What more is needed of the citizen?' October, 358-379.
- *BWP* 13 (1943) 'The family and neighbourhood', December, 380-401.
- *BWP* 14 (1944) 'People at work', January, 402-427.
- *BWP* 16 (1944) 'You and the Empire', March, 458-493.
- *BWP* 17 (1944) 'You and the Colonies', April, 494-519.
Dobash, R.E. and Dobash, R. (1980) *Violence Against Wives: A Case Against the Patriarchy*, Open Books.
Donnison, J. (1977) *Midwives and Medical Men*, Heinemann.

Douglas, M. (1970) *Purity and Danger: an analysis of concepts of pollution and taboo*, Penguin.
Douie, V. (1949) *Daughters of Britain: An Account of the Work of British Women in the Second World War*, George Ronald.
Easthope, G. (1974) *A History of Research Methods*, Longmans.
Economic Council of Canada (1980) *Newfoundland: From Dependency to Self-Reliance*.
Edgell, S. (1980) *Middle Class Couples: A Study of Segregation, Domination and Inequality in Marriage*, Allen and Unwin.
Edwards, S. (1977) 'Time to speak out', *Contact*, June 1977, 22.
Edwards, S. (1981) *Female Sexuality and the Law*, Martin Robertson.
Ehrenreich, B. and English, D. (1979) *For Her Own Good: 150 Years of the Experts' Advice to Women*, Pluto Press.
Eichler, M. (1980) *The Double Standard: a Feminist Critique of Feminist Social Science*, Croom Helm.
Einhorn, B. (1981) 'Socialist emancipation: the women's movement in the German Democratic Republic', *Women's Studies International Quarterly*, **4**(4), 345-452.
Elias, E. and Scotson, J. (1965) *The Established and the Outsiders: a Sociological Enquiry into Community Problems*, Cass.
Ellis, R. (1983) 'The way to a man's heart...', in A. Murcott (ed.), *The Sociology of Food and Eating*, Gower.
Elshtain, J.B. (1981) *Public Man, Private Woman*, Martin Robertson.
Equal Opportunities Commission (EOC) (1981) *The experience of caring for elderly and handicapped dependants: Survey report*, EOC.
Ettore, B. (1980) *Lesbians, Women and Society*, Routledge and Kegan Paul.
Evers, H. (1981) 'Care or custody? the experiences of women patients in long stay geriatric wards', in G. Williams and B. Hutter (eds.), *Controlling Women – the normal and the deviant*, Croom Helm.
van der Eyken, W. (1974) *The Pre-school Years*, 3rd edn. Penguin.
Faraday, A. and Plummer, K. (1979) 'Doing life histories', *Sociological Review*, **27**(4), 773-798
Faris, J. (1972) *Cat Harbour*, ISER.
Ferri, E. and Niblett, R. (1977) *Disadvantaged Families and Playgroups*, NFER.
Filmer, P., Phillipson, M., Silverman, D. and Walsh, D. (1972) *New Directions in Sociological Theory*, Collier Macmillan.
Finch, J. (1983a) 'A first class environment? working class playgroups as pre-school education', *British Education Research Journal*, November.
Finch, J. (1983b) *Married to the Job: Wives' Incorporation in Men's Work*, Allen and Unwin.
Firestone, M. (1967) *Brothers and Rivals*, ISER.
Flew, A. (1980) 'Looking after Granny: the reality of community care', *New Society*, **54**(934).
Fox, B. (ed.) (1980) *Hidden in the Household*, Toronto: Women's Press.
Frere, W.H. (1910) *Visitations, Articles and Injunctions of the Period of the Reformation*, Longmans, Green and Co.
Galtung, J. (1967) *Theory and Methods of Social Research*, Allen and Unwin.
Gardiner, J. (1975) 'Women's domestic labour', first published in *New Left Review*, **89**, 47-58, reprinted in Z.R. Eisenstein (ed.) (1979), *Capitalist Patriarchy and the Case for Socialist Feminism*, Monthly Review Press.
Garnsey, E. (1978) 'Women's work and theories of class stratification', *Sociology*, **12**(2), 223-243.
Gluckman, M. (1954) *Rituals of Rebellion in South-East Africa*, Manchester University Press.
Good Housekeeping (1943) Ann Blythe, 'Living alone is fun...but...don't enjoy it too much', February 22.
Graham, H. (1976) 'The social image of pregnancy: pregnancy as spirit possession', *Sociological Review*, **24**(2), 291-308.

Graham, H. (1979) ' "Prevention and health: every mother's business": a comment on child health policies in the 1970's', in C. Harris *et al.* (eds.), *The Sociology of the Family: New Directions for Britain*, Sociological Review Monograph no. 28, University of Keele.

Graham, H. amd McKee, L. (1980) *The First Months of Motherhood*, Monograph no. 3, Health Education Council.

Gray, R.Q. (1974) 'The labour aristocracy in the Victorian class structure', in F. Parkin (ed.), *The Social Analysis of Class Structure*, Tavistock.

Hacker, M.H. (1951) 'Women as a minority group', *Social Forces*, **30**, 60–69.

Hair, P. (1972) *Before the Bawdy Court*, Elek.

Hall, C. (1981) 'Gender divisions and class formation in the Birmingham middle class, 1780–1850', in R. Samuel (ed.), *People's History and Social Theory*, History Workshop Series, Routledge and Kegan Paul.

Hanmer, J. (1978) 'Violence and the social control of women', in G. Littlejohn, B. Smart, J. Wakeford and N. Yuval-Davis (eds.), *Power And The State*, Croom Helm.

Hanmer, J. and Leonard, D. (forthcoming) 'Negotiating the problem: the DHSS and research on violence in marriage', in C. Bell and H. Roberts, (eds.), *Social Researching: Problems, Politics and Practice*, Routledge and Kegan Paul.

Hanmer, J. and Saunders, S. (forthcoming) *We Are The Subject Of Our Own Research: A Community Study of Violence to Women*, Women's Research and Resources Centre pamphlet, Hutchinson.

Hart, N. (1976) *When Marriage Ends*, Tavistock.

Hartmann, H. (1981a) 'The family as the locus of gender, class and political struggle: the example of housework', *Signs*, **6**(3), 366–394.

Hartmann, H. (1981b) 'The unhappy marriage of Marxism and feminism: towards a more progressive union', in L. Sargent (ed.), *Women and Revolution: A Discussion of the Unhappy Marriage of Marxism and Feminism*, Pluto Press.

Hastrup, K. (1978) 'The Semantics of Biology: Virginity' in S. Ardener (ed.), *Defining Females: The Nature of Women in Society*, Croom Helm.

Hatch, S. (1981) 'The voluntary sector: a larger role?', in E.M. Goldberg and S. Hatch (eds.), *A New Look at the Personal Social Services*, Discussion Paper no. 4, Policy Studies Institute.

Hawkins, T.H. and Brimble, L.J. (1947) *Adult Education – The Record of the British Army*, Macmillan.

Hélias, P-J. (1978) *The Horse of Pride: Life in a Breton Village*, Yale University Press.

Henderson, W. (1979) *Notes on the Folk-Lore of the Northern Counties of England and the Borders*, 2nd edn. The Folk-Lore Society.

Hertz, R. (1973a) 'The hands', in M. Douglas (ed.), *Rules and Meanings – The Anthropology of Everyday Knowledge*, Penguin.

Hertz, R. (1973b; original edition in French, 1909) 'The pre-eminence of the right hand', transl. in R. Needham (ed.), *Death and the Right Hand*, Cohen and West.

Hill, C. (1974) *Continuity and Change in Seventeenth-Century England*, Weidenfeld and Nicolson.

Hirschon, R. (1978) 'Open body/closed space – the transformation of sexuality', in S. Ardener, (ed.) *Defining Females: The Nature of Women in Society*, Croom Helm.

Hoinville, G., Jowett, R. and Associates (1977) *Survey Research Practice*, Heinemann Educational Books.

Home Chat, (1942) 'Why the row began', 19 December, 446.

Home, E. (1942) *Woman*, 26 December.

Home, E. (1943) *Woman*, 13 March, 1 May.

Hornell, J. (1980) *Fishing in Many Waters*, Cambridge University Press.

Hubert, J. (1974) 'Belief and reality: social factors in pregnancy and childbirth', in M.P.M. Richards (ed.), *The Integration of the Child into a Social World*, Cambridge University Press.

Hughes, E.C. (1971) 'The humble and the proud', in *The Sociological Eye: Selected Papers*, Aldine-Atherton.

Hughes, J.A. (1976) *Sociological Analysis: Methods of Discovery*, Nelson.
Hughes, M., Mayall, B., Moss, P., Perry, J., Petrie, P. and Pinkerton, G. (1980) *Nurseries Now: a Fair Deal for Parents and Children*, Penguin.
Humphries, J. (1981) 'Protective legislation, the capitalist state, and working class men: the case of the 1842 Mines Regulation Act', *Feminist Review*, 7, spring 1981, 1-33.
Hunt, A. (1970) *The Home Help Service in England and Wales*, HMSO.
Hunt, P. (1980) *Gender and Class Consciousness*, Macmillan.
Imray, L. (1981) 'Women and stratification', paper presented at the Women and Society Seminar, University of Bradford, 19 March 1981.
Jones, D. (1980) 'Gossip: notes on women's oral culture', *Women's Studies International Quarterly*, 3(2/3), 193-198.
Joseph, A. and Parfitt, J. (1972) *Playgroups in an Area of Social Need*, NFER.
Kadushin, A. (1972) *The Social Work Interview*, Columbia University Press.
Kent, R.A. (1981) *A History of British Empirical Sociology*, Gower.
Komarovsky, M. (1962) *Blue-Collar Marriage*, Random House Inc.
Kramer, H. and Sprenger, J. (1971) *Malleus Maleficarum*, trans. by M. Summers, Arrow/Hutchinson.
La Fontaine, J.S. (1972) 'Ritualization of women's life-crises in Bugisu', in J.S. La Fontaine (ed.), *The Interpretation of Ritual: Essays in Honour of A.I. Richards*, Tavistock.
Land, H. (1977) 'Inequalities in large families: more of the same or different', in R. Chester and J. Peel, *Equalities and Inequalities in Family Life*, Academic Press.
Land, H. (1978) 'Who cares for the family?' *Journal of Social Policy*, 7(3), 257-284.
Land, H. (1981) *Parity Begins at Home*, EOC/SSRC Joint Panel on Equal Opportunities.
Leach, E. (1976) *Culture and Communication*, Cambridge University Press.
Leonard, D. (1980) *Sex and Generation*, Tavistock.
Lévy-Bruhl, L. (1975) *The Notebooks on Primitive Mentality*, trans. by P. Rivière, Basil Blackwell.
Lewis, I.M. (1971) *Ecstatic Religion: An Anthropological Study of Spirit Possession and Shamanism*, Penguin.
Lloyd, P.C. (1965) 'The Yoruba of Nigeria', in J.L. Gibbs (ed.), *Peoples of Africa*, R. and W. Holt.
Loftland, L.H. (1975) 'The "thereness" of women: a selected review of urban sociology', in M. Millman and R.M. Kanter (eds.), *Another Voice: Feminist Perspectives on Social Life and Social Science*, Anchor Books.
London Edinburgh Weekend Return Group (1979) *In and Against the State*, Conference of Socialist Economists.
Lowell, R. (1974) *New Priest in Conception Bay*, McLelland and Stewart.
McCay, B.J. (1979) ' *"Fish is scarce"*: fisheries modernization on Fogo Island', in R.A. Anderson, (1979).
McGregor, O.R. (1957) 'Social research and social policy in the nineteenth century', *British Journal of Sociology*, 8, 146-157.
McKenzie, H. (1980) *You Alone Care*, SPCK.
McIntosh, M. (1978) 'The state and the oppression of women', in A. Kuhn and A.M. Wolpe (eds.), *Feminism and Materialism*, Routledge and Kegan Paul.
McIntosh, M. (1981) 'Feminism and Social Policy', *Critical Social Policy*, 1(1), 32-42.
McNally, F. (1979) *Women for Hire: A Study of the Female Office Worker*, Macmillan.
McRobbie A. (1978) 'Working class girls and the culture of femininity', in Women's Studies Group, CCCS, *Women Take Issue: Aspects of Women's Subordination*, Hutchinson.
Mannion, J. (1978) *Irish Settlements in Eastern Canada*, University of Toronto Press.
Mathieu, N-C. (1978) 'Man-culture and woman-nature?', *Women's Studies International Quarterly*, 1(1), 55-65.
Matthews, A.M. (1980) 'The Newfoundland migrant wife: a power and powerlessness theory of adjustment' in A. Heindfarb and C.J. Richardson (eds.), *People, Power and Process*, McGraw Hill.

Maybury-Lewis, D. (1967) *Askwẽ-Shavante Society*, Clarendon Press.
Maynard, M. (forthcoming) 'The response of social workers to domestic violence', in J. Pahl (ed.), *Private Violence and Public Policy*, Routledge and Kegan Paul.
Mead, M. (1943) 'Science, women and the problem of power', in *Women at Work. The Bulletin of the British Federation of Business and Professional Women*. 4 September, **4**.
Middleton, A. (1981) 'Who pulls the strings? Male control of the ethnographer in a Yorkshire village', paper presented at a meeting of the British Sociological Association's Sexual Divisions Study Group, on the Social Control of Women, University of Bradford, 16 February 1981.
Middleton, A. (1982) 'An endangered species: feminist ethnography in a rural setting'. Paper presented at a meeting of the British Sociological Association's Ethnography Study Group, University of Manchester, 23–24 January 1982.
Middleton, C. (1974) 'Sexual inequality and stratification theory', in E. Parkin (ed.), *The Social Analysis of Class Structure*, Tavistock.
Millman, M. and Kanter, R.M. (1975) *Another Voice: Feminist Perspectives on Social Life and Social Science*, Anchor Books.
Mills, C.W. (1971) 'Situated actions and vocabularies of motive', in B.R. Cosin, (ed.), *School and Society*, Routledge and Kegan Paul.
Morgan, D.H.J. (1975) *Social Theory and the Family*, Routledge and Kegan Paul.
Morgan, D. (1981) 'Men, masculinity and the process of sociological enquiry', in H. Roberts (ed.), *Doing Feminist Research*, Routledge and Kegan Paul.
Moser, C.A. and Kalton, G. (1971) *Survey Methods in Social Investigation*, Heinemann.
Muller, V. (1977) 'The formation of the state and the oppression of women: some theoretical considerations and a case study in England and Wales', *Review of Radical Political Economics*, **9**(3), 17–21.
Murcott, A. (1982a) 'On the social significance of the "cooked dinner in South Wales" ' *Social Science Information*, **21**(4/5), 677–695.
Murcott, A. (1983a) 'Women's place: cookbook's image of technique and technology in the British Kitchen', *Women's Studies International Forum*, **6**(2) (forthcoming).
Murcott, A. (ed.) (1983b) *The Sociology of Food and Eating*, Gower.
Murcott, A. (1983c) 'Cooking and the cooked', in A. Murcott (ed.), *The Sociology of Food and Eating*, Gower.
Murcott, A. (1983d) 'Menus, meals and platefuls', *International Journal of Sociology and Social Policy* (forthcoming).
Murdock, G.P. and Provost, C. (1973) 'Factors in the division of labour by sex: a cross-cultural analysis', *Ethnology*, **XII**(2), 203–225.
Murphy, R.F. (1958) *Mundurucú Religion*, University of California Publications in American Archaeology and Ethnology, **49**.
Murray, H. (1979) *More than 50%: Woman's Life in a Newfoundland Outport 1900–1950*, Breakwater Press.
Needham, R. (1979) *Symbolic Classification*, Goodyear Publishing Co.
Nelson, L. (1980) 'Household Time: a cross-cultural example', in J.F. Berk (ed.), *Women and Household Labour*, Sage Books.
New English Bible (1970) Cambridge University and Oxford University Presses.
Newson, J. and Newson, E. (1965) *Patterns of Infant Care in an Urban Community*, Penguin.
Nissel, M. (1980) 'Women in government statistics: basic concepts and assumptions', *EOC Research Bulletin* no. 4, Equal Opportunities Commission.
Nissel, M. and Bonnerjea, L. (1982) *Family Care of the Handicapped Elderly: Who Pays*, Policy Studies Institute paper no. 602, PSI.
NORDCO (1981) *It Were Well to Live Mainly Off Fish: The Place of Northern Cod in Newfoundland's Development*.
Oakley, A. (1974a) *Housewife*, Penguin.
Oakley, A. (1974b) *The Sociology of Housework*, Martin Robertson.
Oakley, A. (1979) *Becoming a Mother*, Martin Robertson.

Oakley, A. (1980) *Women Confined: Towards a Sociology of Childbirth*, Martin Robertson.
Oakley, A. (1981) 'Interviewing women: a contradiction in terms', in H. Roberts (ed.), *Doing Feminist Research*, Routledge and Kegan Paul.
Obelkevich, J. (1976) *Religion and Rural Society: South Lindsey, 1825-1875*, Clarendon Press.
Okin, S.(1980) *Women in Western Political Thought*, Virago.
Ortner, S. (1974) 'Is female to male as nature is to culture?', in M.Z. Rosaldo and L. Lamphere (eds.), *Woman, Culture and Society*, Stanford University Press.
Owen, L. (1974) 'The welfare of women in labouring families', in M. Hartman and L.W. Banner (eds.), *Clio's Consciousness Raised: New Perspectives on the History of Women*, Harper and Row.
Pahl, J. (1980) 'Patterns of money management within marriage', *Journal of Social Policy*, **9**(3), 313-35.
Pahl, J. (1982) 'The allocation of money and the structuring of inequality within marriage', Board of Studies in Social Policy and Administration, University of Kent. mimeo.
Parker, R.A. (1980) *The State of Care: The Richard M. Titmuss Memorial Lecture 1979-80*, Joint (JDC) Israel Brookdale Institute of Gerontology and Adult Human Development in Israel. Also published as 'Tending and social policy', in E.M. Goldberg and S. Hatch (eds.) (1981) *A New Look at the Personal Social Services*, PSI.
Phillimore, R. (1873) *Ecclesiastical Law*, London.
Pickering, W.S.F. (1974) 'The persistence of rites of passage: towards an explanation', *British Journal of Sociology*, **25**(1), 63-78.
Picture Post (1941) Letter from R.D. Sieff, Chairman of the Women's Publicity Planning Association, **10**(10), 8 March, 5.
Picture Post (1944) 'Wages for wives', by E. Hulton, **22**(6), 5 February, 26.
Pierce, S. (1979) 'Ideologies of female dependence in the welfare state', paper presented to the Annual Conference of the British Sociological Association, mimeo.
Piotrkowski C.S. (1978) *Work and the Family System* The Free Press.
Plowden, Lady B. (1973) 'The playgroup movement: a cycle of opportunity', in Preschool Playgroups Association, *Focus on the Future of Playgroups*, PPA.
Pollert, A. (1981) *Girls, Wives and Factory Lives*, Macmillan.
Porter M. (1978) 'World's apart: the class consciousness of working class women', *Women's Studies International Quarterly*, **1**(2), 175-188.
Porter, M. (1983) 'The tangly bunch: the political culture of outport women', under consideration.
Preschool Playgroups Association (1980) *Playgroups in the Eighties: Opportunities for Parents and Children*, PPA.
Price, M. (1981) 'British restaurants (1940-1946): from collectivism to consumerism', paper given at Women and Housing Policy Conference, University of Kent; to be published in *Making Space*, Pluto Press.
Public Record Office
 - (1941) WO 32/9735, Minute 3A, June
 - (1943) WO 32/10455, Minute 18, January
 - (1945) PIN 8/69, Letter from P.N. Harvey to Sir Thomas Phillips, 4 April.
Purcell, K. (1979) 'Militancy and acquiescence amongst women workers', in S. Burman (ed.), *Fit Work for Women*. Croom Helm.
Purvis, J.S. (1948) *Tudor Parish Documents of the Diocese of York*, Cambridge University Press.
Radford, E. and M.A. (1978) *Superstitions of Love and Marriage*, edited and revised by C. Hole, Arrow/Hutchinson.
Raine, J. (1850) *The Injunctions and Other Ecclesiastical Proceedings of Richard Barnes, Bishop of Durham from 1575 to 1587*, Vol. **22**, Surtees Society.
Raine, J. (1888) *Churchwardens' Accounts of Pittington and Other Parishes in the Diocese of Durham from 1580 to 1700*, Vol. **48**, Surtees Society.
Reinharz, S. (1979) *On Becoming a Social Scientist*, Josey Bass.

Reiter, R.R. (1975) 'Men and women in the south of France: public and private domains', in R.R. Reiter (ed.), *Toward an Anthropology of Women*, Monthly Review Press.
Rich, A. (1977) *Of Woman Born: Motherhood as Institution and Experience*, Virago.
Rich, A. (1980) *On Lies, Secrets and Silences*, Virago.
Richards, A.I. (1956) *Chisungu: a girl's initiation ceremony among the Bemba of Northern Rhodesia*, Faber and Faber.
Richardson, M.A. (1842) *The Local Historian's Table Book - Legendary Division*, Vol. **1**, Newcastle.
Roberts, H. (1978) *Women and Their Doctors: A Sociological Analysis of Consulting Rates*, paper presented at the SSRC Workshop on qualitative methodology.
Roberts, H.,(ed.) (1981) *Doing Feminist Research*, Routledge and Kegan Paul.
Roberts, H. and Woodward, D. (1981) 'Changing patterns in women's employment in sociology: 1950-1980', *British Journal of Sociology*, **XXXII**(4), 531-546.
Rodgers, S. (1981) 'Women's space in a men's house: the British House of Commons', in S. Ardener (ed.), *Women and Space: Ground Rules and Social Maps*, Croom Helm.
Rogers, S.C. (1978) 'Woman's place: a critical review of anthropological theory', *Comparative Studies in Society and History*, **20**(1), 123-162.
Rosaldo, M.Z. (1974) 'Woman, culture and society: a theoretical overview', in M.S. Rosaldo and L. Lamphere (eds.), *Woman, Culture and Society*, Standford University Press.
Rosaldo, M.Z. (1980) 'The use and abuse of anthropology: reflections on feminism and cross-cultural understanding', *Signs: Journal of Women in Culture and Society*, **5**(3), 389-417.
Rosaldo, M.Z. and Lamphere, L. (eds.) (1974) *Woman, Culture and Society*, Stanford University Press.
Rosser, C. and Harris, C. (1965) *The Family and Social Change*, Routledge and Kegan Paul.
Rotenberg, R. (1981) 'The impact of industrialisation on meal patterns in Vienna, Austria', *Ecology of Food and Nutrition*, **11**(1), 25-35.
Rowbotham, S. (1972) *Women, Resistance and Revolution*, Allen Lane.
Rowbotham, S. (1973) *Woman's Consciousness, Man's World*, Penguin.
Rowntree, B.S. (1901) *Poverty, A Study of Town Life*, Macmillan.
Rushton, P. (1980) 'A Note on the Survival of Popular Christian Magic', *Folklore*, **91**(1), 115-118.
Rushton, P. (1982) 'Women, witchcraft and slander in early modern England: cases from the Church Courts at Durham, 1560-1675', *Northern History*, **XVIII**, 116-132.
Sanday, P.R. (1981) *Female Power and Male Dominance: On the origins of Sexual Inequality*, Cambridge University Press.
Saunders, P. (1979) *Urban Politics: A Sociological Interpretation*, Hutchinson.
Seccombe, W. (1973) 'The housewife and her labour under capitalism', *New Left Review*, **83**, 3-24.
Shapland, J., Willmore, J. and Duff, P. (1981) *The Victim in the Criminal Justice System*, Final Report to Home Office, Centre for Criminological Research, University of Oxford.
Sharpe, J.A. (1980) *Defamation and Sexual Slanders in Early Modern England: The Church Courts at York*, Borthwick Papers no. 58, St. Anthony's Press.
Shaw, M. and Miles, I. (1979) 'The social roots of statistical knowledge', in J. Irvine, I. Miles and J. Evans, (eds.), *Demystifying Social Statistics*, Pluto.
Shinman S. (1981) *A Chance for Every Child? Access and Response to Pre-school Provision*, Tavistock.
Sinclair, P. (1981) 'Fishermen divided: conflict in the fisheries in N.W. Newfoundland', unpublished paper.
Sinclair, P. (1981) 'Hunting the cod and harvesting spuds: rural production and social change in Atlantic Canada', unpublished paper.
Skogan, W.G. (1981) *Issues in the Measurement of Victimization*, U.S. Department of Justice, NCJ-74682.
Slater, E. and Woodside, M. (1951) *Patterns of Marriage*, Cassell and Co.

Smith, D.E. (1974) 'Women's perspective as a radical critique of sociology', *Sociological Enquiry*, **44**(1), 7-13.
Smith, D.E. (1978) 'A peculiar eclipsing: woman's exclusion from man's culture', *Women's Studies International Quarterly*, **1**(4), 281-295.
Smith, D.E. (1979) 'A sociology for women', in J. Sherman and E. Peck (eds.), *The Prison of Sex: Essays in the Sociology of Knowledge*, University of Wisconsin Press.
Smith, M. Estelle (ed.) (1977) *Those Who Live From the Sea: A Study in Maritime Anthropology*, West Publishing Co.
Smith, T. (1980) *Parents and Preschool*, Grant MacIntyre.
Sparks, R., Genn, H. and Dodd, D. (1977) *Surveying Victims*, Wiley.
Spender, D. (1980) *Man Made Language*, Routledge and Kegan Paul.
Spender, D. (1981) 'The gatekeepers: a feminist critique of academic publishing' in H. Roberts (ed.), *Doing Feminist Research*, Routledge and Kegan Paul.
Spradley, J.O. and Mann, B.J. (1975) *The Cocktail Waitress: Women's Work in a Man's World*, John Wiley.
Spring-Rice, M. (1939) *Working Class Wives*, Penguin Books.
Stacey, M. (1960) *Tradition and Change: a Study of Banbury*, Oxford University Press.
Stacey, M. (1981) 'The division of labour revisited, or overcoming the two Adams', in P. Abrams *et al.* (eds.), *Development and Diversity: British Sociology 1950-1980*, Allen and Unwin.
Stacey, M. and Price, M. (1981) *Women, Power and Politics*, Tavistock.
Stanley, L. and Wise, S. (1979) 'Feminist research, feminist consciousness and experiences of sexism', *Women's Studies International Quarterly*, **2**(3), 359-374.
Stanko, E.A. (1982) 'Would you believe this woman? Prosecutorial screening for "Credible" witnesses and a problem of justice', in N.H. Rafter and E.A. Stanko (eds.), *Judge, Lawyer, Victim, Thief: Woman, Gender Roles, and Criminal Justice*, Northeastern University.
Stark, E., Flitcraft, A. and Frazier, E. (1979) 'Medicine and patriarchal violence: the social construction of a "Private" Event', *International Journal of Health Services*, **9**(3), 461-492.
Staton, M.W. (1980) 'The rite of churching: a sociological analysis with special reference to an urban area in Newcastle upon Tyne', unpublished M.A. Thesis, Newcastle University.
Stephens, W.N. (1963) *The Family in Cross-Cultural Perspective*, Holt, Rinehart and Winston.
Stewart, W.F.R. (1979) *The Sexual Side of Handicap: a Guide for the Caring Professions*, Woodhead-Faulkner.
Stiles, G. (1971) 'Fishermen, wives and radios: aspects of communication in a Newfoundland fishing village', in R.A. Anderson (ed.) (1979).
Strathern, M. (1972) *Women In Between: Female Roles in a Male World: Mount Hagen, New Guinea*, Seminar Press.
Strawmullion (1980) *Hens in the Hay*, Strawmullion Co-operative Ltd.
Sudnow, D. (1967) *Passing On: The Social Organization of Dying*, Prentice-Hall.
Summerfield, P. (1976) 'Popular radicalism in the Second World War: the case of the armed forces', unpublished paper read at the History Work in Progress Seminar, University of Sussex.
Summerfield, P. (1981) 'Education and politics in the British armed forces in the Second World War' *International Review of Social History*, **26**(2), 133-158.
Szala, K.V. (1952) 'Clean women and quiet men: marriage in Shepherd's Harbour', unpublished paper, Newfoundland Centre.
Szala, K. (1978) 'Family as a source for metaphor: a Newfoundland account', in R.J. Preston (ed.), *Canadian Ethnology*, **40**, Ottawa.
Tanner, A. (1978) 'Putting out and taking out: the social formation of non-capitalist enclaves', unpublished paper.
Taylor, L. (1972) 'The significance and interpretation of replies to motivational questions: the case of sex offenders', *Sociology*, **6**(1), 23-39.

Thomas, K. (1973) *Religion and the Decline of Magic: Studies in Popular Beliefs in Sixteenth and Seventeenth-Century England*, Penguin.
Thompson, E.P. (1967) 'Time, work-discipline and industrial capitalism', *Past and Present*, **38**(197), 56-97.
Tolson, A. (1977) *The Limits of Masculinity*, Tavistock.
Townsend, P. (1979) *Poverty in the United Kingdom: A survey of household resources and standards of living*, Penguin.
Tunstall, J. (1962) *The Fishermen*, MacGibbon and Kee.
Turnbull, C. (1961) *The Forest People*, Cape.
Turner, V.W. (1974) *The Ritual Process: Structure and Anti-Structure*, Penguin.
Ungerson, C. (1981) *Women, work and the 'caring capacity of the community': a report of a research review*, Report to the SSRC.
Ungerson, C. (1983) 'Why do women care?', in J. Finch and D. Groves (eds.), *A Labour of Love: Women, Work and Caring*, Routledge and Kegan Paul.
Vallance, E.M. (1979) *Women in the House: A Study of Women Members of Parliament*, Athlone Press.
Van Gennep, A. (1960) *The Rites of Passage*, trans. by M.B. Vizedom and G.L. Caffee, Routledge and Kegan Paul.
Wadel, C. (1973) *Now Whose Fault is That*, ISER.
Wajcman, J. (1981) 'Work and the family: who gets "the best of both worlds?" ', in Cambridge Women' Studies Group, *Women in Society*, Virago.
Warne, A. (1969) *Church and Society in Eighteenth Century Devon*, David and Charles.
West, J. (1980) 'A political economy of the family in capitalism: women, reproduction and wage labour', in T. Nichols (ed.), *Capital and Labour A Marxist Primer*, Fontana.
Whitehead, A. (1976) 'Sexual antagonism in Herefordshire', in D.L. Barker and S. Allen (eds.), *Dependence and Exploitation in Work and Marriage*, Longman.
Whitehead, B. (1911) *Church Law: Being a Concise Dictionary of Statutes, Canons, Regulations and Decided Cases Affecting the Clergy and Laity*, London.
Whyte, W.F. (1948) *Human Relations in the Restaurant Industry*, McGraw Hill.
Wilkin, D. (1979) *Caring for the Mentally Handicapped Child*, Croom Helm.
Wilson, E. (1977) *Women and the Welfare State*, Tavistock.
Wilson, E. (1980) *Only Half Way to Paradise: Women in Postwar Britain 1945-1968*, Tavistock.
Wilson, N.S. (1949) *Education in the Forces 1939-46: The Civilian Contribution*, Evans Brothers.
Woman's Outlook (1942) Editorial Chat, 'Should wives have economic independence?' 5 December, 1.
Woodforde, J. (1935) *Passages from the Five Volumes of the Diary of a Country Parson, 1758-1802, The Reverend James Woodforde*, edited by J. Beresford, Oxford University Press.
Young, M. and Willmott, P. (1962) *Family and Kinship in East London*, Penguin.
Young, M. and Willmott, P. (1975) *The Symmetrical Family*, Penguin.

Index

Acker, J., 106
Acker, J. and Esseveld, J., 135, 142
Ackroyd, S. and Hughes, J.A., 138, 140
Adams, M., 144
Allatt, P., 48, 55, 60
Anderson, M., 112
Anderson, R., 92
Anderson, R. and Wadel, C., 92
Antler, E., 92, 93
Aquaforte, 94–103
Ardener, E., 118, 120, 135
Ardener, S., 19, 133
Armstrong, P., 140
Army Bureau of Current Affairs (ABCA), 49–59
Astor, N., 20
Auxiliary Territorial Service, 50

Balswick, J. and Peek, C., 153
Barker, D.L., 85
Barrett, M. and Roberts, H., 137
Barrow, H., 122
Bart, P.E., 133
Bateson, G., 18
Batstone, E., 83
Bayley, M., 62, 72
Becker, H., 140
Beechey, V., 106
Bell, C., 160
Bell, C. and Newby, H., 89, 110
Bentley, P., 52, 53, 57
Bentovim, A., 68
Berk, S.F., 136
Bernard, J., 135
Beveridge, W.H., 60
Binney, V., Harkett, G. and Nixon, J., 32
Blackstone, T. and Fulton, O., 9

Blunt, J.H., 122, 125
Booth, C., 145
Borkoski, M., Murch, M. and Walker, V., 29
Bott, E., 83
Bowley, F.L. and Burnett, Hurst, A.R., 138–9
Bradbrook, P., 93
Braverman, H., 44
Brighton Women and Science Group, 133
Broverman, I.K. *et al.*, 144
Brown, G. and Harris, T., 142
Brown, P. and Jordanova, L.J., 120
Brox, O., 92
Bruner, J., 107
Bullock, A., 48
Bulmer, M., 145
Burley, S., 150
Burton, R., 129
BWP (see Directorate of Army Education)

Calder, A., 49, 57
Callaway, H., 15, 120
Capitalism and sexual division of labour, 4, 102–103
   and women, 145
Caplan, P. and Burja, J., 91
Chartered Society of Physiotherapy, 72
Cicourel, A.V., 133, 144
Citizenship in Forces' Education programme in Second World War, 47–61
Clarke, D., 124
Class struggle, 103
Class and women, 106–17
Cowie, C. and Lees, S., 116

Croll, E., 91
Cunnison, S., 26

Dalla Costa, M. and James, S., 14
Davidoff, L., 112
Davies, C. and Roche, S., 140, 142–3
Davis, D., 93, 105
De Bruyn, L., 121
Delamont, S., 111
Delphy, C., 106
Denzin, N., 143
Directorate of Army Education, *The British Way and Purpose* (BWP), 49–50, 55–8
Dobash, R.E. and Dobash, R., 32, 44
Domestic labour debate, 14, 64
Donnison, J., 64
Douglas, M., 19, 25, 27, 74, 76, 122, 127
Douie, V., 48, 58

Easthope, G., 137
Edgell, S., 79, 87–9
Edwards, S., 106, 128, 129
Educational programmes for Forces in Second World War, 47–61
Ehrenreich, B. and English, D., 64
Eichler, M., 106
Einhorn, B., 15
Elias, E. and Scotson, J., 114
Ellis, R., 88
Elshtain, J.B., 133, 137, 146
Elston, M.A., 160
Equal Opportunities Commission, 140
Equal Pay Act, 16, 17
Ettore, B., 130
Evers, H., 66

Family
  and family wage, 16
  and functionalism, 2
  and industrialisation, 4, 79
  and sexual division of labour, 72–3, 78–89
  and society, 2–3, 60
  and sociological theory, 1–3
Faraday, A. and Plummer, K., 158
Faris, J., 92, 101, 104
Fatherhood, 147–61
Feminism and sociological theory, 1–6, 7–11, 62–3
Filmer, P., Phillipson, M., Silverman, D. and Walsh, D., 133
Finch, J., 106, 115

Firestone, M., 104
Fishing and the sexual division of labour, 91–105
Flew, A., 67, 74
Fox, B., 79
Frere, W.H., 123

Galtung, J., 139, 141, 142, 143
Gardiner, J., 14
Garnsey, E., 106
Ginsberg, M., 10
Gluckman, M., 24
Good Housekeeping, 48
Graham, H., 63, 128, 129
Graham, H. and McKee, L., 137, 140

Hacker, M.H., 60
Hair, P., 123, 124
Hall, C., 17
Handicapped adults and tending, 62–77
Hanmer, J., 46
Hanmer, J. and Leonard, D., 28
Hanmer, J. and Saunders, S., 29
Hartmann, H., 14, 16, 26, 139
Hastrup, K., 121
Hatch, S., 107
Hawkins, T.H. and Brimble, L.J., 50, 57
Hélias, P-J., 131
Henderson, W., 125
Hertz, R., 27, 120
Hill, C., 131
Hirschon, R., 131
Home Chat, 48
Hornell, J., 104
Hubert, J., 126, 128
Hughes, E.C., 86
Hughes, J.A., 141, 144
Hughes, M., Mayall, B., Moss, P., Perry, J., Petrie, P. and Pinkerton, G., 107
Humphries, J., 26
Hunt, A., 75
Hunt, P., 10, 137

Ideology
  of caring and tending, 62–77
  of housework, 62–77
  of reproduction, 118–131
Imray, L., 17
Ince, G.H., 57
Incest taboos, 74–5

Jones, D., 143

Kadushin, A., 150

Kent, R.A., 137
Komarovsky, M., 153, 156

La Fontaine, J.S., 119
Land, H., 62, 139
Leach, E., 130
Leisure
  as a concept, 134
  village cricket, 22-5
  women's hockey team, 25
Leonard, D., 79, 82
Lewis, I.M., 129
Lloyd, P.C., 15
Loftland, D., 79, 82
London Edinburgh Weekend Return Group, 63

Markham, S., 7
Marxism and the family, 2-3
  and analysis of women's position, 14-16
Masculinity, social construction of, 47-61, 147-61
Maybury-Lewis, D., 18
Maynard, M., 29, 44
McGregor, O.R., 137
McKenzie, H., 67
McIntosh, M., 63
McKee, L. and O'Brien, M., 142
McNally, F., 26
McRobbie, A., 116
Mead, M., 12, 53
Men
  and control over women in domestic sphere, 78-90, 41-2,
  and control over women in public sphere, 16-26, 118-31
Methods
  ethnography, 22-5, 94
  interviews, 147-61
  observation, 106
  male bias, 132-37
  survey method, 137-46
Middleton, A., 22, 27
Middleton, C., 79
Millman, M. and Kanter, R.M., 136
Mills, C. Wright, 126
Morgan, D.H.J., 60, 116, 132, 134, 136, 147, 159
Moser, C.A. and Kalton, G., 138
Motherhood, 63-5, 122-27
Muller, V., 26
Murcott, A., 79, 80, 82, 83, 85, 90
Murdock, G.P. and Provost, C., 78, 92

Murphy, R.F., 27
Murray, H., 93

Needham, R., 118
Nelson, L., 145
New English Bible, 122
Newsom, J. and Newsom, E., 73
Nissell, M., 139, 144
Nissell, M. and Bonnerjea, L., 62, 70, 72, 75

Oakley, A., 62, 64, 70, 73, 79, 83, 86, 87, 133, 134, 137, 140, 142
Obelkevich, J., 125, 126
Okin, S., 133
Ortner, S., 120

Pahl, J., 89, 139
Parker, R.A., 63
Patriarchy, 2, 3, 14-16, 26, 141-42
Phillimore, R., 126
Pickering, W.S.F., 118, 127
Picture Post, 48
Pierce, S., 53
Piotrkowski, C.S., 154, 161
Plowden, Lady, 106
Pollert, A., 26, 137, 142
Political life and women, 18-22
Porter, M., 105, 106
Power relationships, 107-17
Power relationships between men and power, 60, 86-9, 101-3, 130-1, 134-9, 152-3, 156-8
Price, M., 48
Pregnancy, 20, 128-30, 151-2
Purcell, K., 26
Public and private: discussion of the relationship between the two spheres, 1-5, 12-26, 42-6, 57-60, 76-7, 81, 89, 102-3, 115-17, 121-2, 145-6, 159
Purvis, J.S., 131

Radford, E. and M.A., 125, 129
Raine, J., 122
Reinharz, S., 136
Reiter, R.R., 131
Rich, A., 9, 135, 143, 144
Richardson, M.A., 124
Rites de passage, 118-19
Roberts, H., 134, 135, 136
Roberts, H. and Woodward, D., 9
Rodgers, S., 18, 19, 20, 21, 22, 26
Rogers, S.C., 120

Rosaldo, M.Z., 12, 13, 25
Rosser, C. and Harris, C., 85
Rotenberg, R., 89
Rowbotham, S., 15, 91, 143
Rowntree, B.S., 138, 139, 140
Rushton, P., 122

Saunders, P., 141
Seecombe, W., 14
Sexism and sociology, 9, 132–45
see also sociology
Shapland, J., Willmore, J. and Duff, P., 38
Shaw, J.A. and Miles, I., 144
Shinman, S., 107
Skogan, W.G., 29
Slater, E. and Woodside, M., 48
Smith, D.E., 7, 132, 133, 134, 145
Sociological theory
and feminism, 2–4, 7–11, 62–4, 76–7, 145
as male dominated, 1–6, 7–11, 133–7
Sparks, R., Genn, H., and Dodd, D., 36
Spender, D., 15, 134, 135, 143
Spradley, J.O. and Mann, B.J., 86
Spring-Rice, M., 59
Stacey, M., 1, 6, 7, 62, 76, 107, 110, 111, 112, 132, 133, 135
Stacey, M. and Price, M., 27, 144
Stanley, L. and Wise, S., 132, 134, 142
Stanko, E.A., 42
Stark, E., Flitcraft, A. and Frazier, E., 44
State and the social sciences, 7–11
Staton, M.W., 122, 125, 127
Stephens, W.N., 78
Stewart, W.F.R., 65
Strathern, M., 15
Sudnow, D., 120
Summerfield, P., 48, 49, 51, 52
Szala, K.V., 93

Taboos about human dirt, 72–75
about incest, 74–75

Taylor, L., 126
The Well Fed Bridegroom, 80
Thomas, K., 122, 123
Thompson, E.P., 138, 145
Tolson, A., 79
Townsend, P., 140, 141
Trade unions, 16–17
Tunstall, J., 104
Turnbull, C., 27
Turner, V.W., 24

Ungerson, C., 62, 63
Unwaged work
and women, 23–5, 62–77, 78–89
and men, 147–56

Vallance, E.M., 20
Van Gennep, A., 119, 121, 127, 128
Violence
definitions of 29–31
at home 34, 41
towards women 28–46

Wadel, C., 104
Wajcman, J., 79
Warne, A., 124
West, J., 79
Whitehead, B., 125
Whyte, W.F., 86
Wilkin, D., 62, 68, 69, 70, 72, 75
Wilson, E., 62
Wilson, N.S., 49, 50, 51
Women
as academics, 10
and biological reproduction, 2, 13, 73–4
fighting like a woman, 7–11
and subordination, 26, 102
in other cultures, 15–16, 18, 91–103
Woman's Outlook, 48
Woodforde, J., 124

Young M. and Willmott, P., 78, 126